D0221141

UTSA DT LIBRARY RENEWALS 458-2440

DATE DUE

GAYLORD			PRINTED IN U.S.A.

YOUTH DRINKING CULTURES

Youth Drinking Cultures
European Experiences

Edited by

MARGARETHA JÄRVINEN
University of Copenhagen, Denmark
and the Danish National Institute of Social Research
and
ROBIN ROOM
University of Melbourne, Australia

WITHDRAWN
UTSA LIBRARIES

ASHGATE

© Margaretha Järvinen and Robin Room 2007

All rights reserved. No part of this publication may be reproduced, stored in a retrieval system, or transmitted in any form or by any means, electronic, mechanical, photocopying, recording or otherwise without the prior permission of the publisher.

Margaretha Järvinen and Robin Room have asserted their right under the Copyright, Designs and Patents Act, 1988, to be identified as the editors of this work.

Published by
Ashgate Publishing Limited
Gower House
Croft Road
Aldershot
Hampshire GU11 3HR
England

Ashgate Publishing Company
Suite 420
101 Cherry Street
Burlington, VT 05401-4405
USA

Ashgate website: http://www.ashgate.com

British Library Cataloguing in Publication Data
Youth drinking cultures : European experiences
    1. Youth - Alcohol use - Europe - Cross-cultural studies
    2. Youth - Europe - Social conditions - Cross-cultural
    studies 3. Drinking of alcoholic beverages - Social aspects
    - Europe - Cross-cultural studies
    I. Järvinen, Margaretha II. Room, Robin
    362.2'92'0835'094

Library of Congress Cataloging-in-Publication Data

Youth drinking cultures : European experiences / edited by Margaretha Järvinen and Robin Room.
        p. cm.
    Includes index.
    ISBN: 978-0-7546-4996-0
    1. Youth--Alcohol use--Europe. 2. Teenagers--Alcohol use--Europe. 3. Drinking of alcoholic beverages--Europe. I. Järvinen, Margaretha. II. Room, Robin.
    HV5135.Y694 2007
    306'.1--dc22

                                                                        2007011101

ISBN: 978-0-7546-4996-0

Library
University of Texas
at San Antonio

Printed and bound in Great Britain by Antony Rowe Ltd, Chippenham, Wiltshire.

Contents

List of Figures

List of Tables

Notes on Contributors

Main authors (detailed information) and co-authors.

Salme Ahlström is a PhD and research professor at the National Research and Development Centre for Welfare and Health in Helsinki, Finland. Her research interests include comparative studies on drinking among young people and women. Among her most recent works are *The ESPAD-report. Alcohol and other Drug Use among Students in 35 European Countries* (together with B. Hibell, B. Andersson and others, 2004), 'International Perspectives on Adolescent and Young Adult Drinking' (with E. Österberg) in *Alcohol, Research and Health* (NIAAA 2005) and 'Self-determination in the Home or Written Law', in *Adult Parenthood – Upbringing Regained* (ed. by E. Hermanson and R. Martsola, in Finnish, 2006). Salme.Ahlstrom@stakes.fi

Barbro Andersson has been a sociologist and for 20 years. She was research associate at the Swedish Council for Information on Alcohol and Other Drugs (CAN) in Stockholm, from which she retired in 2006. She has been responsible for the annual Swedish school surveys on alcohol and other drugs and for the European School Survey Project on Alcohol and Other Drugs (ESPAD) that she initiated and coordinated with Björn Hibell. barbro.andersson@can.se

Kim Bloomfield, Dr PH, associate professor, Unit for Health Promotion Research, University of Southern Denmark.

Rebecca N.H. de Leeuw, MA, PhD student, Behavioural Science Institute, Radboud University Nijmegen, The Netherlands.

Nanne K. de Vries, PhD, professor, Department of Health Education and Promotion, Maastricht University, The Netherlands.

Rutger Engels is a full professor at the Behavioural Science Institute, Radboud University Nijmegen, The Netherlands. He obtained his PhD in 1998, at the Department of Medical Sociology, Maastricht University. At the time of writing, he is involved in research on risk, social and health behaviors of children and adolescents. Theoretical models are tested through various research designs ranging from epidemiological survey studies, lab experiments, systematic observational studies to genetic research. He recently co-edited a book on peer relations (with M. Kerr and H. Stattin), *Friends, Lovers and Groups: Who is Important in Adolescence and Why* (2007). R.Engels@bsi.ru.nl

Björn Hibell is a PhD and assistant professor (docent) in sociological alcohol research. He is the Managing Director of the Swedish Council for Information on Alcohol and Other Drugs (CAN) in Stockholm. CAN is an alcohol and drug information centre and the responsibilities also include research-oriented activities like annual nationwide surveys about alcohol and drug habits among students and military conscripts. His main area of interest includes alcohol and drug surveys and an example of such surveys is the ESPAD-study that he initiated and coordinates together with Barbro Andersson. ESPAD covers about 40 European countries and the fourth data collection will be carried out in 2007. bjorn.hibell@can.se

Klaus Hurrelmann, PhD, professor at the University of Bielefeld, School of Public Heath, Department of Prevention and Health Promotion, Germany.

Margaretha Järvinen is a PhD and professor at the Department of Sociology, University of Copenhagen and at the Danish National Institute of Social Research. Her research interests include alcohol and drugs, social marginalisation, general sociological theory and qualitative methods. Among her most recent works are *Young People, Parties and Alcohol* (ed. with P. Gundelach 2006, in Danish), 'Constructing Maturity through Alcohol Experience' (with J. Demant), *Addiction Research and Theory* (2006) and 'Teenage Drinking, Symbolic Capital and Distinction' (with P. Gundelach), *Journal of Youth Studies* (2007). margaretha.jarvinen@sociology.ku.dk

Anja Leppin, PhD, associate professor at the University of Southern Denmark, Faculty of Health Sciences, Institute of Public Health, Unit for Health Promotion Research.

Patrick Miller is a PhD and retired senior research fellow, Department of Psychiatry, University of Edinburgh and University of the West of England, Bristol. His research interests have included the determinants of schizophrenia, life events and depression in the community. At the time of writing, he is involved in the UK part of the ESPAD study. Publications include a book on Social Science methods, many mental health research articles and many more on substance use in teenagers.

Saoirse Nic Gabhainn, PhD, senior lecturer in Health Promotion and Deputy Director of the Health Promotion Research Centre, National University of Ireland, Galway, Ireland.

Gert A. Nielsen, PhD, Department of Cancer Prevention and Documentation, Danish Cancer Society, Copenhagen.

Howard Parker is a PhD and professor emeritus in the School of Law at Manchester University, UK. He is the author of eight books and over 50 journal articles. His most recent books include *Illegal Leisure: The Normalisation of*

Adolescent Recreational Drug Use and *UK Drugs Unlimited: New Research and Policy Lessons on Illicit Drug Use*. Howard Parker is now undertaking local research, development and training for drug and alcohol services in England.
Howard.Parker@manchester.ac.uk

Martin Plant is a PhD and professor of Addiction Studies at the University of the West of England, Bristol, United Kingdom. His research interests include the social and behavioural aspects of alcohol and other psychoactive drug use and alcohol control policies. Martin Plant is director of the UK part of the European School Survey Project on Alcohol and other Drugs (ESPAD). His publications include *Alcohol: Minimising the Harm: What Works* (ed. with E. Single and T. Stockwell, 1997), *The Alcohol Report* (ed. with D. Cameron, 2000) and *Binge Britain: Alcohol and the National Response* (with M. Plant, 2006).
Martin.Plant@uwe.ac.uk

Evelien A.P. Poelen, PhD student, Behavioural Science Institute, Radboud University Nijmegen, The Netherlands

Matthias Richter is a PhD and assistant professor at the University of Bielefeld, School of Public Heath, Department of Prevention and Health Promotion, Germany. His main research areas are health and health behaviour in adolescence, social epidemiology, health promotion and prevention. His most current publications are *Health Inequalities. Principles, Problems and Challenges* (ed. with K. Hurrelman, in German, 2006), 'Risk Behaviour in Adolescence – The Relationship between Developmental and Health Problems' (with K. Hurrelman), *Journal of Public Health* 2006, 'Trends in Socio-Economic Differences in Tobacco Smoking among German Schoolchildren 1994–2002' (with A. Leppin), *European Journal of Public Health* (in press).
matthias.richter@uni-bielefeld.de

Robin Room is a PhD and a professor both at the School of Population Health, University of Melbourne and at the Centre for Social Research on Alcohol and Drugs, Stockholm University. He is also the Director of the AER Centre for Alcohol Policy Research, Turning Point Alcohol and Drug Centre, Fitzroy, Victoria, Australia. He is a sociologist who has worked on alcohol as well as drugs and gambling in terms of norms and patterns of use, problems and social responses, and the formation and effects of policies. Recent books of which he is a coauthor or coeditor include *The Effects of Nordic Alcohol Policies: What Happens to Drinking and Harm When Alcohol Controls Change?* (2002), *Alcohol in Developing Societies: A Public Health Approach* (2002), *Alcohol, Gender and Drinking Problems: Perspectives from Low and Middle Income Countries* (2005), and *Sober Reflections: Commerce, Public Health and the Evolution of Alcohol Policy in Canada, 1980–2000* (2006).
RobinR@turningpoint.org.au

Haske Van der Vorst, post-doctoral student, Behavioural Science Institute, Radboud University Nijmegen, The Netherlands.

Carmen Van der Zwaluw, PhD student, Behavioural Science Institute, Radboud University Nijmegen, The Netherlands.

Jan Van Leeuwe, statistical consultant, Behavioural Science Institute, Radboud University Nijmegen, The Netherlands.

Kirsten Verkooijen holds a masters degree in Health Education and Promotion and in Mental Health Sciences, both received from Maastricht University, The Netherlands. She completed her doctoral studies at the Faculty of Health Sciences, University of Southern Denmark. She defended her PhD thesis 'Identity and Health Risk Behaviour in Adolescence' in January 2007). Since then, she has continued her work in the field of Health Psychology as a post-doctoral student at the same research unit. Her main research interests are determinants of health behaviour, social identity, self-perception, and implicit cognition. KVerkooijen@health.sdu.dk

Foreword

The work with this volume started in August 2005 when 25 researchers met at a conference in Copenhagen, Denmark in order to discuss adolescent drinking. The aim of the meeting was to analyse alcohol consumption patterns among young people in Europe, with a specific focus on youth cultures with high levels of drunkenness. The conference was arranged by Margaretha Järvinen and Peter Gundelach, and was part of a research project funded by the Rockwool Foundation in Denmark. The background for the Danish initiative was the extraordinary high levels of drinking among 15–16 year olds in Denmark. In fact Danish adolescents have for many years – often together with British teenagers – held the European record on heavy drinking and drunkenness. Among the questions discussed at the conference were these: How are the youth drinking cultures in Europe related to national characteristics of different countries? What is the relationship between adolescent drinking and variables such as gender, family background and peer networks? Should heavy drinking be conceptualised as a mainstream cultural phenomenon or a phenomenon associated with specific subcultures, social problems and social vulnerability?

In 2006 some of the participants at the conference revised their papers and developed them into chapters for this volume. By and large the book follows the initial idea behind the conference, the aim being to describe different youth drinking cultures and to understand why young people in northern and north-western Europe drink so much and with such a strong focus on drunkenness.

The editors want to thank the Rockwool Foundation for supporting the conference and the Danish part of the work with this volume. We also want to thank Peter Gundelach for his contribution to the work with the conference and the initial editing of the book. Thanks also to Ditte Schlüntz and Signe Ravn for practical help with the project and to all the participants at the Copenhagen conference for contributing with comments on the papers that later became the chapters of this book.

Margaretha Järvinen and Robin Room
Copenhagen and Melbourne, February 2007

Chapter 1

Youth Drinking Cultures: European Experiences

Margaretha Järvinen and Robin Room

Introduction

The aim of the book is to analyse drinking patterns among young people, with particular emphasis on experiences in different European societies. Among the world regions, Europe has the highest levels of alcohol consumption (Rehm et al., 2004). The production of alcoholic beverages is important economically and given a high cultural value in a number of European countries, and drinking is enmeshed in diverse ways in cultural symbolism and practices all over Europe. These general social patterns are reflected in high levels of drinking, and of alcohol-related problems, among teenagers and young adults (Rehm et al., 2001). Foremost among the problems related to drinking for young people are injuries and other health and social problems related to alcohol intoxication.

Within the relatively high levels of alcohol consumption in Europe, there are nevertheless wide variations between different societies. The fact of such variations has been noted by travellers through the centuries, although there have been some changes over time in the comparisons reported. Thus, the Roman historian Tacitus noted about the habits of life in *Germania*, contrasting them with the civilised life style of the Romans: 'Drinking bouts, lasting day and night, are not considered in any way disgraceful .... People satisfy their hunger without elaborate preparation and without delicacies, and in drinking they show no self-control. You have only to indulge their intemperance by supplying all that they crave, and you will gain as easy a victory through their vices as through your own arms' (from Tacitus' *Germania*, cited in Rosberg, 1931, p. 3ff).

Similarly, Martin Luther complained of 'the abuse of eating and drinking' of his fellow-Germans, noting that 'the Italians call us gluttonous, drunken Germans and pigs because they live decently and do not drink until they are drunk. Like the Spaniards, they have escaped this vice' (Austin, 1985, p. 147). A few decades later, the English traveller Fynes Moryson agreed with Luther about the Germans: 'let the Germans pardon me to speak freely: ... to their drinking they can prescribe no mean nor end'. On the other hand, in his view 'drunkenness is reproachful among the French, and the greater part drink water mingled with wine'. He also saw British drinking in his era as mostly moderate: 'in general the greater and better part of the English hold all excess blameworthy, and drunkenness a reproachful vice'. Moryson found heavy drinking, on the other hand, among the Irish: 'especially at feasts, both men and women use excess' of whiskey, he reported; he had not seen heavy drinking as 'a woman's vice' anywhere else, 'but only in Bohemia' (now in the Czech Republic; MacManus, 1939, pp. 19–20; Austin, 1985, pp. 211–213).

Also Scandinavians and Finns have traditionally been portrayed as hard drinkers, as 'proud and self-willed people' with a tendency to 'go berserk' when drinking alcohol, 'either because they put porse in their brew or because they carry liquors badly' (Rosberg, 1931, p. 5). And as noted by the Swedish historian Carl Gimberg in the beginning of the twentieth century: 'In Finland berserk is still very wide-spread, and usually caused by spirits, especially spirits of poor quality … Like madmen [the drinkers] draw their sheath-knives and start swinging them while jumping or running with soft knees and cat-like movements. This condition should not be mistaken for *sisu* [the Finnish variant of a never-say-die attitude], although people with *sisu* are probably more prone to show this kind of behaviour than are others' (Rosberg, 1931, p. 4).

As Ahlström briefly reviews in her chapter in this volume, contrasts between European drinking cultures have figured quite heavily in the modern literature on variations in the cultural position of alcohol. The most important contrast has been between the southern European wine cultures and 'the rest'. Recurrently, southern European drinking cultures have been held out as a model by those critiquing their own country's drinking culture, whether it be American scholars holding up the ideal of an 'integrated drinking culture' (Ullman, 1958), Swedish newspaper columnists whose 'dream of a better society' centres on 'continental' styles of drinking (Olsson, 1990), or present-day British politicians seeking to reform 'binge Britain' into a 'café drinking' culture (Parker, 2003). Often a further division has been made in terms of the traditionally dominant beverage: not only 'wine cultures', but also 'beer cultures' stretching from Ireland to the Czech Republic, and 'spirits cultures' north of the Baltic and in eastern Europe. The fact that analyses in the European Comparative Alcohol Study (ECAS; Leifman, 2001) were forced to rename the countries north of the Baltic the 'former spirits-drinking' countries is an indication that this way of dividing up Europe is no longer so neat, in an era of some homogenisation in drinking; in terms of the most-used beverage (in pure-alcohol terms), Sweden became first a beer-drinking country, and now a wine-drinking country.

The contrasts between European drinking cultures have been implicitly focused on adult drinking; in fact, one might guess that the implicit contrasts are often of middle-aged male groups (for example Csikszentmihalyi, 1968). In terms of the analyses in several of the chapters which follow, one contribution of this volume is to bring these traditions of thinking about differences in the cultural position of drinking to bear on samples of younger respondents, and in particular on those in their mid-teenage years. How far can the ideal-type differences in drinking cultures described in the literature, oriented to adult drinking and resting often on a limited empirical base, be found already as contrasts in the patterns of youngsters at the beginning of their drinking career? The ability to undertake such analyses now reflects the emergence in recent years of two separate cross-national traditions of data-collection which have transformed our ability to make quantitative cross-national comparisons. These are the 'European School Survey Project on Alcohol and Other Drugs' (ESPAD), most recently carried out in 35 European countries in 2003 (see Andersson and Hibell in this volume), and the 'Health Behaviour in School Aged Childen Study' (HBSC) of 11–15-year-olds, including data from 26 European countries in 2001/02 (see Richter et al. in this volume).

In forms such as the analyses in this volume, the ESPAD and HBSC data-sets have made a very substantial contribution in advancing our ability to conduct cross-cultural analyses of youth drinking, and in particular youth drinking across Europe. But the ESPAD dataset, and to a lesser extent also the HBSC dataset, have also made contributions to the cultural politics of alcohol. Like other cross-cultural comparisons, the main form in which their results appear in the public media is in the 'league table': which country's 15-year-olds top the charts, for instance, in terms of rate of 'binge drinking'? As can be seen in the chapters by Andersson and Hibell and by Ahlström, Denmark, constituent parts of the UK, Ireland and Finland tend to top the ESPAD charts on intoxication and reported alcohol problems; in the HBSC results (the chapter by Richter et al.), Ireland ranks lower but Ukraine is added to the top tier. Such results have raised the profile of youth drinking as a fundable research problem in Denmark, the UK and Finland. That half of the substantive chapters in this volume are by researchers from these three countries may well partly reflect this policy effect of the international comparisons.

As can be seen from the contents of this book, the effect of the availability of the ESPAD and HBSC comparisons has been to give a substantial boost to quantitative research, and particularly to quantitative comparative research, on youth drinking. In the meantime, there has also been a substantial growth in the qualitative literature on youth drinking, both in Europe and elsewhere. Instances can be found in the literature of explicitly comparative qualitative analyses (for example Pyorälä, 1995; Beccaria and Sande, 2003), but such studies are inherently hard to do and thus not common. In this introduction, we draw upon this literature to complement the quantitative studies in the volume.

Differences in Youth Drinking Cultures

The cross-national surveys of adolescent drinking – ESPAD and HBSC – show that big differences persist between European countries in drinking and drunkenness. In the wine-producing countries, adolescents' drinking can be described as relatively frequent but modest on each occasion. In the Nordic countries (Finland, Iceland, Norway and Sweden) adolescents consume alcohol more seldom, but when they drink, they typically drink a lot. In the beer-countries Denmark, Ireland and the UK, adolescents both drink frequently and to intoxication. This pattern, though, cannot be found in all beer-countries. Adolescents in Germany and Belgium for instance, report intoxication far more seldom than adolescents in Denmark, Ireland and the UK (Ahlström et al., 2001; Hibell et al., 2004).

An interesting feature in some of the youth cultures in the northern and north-western parts of Europe is that gender differences in drinking are relatively small. While 15–16-year-old boys in France and Portugal report drunkenness rates four times higher than girls' rates, the drunkenness rates in the UK and some of the Nordic countries are gender equal (in some countries girls even outrank boys).

Regression analyses of data from the ESPAD-study show that across European countries, beer and spirits consumption are the most important predictors for heavy drinking or 'binge drinking' (five or more drinks on one drinking occasion) (Kuntsche et al., 2004). Binge drinking in turn is likely to be part of multiple substance use (cigarettes, marijuana and other illegal drugs), a relationship that has been demonstrated in many studies from different countries.

The ESPAD data also show an association between heavy drinking and risk perception at country level (Morgan et al., 1999). First of all, the perception of risk associated with binge-drinking varies greatly between countries, with only 12–13 per cent of adolescents regarding binge drinking as risky in Wales and Denmark compared to more than half of the adolescents in some Mediterranean countries (Portugal, Cyprus, Turkey). Second, the country level of risk conception is explicitly related to heavy use of alcohol – the lower the risk awareness level, the higher the drunkenness rates – and less clearly associated with the broad measures such as lifetime prevalence of drinking in the country's teenage population.

The drunkenness rates in different ESPAD-countries are also strongly associated with young people's positive expectancies in relation to alcohol (see Andersson and Hibell in this volume). Thus, the countries with high drunkenness figures (for instance Finland, Ireland, UK and Denmark) are also those where adolescents expect most positive consequences of drinking (to feel relaxed, happy, more friendly and outgoing, to have fun and forget problems). On the other hand, the expected negative consequences of drinking (get a hangover, do something one regrets later, feel sick, etc.) are highest in countries such as Romania, Italy, Portugal and Turkey, where the drunkenness figures are low. Although adolescents in the northern and north-western parts of Europe do not *expect* negative consequences of alcohol, they obviously *experience* such consequences relatively often. When students in the 35 ESPAD-countries were asked how often they had actually encountered alcohol-related problems (school problems, problems with parents or friends, sexual problems and problems related to violence and crime), the students from these countries were at the top of the list. The highest sums of problem items were found in Denmark and Isle of Man, followed by Finland, Ireland, the UK and the Baltic states.

A New Culture of Intoxication?

Reports from different countries indicate that young people today drink more, and with a clearer focus on drunkenness, than earlier generations. In general, time-trends suggest that youth alcohol consumption has increased over the last 30–35 years (Gabhainn and François, 2000; Johnston et al., 2002; Schmid and Gabhainn, 2004). It has been claimed that the increasing alcohol and drug use among teenagers and young adults represents an escalation of the 'psychoactive revolution' – the tendency for people everywhere in the late modern world to develop more and more potent means of altering their ordinary waking consciousness (Courtwright, 2001, p. 2).

The decade when 'a new culture of intoxication' (cf. Parker et al., 1998) seems to have manifested itself was the 1990s. For this period research from different countries showed an escalation in the use of both legal and illegal drugs among young people (Settertobulte et al., 2001). In Britain, for instance, the 1970s and 1980s were decades of apparent stability in young people's drinking, while the weekly consumption by young people doubled across the 1990s (Parker et al., 1998; Measham, 2004). According to British school surveys, the average alcohol consumption of young adolescents (11–15 years) increased from 5.3 units per week in 1990 to 10.4 units in 2000 – and has fluctuated around this level since then (Department of Health, 2005). The increase in young people's alcohol consumption in the 1990s was accompanied by a dramatic rise in the use of illegal drugs, primarily of cannabis, LSD and the 'dance drugs' amphetamine and ecstasy (Parker et al., 1998). From the 1980s to the mid and late 1990s the proportion of persons reporting experience with illegal drugs almost tripled in the UK (ibid., p. 13). One of the central messages in Parker et al.'s work is that young people's use of illegal drugs cannot be understood separately from their use of alcohol. Drinking, and drinking heavily, is the 'underpinning' of their psycho-active substance careers. According to Measham and Brain (2005, p. 267), alcohol and drug use today 'intertwine and celebrate cultures of hedonistic consumption'. In the interviews conducted by these British researchers, the majority of young people conceived of their nights out not just to go out drinking but to get drunk. Measham and Brain point out that certain individual and social constraints surrounding drunkenness, for instance norms condemning heavy female drinking and a visible loss of self-control, seem to have disappeared from the youthful drinking scenes. Instead young people of both genders are said to pursue a 'determined drunkenness' tied to a 'wider drug-wise and consumption-oriented leisure time culture' (ibid.).

In Denmark as well, the drinking and drunkenness levels among teenagers rose in the 1990s. Here, the increase started in the 1980s and escalated in the 1990s (Gundelach and Järvinen, 2006). In the past five years the increase has stopped, but Danish 15–16 year olds have retained their position (together with British teenagers) as European record-holders when it comes to drinking and (especially) drunkenness.

In Finland, the development is very reminiscent of that in Denmark and the UK, although Finnish youths started out from a much lower consumption level. Alcohol use among teenagers increased continually from the beginning of the 1980s to the late 1990s. From 1999 to 2003 the numbers decreased somewhat for boys but not for girls (Rimpelä et al., 2003). In parallel with the development in alcohol consumption, the attitudes toward drunkenness changed so that twice as many teenagers in 1999 (as compared to 1979) were of the opinion that 'it's important to drink oneself intoxicated now and then'. Also Finnish teenagers' experience with illegal drugs increased dramatically in this period, although the rates of reported use remain considerably lower than in the UK or Denmark. When Rimpelä et al. (2003) used an indirect measure of young people's contacts with the illegal drug scene, asking them about their friends' drug use, the results showed a very clear change. While 13 per cent of the 16-year-old boys and 18 per cent of the girls in 1981 said that (at least) one of their acquaintances had used drugs, in 2001 these numbers had climbed to 49 and 66 per cent respectively (ibid.).

In the southern part of Europe, there has also been a substantial rise in concern about youth drinking in recent years. However, most of the data on what actual changes have occurred are qualitative, leaving open the question of how much the concern is a matter of shifting adult perceptions. One clear trend is that in all the 'wine cultures', there has been a shift by young drinkers away from wine, and often towards beer drinking. This in itself, of course, has been seen as a break in tradition. Along with it have come worries that youth drinking styles are taking on 'anglo-saxon' characteristics, as they are often described: young drinkers are seen as breaking with tradition by drinking for the intoxication value of alcohol. A French study which mixes qualitative and quantitative methods, interviewing technical students in their 20s in the Paris region, gives some substance to these concerns (Freyssinet-Dominjon and Wagner, 2003). A plurality of the drinkers in the study (40 per cent) describe themselves as 'VSD drinkers', that is Friday, Saturday, Sunday drinkers, of beer or white wine or spirits drinks. For them, drinking daily would be a sign of alcoholism – as drinking red wine would also be. Alternatively, daily drinking and red wine drinking are identified by them with their parents' generation. What they are seeking from the drinking is indeed a mild intoxication – only a minority, seen as still stuck in a teenage mentality, are looking for full intoxication.

In Spain, the worries have been about the specific new custom of *el botellón* (the big bottle; http://en.wikipedia.org/wiki/Botellon; Tremlett, 2002; Rowe and Gomez, 2003; Keeley and Bagenal, 2006), whereby teenagers sit around in Spanish town squares until late on weekend nights passing around cheap alcoholic drinks (for example red wine or spirits mixed with cola). As *el botellón* spread from town to town in Spain, municipalities have attempted to legislate against it, and it has taken on overtones of a generational conflict (Baigorri et al., 2004).

Beccaria and Guidoni (2002) report that 'northern drinking habits' have spread to Italy so that young Italians today show a growing consumption of beer and spirits, a greater concentration of alcohol consumption at the weekends, a reduction of the differences between female and male drinking and an increased search for risk through alcohol use. Still, however, there is a very significant difference between southern and northern Europe, when it comes to intoxication among teenagers. According to ESPAD-data, teenagers in the north report drunkenness rates that are three to five times as big as their peers in the Mediterranean countries (for instance Italy), although the differences in reported rates of drinking five or more drinks on an occasion are considerably less (see Room in this volume). As Beccaria and Guidoni (2002) point out, there still seems to be drinking norms in Italy protecting teenagers from heavy drinking. In the qualitative study reported by these authors, 'drinking to get drunk' and 'going overboard' were behaviours voiced in terms of disapproval among young Italians.

Beccaria and Guidoni's data may be compared with qualitative data from the UK. In interviews with 14–15-year-old Britons, Coleman and Cater (2005) found no condemnation of drunkenness. The teenagers interviewed in their study pronounced the normality of binge drinking and intoxication and tended to focus on the positive effects of drunkenness (social facilitation, forgetting problems, drinking at the same level as the others) and ignore the negative. Similarly, Danish qualitative data show that intoxication is described in unambiguously positive terms by 15–16 year olds (Demant and Järvinen, 2006). Danish teenagers tend to regard binge drinking as natural and to associate drunkenness with sociability, romantic relations and 'time out'. There is no indication at all in the Danish data of the type of condemnation of drunkenness Beccaria and Guidoni found in Italy. In Finland as well, high school students' images of alcohol have been shown to systematically imply drunkenness (Jaatinen, 2000). For the Finnish adolescents interviewed by Jaatinen, drunkenness symbolised a progress from childhood to cultured worlds of adults: the city centre, money, sexuality, etc.

In a comparative analysis of drinking in Norway and Italy, Beccaria and Sande (2003) demonstrate clear differences between the two countries in young people's attitudes towards drunkenness. While the goal for young Italians was to experiment with intoxication without losing control, young Norwegians associated heavy drinking with a symbolic performance of drunkenness and lack of control of the intoxicated body. According to Beccaria and Sande the Norwegian code of intoxicated performance would in Italy signal alcohol problems and 'bad' behaviour. In contrast, the Italian code of controlled intoxication would among Norwegian young people signal a person unwilling to take part in the fellowship and 'reveal his or her personal identity' (ibid.: 111).

In a qualitative study, Lalander (1997, 1998) identified a 'hedonistic', drunkenness-oriented alcohol life style among some groups of young Swedes. Lalander analyses hedonistic drinking as a 'breaking away' activity in which young people experience a sense of freedom and detachment from different kind of demands in their everyday lives. Heavy drinking is described as 'hitting the pause key' and drunkenness is comprehended as a collective replacement of the 'paramount reality' with another reality (Lalander, 1997, p. 35). For the youths interviewed by Lalander, hedonistic drinking is not only a way to demonstrate that they are entering adulthood but also a way of protesting against adulthood, and all the restrictions and conventions associated with it. Heavy drinking among youths is only meaningful as long at it is a social activity, according to Lalander's informants. Drunkenness is a 'collective cocoon' that transforms the individual into something bigger than him/herself and gives the participant the feeling of being 'where the action is' (Lalander, 1998, p. 139 *ff*).

Though there thus seem to be continuing north-south differences in the meaning and acceptability of intoxication to young drinkers in Europe, the generational change towards an acceptance of intoxication may nevertheless be greater in the south. Among the student informants in Pyörälä's study (1995), the Spanish but not the Finns reported a generational gap, with the older generation less accepting of drinking to intoxication. Indeed, Room (2004) has noted, 'there is much that has changed in the environment of young people in southern Europe in the last half-century which might have lent itself to cultural change. The societies are less authoritarian, marriage and family formation occur later, and there is more money in young people's pockets'. Increasingly, young people in different societies are tied together as a single audience for media and music, and for the promotions of the alcoholic beverage multinationals. On the other hand, the specific practices around youth drinking parties in northern Italy described by Beccaria and Guidoni (2002), for instance, suggest considerable cultural continuity. 'Features of the parties such as traditional drinking games suggest that the parties do not constitute a new cultural innovation' (Room, 2004).

From Problem Behaviour to Risk Management

The 'new culture of intoxication' among young people may be related to another development in recent decades. As demonstrated in different areas of sociology, the late twentieth century brought about a change in the conceptions of risk and how risk should be managed. Today, risk is increasingly comprehended as an integrated part of everyday life, and a part that people should learn to calculate and handle. While earlier the categories of dangerous vs. safe; proper vs. improper behaviour were more clearly defined, and, especially for children and teenagers not up to negotiation, today the picture is more complicated. According to Beck (1992, p. 135), the spheres of life which are 'fundamentally closed to decision-making' are decreasing while the spheres which are 'open and must be constructed personally' are increasing. Simultaneously the sphere of consumption has become more central and is often presented as playing a crucial role in the individual's identity development. A consumerist ethic based on hedonism and gratification has become part of people's way of 'realizing themselves'. Consumption risks are embedded in these individual projects and contribute to the constitution of the individual as calculative and autonomous (cf. Reith, 2004). In late modern society, the locus of control has moved from factors outside the individual (society, tradition, different authorities) to factors inside the individual. This goes for drinking as well as experimenting with illegal drugs – which the term 'recreational' drug use is a clear indication of. Drug use is no longer condemned once and for all. In research as well as public opinion the door has been opened for a more reflexive comprehension of drugs, where the critical line is no longer drawn between use and no-use but between 'controlled' use and 'uncontrolled' use.

In this development towards 'reflexive risk management' young people, and especially teenagers, are seen as both capable and incapable of control, both responsible and (potentially) irresponsible. On the one hand, teenagers are expected to develop their own individual relationship to different types of potentially risky behaviour, for instance alcohol use, handling the risk factors communicated by teachers, parents, etc. rationally and responsibly. On the other hand, young people are not comprehended as fully capable of managing these risks. In the formulation of Kelly (2001, p. 30) 'youth is principally about becoming'; becoming independent, becoming mature, becoming capable of self-control: 'youth, as it is constructed in at-risk discourses, is at-risk of jeopardising, through present behaviours and dispositions, desired futures'. Hence young people's drinking is surrounded by considerable ambivalence and a constant oscillation between risk accentuation and (in many European countries) risk neutralisation. Drinking is thought to have potential negative consequences, yet it is regarded as normal for teenagers to experiment with alcohol. Adolescents are taught that alcohol is dangerous and that it may get the upper hand of the drinker, yet they grow up in alcohol cultures that are more or less 'risk-immune', treating alcohol as a commodity among other commodities.

It is possible, although we do not have direct research evidence of this, that the differences in teenage drinking between European countries partly reflect differences in the conceptions of youth and risk management. Could it be that the countries (in northern and north-western Europe) in which teenagers start to drink heavily at a very early age are also the countries where reflexive – and individualised – risk management is most strongly idealised? Could it be that grown-ups (parents, teachers, other grown-ups in the teenagers' surroundings) in these countries are reluctant to control young people's drinking because they regard control as interference in the development of the teenagers' ability to self management?

Research on other aspects (than alcohol and risk-taking) of parental attitudes lends some support to these suggestions. Juul (2003) compared upbringing ideals among parents from five European countries: Denmark, Italy, Romania, Sweden and the UK. Using survey data from the European Value Study, he showed that Danes (80 per cent) and Swedes (69 per cent) mentioned 'autonomy' as a 'personal quality they want to encourage in their children' more often than respondents in Romania (28 per cent) and Italy (38 per cent), while the respondents from the UK (53 per cent) occupied a medium position. The respondents were also asked to take a stand on the statements 'Children should always honour and love their parents' vs. 'Children do not have to honour and respect their parents, if the parents do not deserve this'. While the majority of Romanian (84 per cent) and Italian (79 per cent) respondents tended to see children's respect and love for their parents as a matter of course, the corresponding numbers in Scandinavia were smaller (Denmark 39 per cent, Sweden 44 per cent). Scandinavian respondents on the other hand were more often of the opinion that parents have to 'earn' their children's respect (Denmark 61 per cent, Sweden 56 per cent) than were Romanian and Italian respondents (16 and 21 per cent respectively). Again British respondents held positions in between the Scandinavians and southern Europeans. A third kind of statement with relevance for the question of individualisation and family values concerned the parents' self-interest vs. identification with their children's interests. The statement the respondents were asked to take a stand on was: 'Parents have their own lives and shouldn't be expected to sacrifice their own well-being for the sake of their children'. Measured this way Italians and Romanians were less in favour of individualisation in the family than were Danes, Swedes and Britons. While 10–11 per cent of the respondents in the two southern

European countries agreed with the statement, the corresponding numbers in Denmark, Sweden and the UK were 32, 22 and 17 per cent respectively (Juul, 2003).

It is not clear, however, what this kind of differences in upbringing ideals and family orientation means for alcohol socialisation. What scattered evidence there is for country differences in alcohol socialisation and for an association between drinking and upbringing ideals comes from the ESPAD-study and from some national studies. Ledoux et al. (2002) compared ESPAD-samples of 15–16 year olds from the UK and France on the association between alcohol and drug usage and family variables, demonstrating some differences of interest for the present discussion. First, the UK teenagers of both genders were far more likely than French teenagers to have consumed alcohol six or more times in the last 30 days, to have had five or more drinks in a row and to have been intoxicated three or more times in the past year. Second, in both countries 'parental awareness', that is parental monitoring of their children's whereabouts on Saturday nights was one of the variables showing the strongest association with the teenagers' use of alcohol, tobacco and illicit drugs. Third, the analysis showed that French parents were significantly more likely than UK parents to know where their children were at Saturday night – a result indicating that national differences in parental monitoring and intervention may indeed be *part* of the explanation of the huge variation in teenage alcohol use and drunkenness across Europe.

Another example indicating that the national level of teenage drinking may be related to parenting styles and socialisation ideals comes from Denmark. In a study combining survey data and focus group interviews, Järvinen and Østergaard (2006) show that Danish parents put very strong emphasis on their teenage children's right to independence and self-determination in relation to drinking. Hence, about half of the parents in the survey were of the opinion that teenagers should be allowed to 'learn how to drink' in the company of their peers, that is outside of the control sphere of parents and other grown ups, and just as many stated that it is 'necessary for young people to transcend limits before they learn how to drink'. In the focus group discussions Danish parents were very sceptical in relation to direct control of teenagers' drinking. A common conception was that external control and monitoring is a hindrance for the teenagers' development of self-control, and that parental rules do not limit teenagers' drinking but on the contrary make them drink more. These conceptions among Danish parents were in direct conflict with the results from the regression analyses in the study, showing that – contrary to the parents' impression – alcohol rules *do* reduce teenagers' drinking. According to these data, the more lenient parents were in relation to their children's drinking and partying (home coming hours and the amount of alcohol the children were allowed to drink), and the more they pronounced teenagers' self-control, the more their children tended to binge drink (Järvinen and Østergaard, 2006).

The Contents of this Volume

As stated in the introduction, the aim of this book is to analyse the varying drinking cultures among European teenagers. The point of departure for the chapters that follow is that teenage drinking – 'heavy' Nordic or Anglo-Saxon drinking as well as the more moderate Mediterranean drinking patterns – cannot be understood independently of adult drinking cultures and traditions. To a very significant degree adolescents' drinking patterns in northern and north-western Europe reflect the traditional 'intoxication cultures' of their forefathers, although the 'psychoactive revolution' of the 1990s seems to have made the drunken component even more distinct. The 'new culture of intoxication' therefore is not entirely new. It is new in the sense that young people obviously have increased their intake of alcohol – and other drugs – and in the sense that girls in many European countries have started to join the boys in heavy drinking. It is old, however, in the sense that the alcohol cultures of northern Europe have always been accused of 'excesses', of 'drinking for the sake of getting drunk' and people 'going berserk' after consuming alcohol (cf. notes made my European travellers quoted earlier in this chapter). In this sense the geographical differences registered in ESPAD, HBSC and other studies is simply a repetition of age-old patterns of cultural symbolism and practices.

The plan of this book looks as follows: in Chapter 2 Robin Room continues the reflections on different drinking cultures in Europe and on the relationship between young people's alcohol usage and the geographic pattern of adult drinking. Room describes the cultural matrix of European drinking, testing some hypotheses about differences in drinking between southern wine cultures, Central European beer countries and northern 'spirits' cultures. The chapter also underlines that drinking has a variety of functions for teenagers, associated with the general tasks of youth and young adulthood and applying to a greater or lesser extent across all societies.

In Chapter 3 Barbro Andersson and Björn Hibell analyse drunken behaviour and consequences of drinking in different European countries as related to young people's expectancies to alcohol. Based on ESPAD-data from 2003 this chapter shows some very marked geographical differences in alcohol expectancies – positive as well as negative – and a strong association between high positive expectations, heavy drinking and high prevalence of negative consequences. Also included in the chapter is an analysis comparing country data for Sweden and Greece.

In Chapter 4 Salme Ahlström uses ESPAD-data to analyse gender differences in youth drinking cultures. While drinking and especially heavy drinking has traditionally been a masculine activity, youth drinking cultures today differ in the extent to which girls have taken up on drinking. While in some countries – and for some drinking variables and some alcohol beverages – girls are almost equal with boys, in other countries girls' drinking still seems to be regulated by strictly gender-specific norms.

Chapter 5, by Matthias Richter et al. is based on the other cross-national study mentioned above, HBSC. The aim of this chapter is to analyse the relationship between socioeconomic background variables (parents' occupation and family affluence) and teenagers' drinking. In much public health research, people with lower socio-economic status have been found to engage in more health-damaging behaviour and to suffer from more illness. In the field of alcohol research, however, the evidence about such a relationship is inconsistent and even contradictory. Richter et al.s' study is the first to examine this association between socioeconomic background, drinking and drunkenness in a wide range of countries using directly comparable measurements.

In Chapter 6 Rutger Engels et al. analyse young people's drinking in relation to peer and parental influences. Parental alcohol behaviours and rules concerning their children's drinking have long been identified as some of the most important factors behind adolescent drinking. Also peer influence is one of the 'classics' when it comes to explaining heavy teenage alcohol consumption. Using Dutch longitudinal data Engels et al. presents a thorough analysis of the association between parents' behaviour, teenage drinking and friendship selection processes, offering new and intriguing insights into these complex relationships.

Chapters 7 and 8 both analyse the drinking and substance use patterns of young Britons. Howard Parker's chapter relies on data from two longitudinal British studies and a large-scale night club study. Rather than focusing on the quantitative nature of England's heavy youth drinking, Parker takes this consumption reality as a fact, and focusses on understanding the dynamics of young heavy drinkers' life styles and their motives for drinking. The chapter of Martin Plant and Patrick Miller in turn is concerned with the question of how to tackle heavy teenage drinking. With the help of ESPAD-data, Plant and Miller address the question of alcohol socialisation in the family. Does British teenagers whose parents have 'taught' them to drink, develop more sensible and moderate drinking habits than other teenagers?

In Chapter 9, Kirsten Verkooijen et al. analyse alcohol use among young people in Denmark from the point of view of their 'self-identity' and 'social identity'. Building on longitudinal Danish data, Verkoojen et al., test the predictor value of teenagers' self-identification with heavy drinking and with different sub-cultural or life style groups. The identity approach offered in the chapter is not only a new way of explaining variations in drinking; it may also represent a fruitful strategy in the prevention of excessive drinking. If heavy alcohol consumption is associated with certain subcultures, health promotion activities could be tailored according to the profiles of these life style groups.

In Chapter 10, finally, the main findings of the books are discussed together with the question of how excessive drinking among young people may be prevented.

References

Ahlström, S. et al. (2001), 'Ungdomars Bruk av Rusmedel i Europa 1995 och 1999' ('Young People's Substance Use in Europe 1995 and 1999'), *Nordisk Alkohol- och Narkotikatidskrift*, **18**, 283–295. [PubMed 16669897,10723844]

Austin, G.A. (1985), Alcohol in Western Society from Antiquity to 1800: A Chronological History (Santa Barbara, CA: ABC-Clio Information Services).

Baigorri, A. et al. (2004), *Botellón: un Conflicto postmoderno*. (*Botellón: a Postmodern Conflict*) (Barcelona: Icaria Editorial). Excerpts at: http://www.unex.es/sociolog/botellon_extractos.pdf.

Beccaria, F. and Guidoni, O.V. (2002), 'Young People in a Wet Culture: Functions and Patterns of Drinking', *Contemporary Drug Problems*, **29**(2), 305–334.

Beccaria, F. and Sande, A. (2003), 'Drinking Games and Rite of Life Projects', *Young: Nordic Journal of Youth Research*, **11**(2), 99–119.

Beck, U. (1992), *Risk Society. Towards a New Modernity* (London: Sage).

Coleman, L. and Cater, S. (2005), 'Underage "Binge" Drinking: A Qualitative Study into Motivation and Outcomes', *Drugs: Education, Prevention and Policy*, **12**(2), 125–136.

Courtwright, D.T. (2001), *Forces of Habit: Drugs and the Making of the Modern World* (Cambridge: Harvard University Press).

Csikszentmihalyi, M. (1968), 'A Cross-Cultural Comparison of some Structural Characteristics of Group Drinking', *Human Development*, **11**, 201–216. [PubMed 5663538].

Demant, J. and Järvinen, M. (2006), 'Constructing Maturity through Alcohol Experience, Focus Group Interviews with Teenagers', *Addiction Research and Theory*, **14**(6), 589–602.

Department of Health (2005), *Drug Use, Smoking and Drinking among Young People in England 2005* (London: NHS Health and Social Care Information Centre). http://www.ic.nhs.uk/pubs/drugsmokedrinkyoungeng2005/finalreport.pdf/file.

Freyssinet-Dominjon, J. and Wagner, A.-C. (2003), *L'Alcool en Fête: Manières de Boire de la Nouvelle Jeunesse Étudiante*. (*Alcohol in Partying: Styles of Drinking of the New Student Youth*) (Paris: L'Harmattan).

Gabhainn, S.N. and François, Y. (2000), 'Substance Use' in *Health and Health Behaviour among Young People*. Currie, C. et al. (eds) (Copenhagen: WHO, European Office), 97–114.

Gundelach, P. and Järvinen, M. (eds) (2006), *Unge, fester og alkohol* (Youth, Parties and Alcohol) (Copenhagen: Akademisk Forlag).

Hibell, B. et al. (2004), *The 2003 ESPAD Report: Alcohol and other Drug Use among Students in 35 European Countries* (Stockholm: Swedish Council for Information on Alcohol and Other Drugs).

Jaatinen, J. (2000), *Viattomuuden tarinoita. Nuoret päihdekulttuurin kuvaajina (Stories of Innocence. Young People's Reflections on the Drinking Culture)*, *Raportti 251* (Helsinki: Stakes).

Järvinen, M. and Østergaard, J. (2006), 'Forældreregler og unges alkoholforbrug' ('Parents' Rules and Young People's Drinking') in *Unge, fester og alkohol (Youth, Parties and Alcohol)*. Gundelach, P. and Järvinen, M. (eds) (Copenhagen: Akademisk Förlag), 126–150.

Johnston, L.D. et al. (2002), *Monitoring the Future: National Survey Results on Drug Use, 1975–2001* (Bethesda, MD: National Institutes on Drug Abuse).

Juul, S. (2003), 'Solidaritet' ('Solidarity') in *Danskernes særpræg. (Characterising Danes)*. Gundelach, P. (ed.) (Copenhagen: Hans Reitzels Forlag), 145–169.

Keeley, G. and Bagenal, F. (2006), 'Young Spaniards Turn to "big bottle" Binge Drinking', *Sunday Times* (London), 1 Jan. http://www.timesonline.co.uk/article/0,,2089-1965183,00.html.

Kelly, P. (2001), 'Youth at Risk: Processes of Individualisation and Responsibilisation in the Risk Society', *Discourse: Studies in the Cultural Politics of Education*, **22**(1), 23–33.

Kuntsche, E. et al. (2004), 'Characteristics of Binge Drinkers in Europe', *Social Science and Medicine*, **59**, 113–127. [PubMed 15087148] [DOI: 10.1016/j.socscimed.2003.10.009]

Lalander, P. (1997), 'Beyond Everyday Order; Breaking Away with Alcohol', *Nordisk Alkohol- och Narkotikatidskrift*, **14**, 33–42. [PubMed 16669897,10723844]

Lalander, P. (1998), *Anden i flaskan. Alkoholens betydelser i olika ungdomsgrupper (The Spirit in the Bottle. The Meaning of Alcohol in Different Youth Groups)* (Stockholm: Brutus Östlings Bokförlag Symposion).

Ledoux, S. et al. (2002), 'Family Structure, Parent-Child Relationships, Alcohol and other Drug Use among Teenagers in France and the United Kingdom', *Alcohol and Alcoholism*, **37**, 52–60. [PubMed 11825858] [DOI: 10.1093/alcalc%2F37.1.52]

Leifman, H. (2001), 'Homogenization in Alcohol Consumption in the European Union', *Nordisk Alkophol- & Narkotikatidskrift*, **18**(English Suppl.), 15–30.

MacManus, M.J. (1939), *Irish Cavalcade: 1550-1850* (London: Macmillan).

Measham, F. (2004), 'The Decline of Ecstasy, the Rise of "Binge" Drinking and the Persistence of Pleasure', *Journal of Community and Criminal Justice*, **51**(4), 309–326.

Measham, F. and Brain, K. (2005), '"Binge" Drinking, British Alcohol Policy and the New Culture of Intoxication', *Crime, Media, Culture*, **3**(1), 262–283. [DOI: 10.1177/1741659005057641]

Morgan, M. et al. (1999), 'The ESPAD-Study: Implications for Prevention', *Drugs: Education, Prevention and Policy*, **6**(2), 243–256. [DOI: 10.1080/09687639997205]

Olsson, B. (1990), 'Alkoholpolitik och alkoholens fenomenologi: Uppfattningar som artikulerats i pressen' ('Alcohol Policy and the Phenomenology of Alcohol: Opinions Expressed in the Press'), *Alkoholpolitik*, **7**, 184–194.

Parker, H. et al. (1998), *Illegal Leisure. The Normalization of Adolescent Recreational Drug Use* (London: Routledge).

Parker, S. (2003), 'Drink and Be Merry', *Guardian* (London) 8 April. http://society.guardian.co.uk/drugsandalcohol/story/0,,931739,00.html.

Pyorälä, E. (1995), 'Comparing Drinking Cultures: Finnish and Spanish Drinking Stories in Interviews with Young Adults', *Acta Sociologica*, **38**(3), 217–229. [DOI: 10.1177/000169939503800301]

Rehm, J. et al. (2001), 'Average Volume of Alcohol Consumption, Drinking Patterns and Related Burden of Mortality in Young People in Established Market Economies of Europe', *European Addiction Research*, **7**, 148–151. [PubMed 11509845] [DOI: 10.1159/000050732]

Rehm, J. et al. (2004), 'Alcohol Use' in *Comparative Quantification of Health Risks. Global and Regional Burden of Disease Attributable to Selected Major Risk Factors, Volume 1.* Ezzati, M. et al. (eds.) (Geneva: World Health Organization), 959–1108.

Reith, G. (2004), 'Consumption and its Discontents: Addiction, Identity and the Problem of Freedom', *The British Journal of Sociology*, **55**(2), 283–300. [PubMed 15233634] [DOI: 10.1111/j.1468-4446.2004.00019.x]

Rimpelä, A. et al. (2003), *Nuorten terveystapatutkimus 2003: Tupakkatuotteiden ja päihteiden käytön nuutokset 1977–2003* (A Study of Young People's Health 2003: Changes in Substance Use 1977–2003). (Helsinki: Stakes).

Room, R. (2004), 'Drinking and Coming of Age in a Cross-Cultural Perspective' in *Reducing Underage Drinking: A Collective Responsibility.* Bonnie, R.J. and O'Connor, M.E. (eds) (Washington, DC: National Academy Press), 654–677.

Rosberg, J.E. (1931), *Nordiskt kynne. Jämförande karakteristiker* (Nordic Disposition. Comparative Characterisations). (Helsingfors: Söderström and Co.).

Rowe, J.E. and Gomez, R. (2003), 'El Botellón: Modeling the Movement of Crowds in a City', *Complex Systems*, **14**, 363–370.

Schmid, H. and Gabhainn, S.N. (2004), 'Alcohol Use' in *Young People's Health in Context*. Currie, C. et al. (eds); HBSC-study: International Report from the 2001/2002 Survey. (Copenhagen: WHO), 73–83.

Settertobulte, W. et al. (2001), *Drinking among Young Europeans* (Copenhagen: WHO).

Tremlett, G. (2002), 'Mayor Starts Party Purge of Night-Time Madness in Madrid', *The Guardian* (London) February 9. http://www.guardian.co.uk/international/story/0,,647436,00.html. [PubMed 12391388,12084903].

Ullman, A.D. (1958), 'Sociocultural Backgrounds of Alcoholism', *Annals of the American Academy of Political and Social Science*, **315**, 48–54. [DOI: 10.1177/000271625831500107].

Chapter 2

Understanding Cultural Differences in Young People's Drinking[1]

Robin Room

Introduction

This chapter is concerned with cultural differences in Europe in drinking, and particularly drinking to intoxication, during adolescence and young adulthood, roughly defined in terms of ages 13–25. A drinker's first experience of alcohol intoxication normally falls within this age period, and in many societies it also roughly corresponds to the age group in which drinking to intoxication is most common, even if the total volume of drinking is often greater at older ages. Thus, for instance, in the ECAS surveys (European Comparative Alcohol Study, Leifman, 2002; Ramstedt and Hope, 2002) drinking at least the equivalent of a bottle of wine on an occasion was more common in the age group 18–29 than among older respondents among men in Finland, Sweden, Germany, the UK, Ireland and France, and among women in the first five of these countries. Only in Italy were such occasions more frequent for an older group (those aged 50–64 among both men and women).

The Common Tasks of Adolescence and Young Adulthood

The period of 'coming of age' is also a period for experimentation and establishing patterns in many other behaviours, expected by older people as well as adolescents themselves to be initiated sometime in the teenage years and early 20s (Paglia and Room, 1998; Room, 2004). Young people are expected to emancipate themselves from their family of origin, and to move towards defining themselves in terms of three major aspects of everyday life: in terms of their work or professional life, in terms of their affectional life and forming partnerships, and in terms of sociability and friendships. In each of these arenas, there is often a generational tug-of-war over the timing of onset of the behaviour, interpreted by all parties in terms of claims to adult status (Room, 2004).

---

1 Prepared for presentation at the conference 'Wet youth cultures', Copenhagen, 29–30 August 2005. Thanks to Sharon Rödner and Kalle Tryggvesson for their helpful comments.

In each of these tasks of adolescence and young adulthood, there is an element of differentiation – not only with respect to their family of origin, but also with respect to other young people. Processes such as schooling during this period may be seen as a society-wide sorting process, where youth are judged against each other as well as in terms of general standards in a fateful process of social differentiation. For many, this is the period of one's life when one is most subject to evaluation and judgement by others – both by older people in charge of the sorting process, and by same-age peers. Few indeed are those who make it through this life period without experiencing humiliation or rejection in some aspect of their lives – whether by a school admissions committee, by a high-status peer group, or by a potential soul mate or lover.

Forming close friendships and adhering to subcultures or social scenes are also characteristic of this stage of life. Most young people learn to share feelings and experiences and get affirmation and solidarity from friendships, cliques and peer groups, defined by common interests, tastes or activities. Courtship – flirting, dating and sexual relationships – also becomes a potential source of identification and affirmation.

Differentiation and attachment are tasks for the individual, but they are also processes at the collective level. The two processes are often linked. A playground clique or followers of a music style are defined as much by their contrast with other cliques or styles as by what the members have in common, and those seeking to join a clique or subculture are often expected to make an exclusive choice. At the individual level, the clique or scene or subculture often becomes part of a young person's identity, but the identity is formed in part in contrast to other alternative identities.

Differentiation and solidarity are to a considerable extent expressed publicly and often theatrically, in front of a double audience: on the one hand those in the solidarity group, and on the other hand 'outsiders'. A variety of behavioural routines and props, including those involving alcohol and drinking, are brought to bear in the performance (Room, 2005).

A specific form of differentiation and attachment is in terms of particular historical age-cohorts. At graduation from high school or with respect to military training, for instance, the cohort is often defined around the specific year of graduation or training. Here the points of reference are the year-groups before and after the cohort. A broader age-cohort may become defined in generational terms, implicitly with reference to a generation a few years older or the generation of their parents. Again, the differentiations from the comparison cohort are at least as important in affiliation and identity formation as the sense of community of the cohort.

Drinking and Intoxication and Young People's Identifications and Identities

Since there are minimum age limits on drinking in most countries, even if they are not rigorously enforced, drinking in itself, particularly when away from parents or adult guardians, is a claim on adult status. A Canadian study found that, apart from the legal limit, both teenagers and adults were willing to specify ages at which having a drink and for that matter getting drunk was OK. Younger teenagers and adults agreed in setting the age a little higher, with those around age 16 setting the lowest age, which was in fact their age (Room and Paglia, 2001). Despite this normative agreement, Canadian teenagers actually began drinking three or four years younger than even the 16-year-olds specified, although the age at which they started getting drunk was closer to the normative age for drinking. In the early stages of initiating drinking, then, Canadian teenagers were staking a claim to maturity which was premature by even their own account.[2]

While there is data from ESPAD (European School Survey Project on Alcohol and Other Drugs) and other studies on age of initiating drinking, no cross-national or European data seem to be available on the normative 'social clock' for drinking and intoxication. A cross-national study of this would be an interesting and fruitful initiative.

Drinking enough to feel psychoactive effects, or drinking more than this, has a variety of functions in relation to the life and what are called here the common tasks of young people. Pharmacologically, alcohol is a depressant, and – at various levels of consumption – can be used as a mood-changer, an anodyne, or as a means to temporary oblivion – the 'quickest way out of Manchester', in a British phrase from the industrial era. Socially, in most European societies, drinking together is an expression of sociability and commensality, and often of *communitas*, to use Victor Turner's (1969) term. Conversely, leaving someone out of a drinking group is often a strong expression of differentiation. Drinking with or in front of someone, and getting drunk with or in front of someone, are highly symbolic behaviours which are often important ways of performing and expressing distinction or community (Room, 1994, 2005).

Besides its other symbolic content, intoxication is also widely viewed in terms of disinhibition: that it explains and may justify behaviour which otherwise would be out of bounds. Drawing on the anthropological literature, MacAndrew and Edgerton (1969) have emphasised the extent of cultural differences in the disinhibitory effects attributed to drinking and intoxication. As we shall discuss, it is unclear, however, how much (and in which direction) European cultures vary in the disinhibitory powers they attribute to alcohol. In the ECAS survey, adult respondents in Italy, France and Germany were actually more likely than respondents in the UK, Sweden and Finland to agree that 'anyone might become violent after drinking too much' (Room and Bullock, 2002).

There are three primary fields of disinhibition with respect to young people and intoxication. One of them, drinking-driving, is usually thought of in terms

---

2   Among adults aged 25 or older (these data were not available for teenagers), the mean ages at which it was OK to 'get drunk on beer at home' (19.4) or 'go to bar with friends and drinking enough to feel the effects' (19.8) were only one-half to one year older than the age when it was OK 'to have a drink of beer' (18.8). For these items, and also for having 'a drink of liquor' (19.3) and buying a six-pack of beer (19.5), the mean age when it was OK for a female was significantly but slightly less than the mean age when it was OK for a male (Paglia and Room, 1998).

of the motor impairment from intoxication which means that a drinking driver is more likely to crash. But disinhibition is also to a greater or lesser extent involved in the offence (Assailly, 2004), since drinking beyond a fixed blood-alcohol level (below frank intoxication) and driving is illegal and well known to be illegal everywhere in Europe.

The second major field of disinhibition related to intoxication is sexuality. A variety of studies suggest that intoxication is a very common accompaniment to sexual play and intercourse among young people, and particularly for a pair's first sexual coupling (Bullock and Room, 2006). For instance, here are 13- and 14-year-old girls in New Zealand describing how intoxication makes it possible to cross the threshold at every stage of intimacy:

> [Informant 1:] It's a lot easier to talk to people like when you're drunk ... just walk up to people, anyone and just say, 'Hi, how are you?' Just go up to them and tell them that you like them 'cause you don't even care what you say to them when you're drunk ....
> [Interviewer:] Tell me about ... when you just meet a guy at a party, and ... sleep with them.
> [Informant 2:] You're just like pissed [drunk] and stuff and like getting with them and ... then, I don't know, it just ... leads into it ....
> [Interviewer:] You just do it 'cause why?
> [Informant 3:] 'Cause, I don't know, I'm drunk (Abel and Plumridge, 2004).

The third major field of disinhibition is violence – including individual fighting and aggression, sexual violence, and collective violence. The recent strengthening of the literature on the role of alcohol in violence (Room and Rossow, 2001) and sexual violence (Leonard, 2001) has underlined the role of intoxication in all the roles – perpetrators, victims, and bystanders – in violent episodes. Frequently, the violence occurs in an environment where all concerned are intoxicated. The lability of the intoxicated occasion and excuse-value of the intoxication means that violence is more likely to occur even within the solidarity drinking occasion (Tryggvesson, 2004). With respect to those outside the solidarity group, there are long historical traditions of intoxication as a prelude, accompaniment and aid (up to a point) in collective violence (for example Haavio-Mannila, 1958; Hunt and Laidler, 2001).

In terms of differentiation and solidarity within the social life of youth, intoxication plays a complicated series of roles. As we have already seen in the specific context of sexuality, intoxication tends to allow people to feel and be closer to each other. This applies also more broadly in terms of bonding and solidarity feelings within a social group, for instance a group of football fans (Estrada and Tryggvesson, 2001). As just noted concerning collective violence, intoxication is also often involved in episodes where boundaries are drawn and dramatised between the group and outsiders.

A generational commitment to drinking and intoxication can play a substantial role in the self-definition of a particular historical cohort in comparison with a preceding cohort or to the parental generation. In some societies, it is particularly in reaction to the great social movements around temperance and prohibition that drinking and intoxication became generational markers, just as a commitment to abstinence may have marked the previous youth generation (Warner, 1970). Thus, Sulkunen (1979) described the post-war generation in Finland as a 'wet generation', and the term has been used also to describe the US generation of the 1930s, reacting against the cultural-political hegemony of US prohibition (Room, 1984).

If one searches today for a cultural political boundary in Europe between abstinence and intoxication, it is Muslim minorities who have taken on the role of a group defining itself in part in terms of abstinence (Pape and Rossow, 2000). In the opposite direction, a recent study of tertiary students in Paris (Freyssinet-Dominjon and Wagner, 2003) found that students defined themselves self-consciously as 'VSD' (Vendredi, Samedi, Dimanche [Friday, Saturday and Sunday]) drinkers, enjoying weekend drinking to the point of 'gaiety' or intoxication, and differentiated themselves sharply from what has usually been regarded as the archetypal French drinking pattern – drinking daily and drinking red wine – regarding both of these as signs of alcoholism, not to mention as being the patterns of their parents. Recent studies at both ends of Europe have also focused on festivals of intoxication as solidarity celebrations of each year-cohort – in the conscription festivals of Piedmont (Beccaria and Guidoni, 2002) and the *russefeiring* marking the end of high school in Norway (Sande, 2002).

The Cultural Matrix: Drinking Cultures in Europe

So far, we have considered drinking and intoxication in the context of the general tasks and characteristics of adolescence and young adulthood, applying to a greater or lesser extent across all societies. Young people's drinking and associated behaviours occur, however, in the context of specific cultural norms and practices concerning drinking. Let us start by considering the literature on variations in the general cultural position of drinking, before considering the relationship between general drinking cultures and youth cultures.

There are wide divergences in drinking norms and practices from place to place in Europe, both between and within countries, reflecting the physical circumstances, the particular historical experiences, and often deep-rooted cultural traits. However, the literature on typologies of the cultural position of drinking (Room and Mäkelä, 2000) has mostly operated at a much broader level, in terms of two or three categories or dimensions. Ahlström-Laakso (1976) contrasted southern and northern Europe on the dimension of integration of drinking with meals (implying relatively frequent drinking), common in southern Europe but not in northern, and in terms of an emphasis on intoxication, with stronger traditions in northern Europe of ostensive drunkenness and its control by formal criminal law. A related contrast has been in terms of 'wetter' vs. 'dryer' cultures (Room, 1989). Apart from the contrast between southern and northern Europe, a similar distinction has been applied in more local circumstances, for instance in Christie's contrast of wetter Denmark with the rest of the Nordic countries (Christie, 1965).

A more programmatic version of much the same contrast has been the American tradition known as the 'sociocultural approach', which contrasts a putatively 'unintegrated' culture of drinking in North America with the 'integrated drinking' to be found, among other places, in southern European wine cultures (Room and Mäkelä, 2000). In its current manifestations, this tradition focusses its critique on the relatively high legal drinking-age in the US, arguing that alcohol problems would diminish if drinking were integrated into family life, with children learning to drink at the family dinner-table as is presented as customary in southern Europe (Room, 2004). A Nordic version of this line of argument presents 'continental drinking' as the ideal to be striven for in what Olsson (1990) describes as Swedish 'dreams of a better society'.

Another common typology, particularly in the European context, has distinguished between 'wine', 'beer' and 'spirits' cultures, in terms of the society's dominant form of alcoholic beverage (for example Sulkunen, 1976). Implicitly, analyses in this frame have often regarded the beer cultures as intermediate between the wine cultures of southern Europe and the spirits cultures of northern and eastern Europe, in terms of the historical social disruption around heavy drinking, the strength of temperance movements in response to the disruption, and the continuing domination of intoxicated drinking among drinking occasions. Since in recent decades beer has become the dominant beverage in all of the Nordic countries, analyses in this tradition have adopted the label 'former spirits-drinking' to describe the Nordic countries north of the Baltic (Leifman, 2001).

A three-category classification of western Europe in terms of 'low', 'medium' and 'high' consumption countries, corresponding to the division into southern wine, central beer and northern former spirits-drinking countries, was used in the mortality analyses of the earlier mentioned ECAS-study (Norström et al., 2001, p. 169). For many of the causes of mortality, there was a north-south gradient, with a greater change in mortality per extra litre of alcohol consumed in the north. In the case of homicide, where the gradient was particularly steep, this raised the issue of the explanatory power of differences in drinking patterns and behaviour. Leifman's (2002) analysis of the ECAS six-country survey, already mentioned, did indeed find that a considerably greater proportion of drinking in Italy and France was in non-heavy drinking occasions, but that the two countries from the 'central' category were split, with Germany close to the southern Europe pattern, but Britain to the northern Europe pattern. The absolute frequency of heavy drinking occasions, however, did not show a clear north-south gradient.

These findings pointed to the salience in a European context of the question already posed in general terms by MacAndrew and Edgerton (1969): is the north-south differential in the effect of changed consumption on homicide rates at least partly attributable to cultural differences in behaviour at a given level of drinking? This was tested in the six-country survey at the level of expectancies and attributions about intoxicated behaviour (Room and Bullock, 2002). However, the results did not generally follow predictions in terms of hypotheses of greater expectation and tolerance of aggression while drunk and of intoxication as an excuse in the north. An earlier cross-cultural study of university students' expectancies of aggression 'after many drinks' (Lindman and Lang, 1994) also did not find a clear north-south gradient.

Some analyses of European variation in drinking have drawn in more general social and historical factors in analysing contrasts. Levine (1992) saw Protestantism as an important precondition of what he termed 'temperance cultures', displaying a great concern about alcohol problems, in contrast to Catholic Europe. However, Zieliński (1994) pointed to the existence of a substantial temperance history in Catholic Poland, besides the contestable case of Ireland.

The most consistent finding across cultures about patterns of drinking is that in all cultures the men drink more than the women (Marshall, 1979). A general expectation in the literature is that the difference in drinking between the genders will be greater in cultures with more gender inequality. By conventional measures of general gender inequality, the Nordic countries show the greatest equality among European countries, and southern European countries the least. The conventional expectation, then, is that gender ratios (male rate/female rate) for drinking indicators would be higher in southern Europe and lower in the Nordic countries. However, computing such ratios for the ECAS six-country survey (Leifman, 2002, p. 536), there is no evidence of such trends. Gender ratios for number of drinking occasions in the last year varied only between 1.5 and 2.0, with Finland and France showing the highest ratio, and Sweden and Italy the lowest. Gender ratios for number of heavy drinking occasions (at least a bottle of wine or equivalent) in the last year varied between 1.2 and 2.0, with Italy showing the lowest ratio and Sweden, Germany and the UK all at or near the top. The gender ratios are substantially lower than the four – to five-fold ratios between the top and bottom country in numbers of drinking occasions and of heavy drinking occasions.

There has also been considerable analysis of trends in drinking in Europe. A consistent theme in the three decades since Sulkunen's initial analysis (1976) has been on the convergence in European drinking, characterised in particular in terms of the addition of new types of alcoholic beverages to a culture's traditional main beverage. Karlsson and Simpura (2001) found that general structural changes in society had rather limited explanatory power in explaining trends in drinking in western Europe. Particular attention has been given to trying to explain the historic decline in alcohol consumption levels in the wine cultures of southern Europe (Gual and Colom, 1997; Simpura, 1998). Focusing on the specific case of France, Sulkunen (1989) emphasised both structural factors such as migration to the cities from the heavier-drinking countryside, and the expression of social differentiations within the society in terms of changing fashions in beverage preferences and drinking styles.

General Drinking Cultures and Youth Drinking Cultures

There has been only limited discussion in the literature of the relation between the culture of drinking among youth in a particular society and the society's general drinking culture. The American literature attacking a high minimum drinking age (Room, 2004) on the grounds that it means that youth drinking is initiated and carried on furtively and oppositionally raises the issue of the relationship, but with little in the way of explicit cross-cultural analysis.

The assumption in much of the literature is that a youth drinking culture expresses the general drinking culture. While the assumption is often unspoken, in some analyses the connection is made explicit. Thus, an analysis of 1998 data from the Health Behaviour of School-Aged Children (HBSC) study noted that 'geographical location' was an important predictor of differences in the drinking of 15-year-olds, and went on to interpret this in terms of the general drinking cultures:

> For both genders, lower numbers of drunkenness occasions were observed in southern European countries, whereas higher numbers were found in Scandinavia, the Baltic countries and Russia .... Geographical location, in fact, may be a proxy for the different drinking cultures found in Nordic and southern European countries (Schmid et al. (2003).

The assumption that youth drinking culture expresses the general drinking culture is in line with the general conclusion in the literature that drinking cultures are quite conservative, that changes in drinking customs 'take decades and even longer to become visible .... The natural time frame for changes in drinking patterns is a generation, rather than a decade or any shorter period' (Simpura, 2001). But Simpura's mention of a generational time frame reminds us that, if a cultural change occurs, it seems most likely to appear first in a specific youth cohort – at least that is the conclusion which might be drawn from the analyses in terms of 'wet generations' mentioned above (Sulkunen, 1979; Room, 1984). As noted above, these and some other analyses (for example Warner, 1970; Freyssinnet-Dominjon and Wagner, 2003) discuss the relationship between the prevailing drinking culture and the new generation's innovations in dialectical terms: the new drinking style in the youth culture is explicitly defined in contrast to the drinking style of preceding generations.

These analyses caution us not to assume that comparisons of youth drinking cultures are simply general cross-cultural comparisons writ small. Other factors may also differentiate cross-cultural comparisons of youth drinking from cross-cultural comparisons of adult patterns. One set of potential factors is effects of the common historical experience of a particular youth generation, in our time communicated in ever broader circles. This is commonly discussed in terms of the innovations and promotions of the increasingly multinational alcohol industries (Jernigan, 1997). If an innovation like 'alcopops' has a success on the youth market in one country, it will not be long before an entrepreneur tries the innovation elsewhere. If an advertisement appeals to youth in a particular culture, variations on it may well appear before long elsewhere. The forces of globalisation – both in terms of marketing and media and in terms of *Wanderjahren* and other youth tourism and travel – are potentially forces to differentiate youth cultures from general national cultures. Less tangible influences of the *Zeitgeist* of a particular historical period may also result in common patterns of change reaching across cultures: the receptive audiences of youth across Europe in 1848 or in 1968 cannot be explained simply in terms of patterns of travel, diffusion of news or shared sociopolitical situations.

A second set of potential factors is the influence of the common tasks of adolescence and young adulthood with which we started. The shared experiences and challenges of being young, whether in terms of biological, psychological or social concomitants, may tend to diminish general cultural differences. In the context of the multicultural US society, ethnic differences in drinking have tended to be stronger among the middle-aged than among young adults – and this was not simply a matter of acculturation of the younger generation (Knupfer and Room, 1967). Specific cultural traits in a multicultural context seem to follow the aphorism of Arthur Noyes: 'as we grow older, we grow more like ourselves'.

Both of these sets of factors, to the extent they are operating, would tend to have the effect of reducing differences in cross-cultural comparisons of youth below the level of general cultural differences in drinking. A factor which might operate in the opposite direction, to increase differences, might be cultural differences in attitudes to youthful sexuality, and particularly sexual activity by unmarried young women. Traditional societies, particularly in southern Europe, limited the autonomy and recreational activities of young women in the interest of keeping them virginal until marriage. Such patterns seem to have been most entrenched in Catholic and Orthodox southern Europe, where societies have been 'more patriarchal and have [had] more "traditional" views on family values and gender roles' (Karlsson and Simpura (2001, p. 96). Karlsson and Simpura note that this might well 'have a bearing on the formation of drinking habits'. In such a traditional frame of reference, intoxication has been forbidden for young women, particularly in any situation where sexuality might come into play. Drinking and even light intoxication is often permitted in such societies, on the other hand, to older women beyond the reproductive years. To the extent that such a mentality survives, particularly in southern European societies, it would tend to produce a stronger gender division on drinking practices in adolescence and young adulthood than in adult society in general.

Some Hypotheses for Testing

There is thus a rich tapestry of influences which could result in contrasts and similarities in young people's drinking in different cultures. Making a comparison at a particular point in time, it will often be difficult to disentangle which threads are crucial, since their interweaving extends over time in each culture. However, it is possible to subject at least some of the conjectures implied by our discussion to the cold light of empirical comparison.

In recent years, empirical resources for such comparisons have become more available. There is at least a scattering of comparative qualitative studies, finding some surprising similarities between youth drinking practices in northern and southern Europe (for example Pyörälä, 1995; Beccaria and Sande, 2003). In terms of social statistics, there is the possibility of comparisons focusing on young age-groups in morbidity and mortality analyses (Rehm et al., 2001) or in police records, although this track appears to have been little pursued. Cross-national university student surveys offer comparisons for a privileged section of youth (for example Steptoe and Wardle, 2001; Steptoe et al., 2004). And survey comparisons of adult populations (for example Hupkens et al., 1993; Ahlström et al., 2001; Leifman, 2002; Bloomfield et al., 2005) offer the possibility of reanalyses focusing on their youngest age-groups.

The most comprehensive sources for cross-national comparisons, however, are the two series of surveys of teenagers mentioned in Chapter 1: the Health Behaviour in School-Aged Children studies of school students aged 11, 13 and 15 (Schmid et al., 2003; Schmid and Gabhainn, 2004), and the ESPAD studies (Hibell et al., 2004) of students aged 15 or 16. These surveys do not offer a full picture of drinking during youth: respondents to them are only started on a drinking career which will, in many cases, become more intense in the years to follow. But the age limits on the studies do offer the advantage of ensuring that a high proportion of the age group in the society is represented in the sample. And the common data-collection methods ensure a higher degree of comparability in the data than is usually available. In what follows, some hypotheses based on the discussion above are presented, and then tested on some of the published data from these two studies.

Following the level of generality of the conceptual discussions of cultural differences in drinking, our tests will primarily be based on three categories aggregated from selected individual country data. The three categories are composed as follows:

- Southern wine cultures: France, Greece, Italy, Malta, Portugal. In 2000, and 2001, wine had become the leading beverage in recorded consumption in Malta (replacing beer), and retained its long-term dominance in the other countries in this category (WHO, 2004).
- Central beer countries: Czech Republic, Denmark, Germany, Ireland, the Kingdom of the Netherlands, UK. Beer remained the dominant beverage in all these countries in 2001 (WHO, 2004).
- Northern 'spirits' countries: Estonia, Finland, Latvia, Lithuania, Norway, Poland, Sweden. As Leifman (2001) noted concerning some of these countries, most of these should be described as 'former spirits-drinking' countries, since in 2001 recorded consumption of spirits is still dominant only in Latvia. In Poland and Estonia in 2001, spirits consumption was marginally higher than beer consumption, while beer was marginally higher in Lithuania. In Finland, Norway and Sweden beer is now dominant (WHO, 2004). But despite the changes in beverage preference, the category retains its utility, as representing the 'hard-drinking' traditions of northern and parts of eastern Europe.

Below are listed the hypotheses for testing.

- The initiation of drinking will come at an earlier age in wine cultures than elsewhere. In wine cultures, there will be more children than elsewhere drinking regularly at a relatively young age.
- In view of the association of drinking with meals in southern Europe, and greater acceptance by parents of drinking at an earlier age, teenagers will be more likely to drink at home in southern Europe.
- Drinking to intoxication will be most common in northern Europe, and least common in southern Europe. The proportion of young people who have been intoxicated or who are consuming substantial amounts of alcohol on an occasion will be highest in the north and lowest in the south.
- Drunkenness will be least acceptable in wine cultures, and most acceptable in 'spirits' cultures.
- There will be more gender differences in drinking, and particularly in heavy drinking, in wine cultures, and less differences in the Nordic countries.
- In view of the strong traditions of drinking in 'pubs' and other drinking places, there will be more drinking in pubs and other public drinking venues in central Europe than in northern or southern Europe.
- To the extent that alcoholic beverages are regarded more as a food than as an intoxicant in southern Europe, expectancies of psychoactive effects of alcohol will be less common in southern Europe than elsewhere. In particular, drinking to forget problems, which tends to involve intoxication, will be more common in northern Europe.
- Rates of problems from drinking will be higher in northern than in southern Europe. This will be particularly marked for rates of drinking-related violence and police trouble. Rates of problems for a given amount of drinking will also be higher in the north than in the south.

Some Results

Hypothesis 1:

- The initiation of drinking will come at an earlier age in wine cultures than elsewhere. In wine cultures, there will be more children than elsewhere drinking regularly at a relatively young age.

The first column of figures in Table 2.1 shows the responses by 15-year-olds in the HBSC study to the question 'at what age ... did you first drink alcohol (more than a small amount)?' On average, children in the southern wine cultures report having initiated drinking at much the same age as children elsewhere in Europe. Consistently, in the three regions, girls report initiating drinking about half a year after boys. Children from the Czech Republic report the lowest initiating age of any of the countries included.

The second column of Table 2.1 shows the responses by 11-year-olds in the HBSC survey to the question 'how many times a week do you usually drink any alcoholic beverage?' The proportion reporting drinking this frequently is low in all segments of Europe, but highest in the wine cultures, although the average is only slightly higher than for the beer cultures. The proportion is definitely lower for the 'spirits' cultures. In all three segments the rate for females in less than half the rate for males.

The idea that the induction of children to drinking alcohol is earlier in wine cultures than elsewhere is only rather weakly supported in the data. It might be argued that the heavily-diluted wine that is sometimes mentioned as offered to children at the family dinner table in wine cultures would not be counted by the respondents as 'drinking alcohol'. But if this is so, by the same fact it seems unlikely that a drink which is not counted by the child as constituting 'alcohol' will be much of a prophylactic against teenage binge drinking.

Hypothesis 2:

• In view of the association of drinking with meals in southern Europe, and greater acceptance by parents of drinking at an earlier age, teenagers will be more likely to drink at home in southern Europe.

The first row of figures in Table 2.2 shows the average proportions of ESPAD survey respondents reporting 'at home' as a place where they drank on 'the last day on which you drank alcohol'. Young people aged 15–16 in southern Europe are not more likely to drink at home than their counterparts elsewhere in Europe. The proportion reporting drinking at home when they last drank is in a fairly narrow range for most countries, between 20 per cent and 27 per cent; the two outliers are the UK (30 per cent) on one side, and Ireland (13 per cent) on the other. The hypothesis is not supported by the data.

Hypothesis 3:

• Drinking to intoxication will be most common in northern Europe, and least common in southern Europe. The proportion of young people who have been intoxicated or who are consuming substantial amounts of alcohol on an occasion will be highest in the north and lowest in the south.

The third column of figures in Table 2.1, from the 15-year-olds in the HBSC study, shows very little variation between segments of Europe in the age at which 15-year-olds report having first become drunk, though it is marginally higher in the wine cultures. It should be noted that the mean ages reported are often not much below the respondent's age; the mean age would undoubtedly rise a little if late starters in terms of intoxication could be taken into account.

The fourth column of figures in Table 2.1, from the ESPAD data, shows the proportion of respondents reporting having been 'drunk from drinking alcoholic beverages' at least three times in their lifetime. Here there is a clear difference between the wine cultures and the rest of Europe, with fewer than half as many boys in the wine cultures, and about one-third as many girls, reporting having been drunk at least three times. Even in terms of the range of responses, the wine

Table 2.1 Drinking patterns among teenagers, southern wine, central beer and northern 'spirits' cultures, by gender. HBSC 2001/2002 and ESPAD 2003 studies

	Age at first drink	11-year-olds: weekly+ drinking (%)	Age when first drunk	Drunk 3+ times in life (%)	Drunk in last 30 days (%)	5+ drinks in last 30 days (%)
Males:						
Wine cultures	12.6	8.7	13.9	25.6#	19.2#	42.6#
	12.2–13.2	*3–19*	*13.5–14.2*	*22–32*	*18–23*	*33–58*
Beer cultures	12.2	7.2	13.6	58.5	46.0	59.5
	10.9–12.8	*4–14*	*13.4–14.8*	*42–75*	*33–65*	*54–67*
'Spirits'	12.5	4.8*	13.6	54.3	37.9	43.9
cultures	*11.6–13.2*	*3–7*	*13.5–13.7*	*42–68*	*33–44*	*35–53*
Females:						
Wine cultures	13.2	3.1	14.2	16.6#	14.8#	30.8#
	12.9–13.7	*0–9*	*13.8–14.5*	*13–23*	*12–22*	*19–43*
Beer cultures	12.7	3.2	13.8	53.8	41.8	51.8
	11.8–13.2	*2–8*	*13.5–14.1*	*27–74*	*20–58*	*41–57*
'Spirits'	13.1	1.6*	13.9	46.7	32.9	35.1
cultures	*12.6–13.5*	*1–3*	*13.6–14.2*	*28–59*	*20–44*	*15–49*

Notes

* without Lithuania; # without Spain; ¤ without France.
1 Figures in italics are the highest and lowest figures for the countries in the category.
2 Age of respondents about 15 except as noted.
3 Southern wine cultures: France, Greece, Italy, Malta, Spain, Portugal.
4 Central beer cultures: Czech Republic, Denmark, Germany, Ireland, Netherlands, United Kingdom (England for HBSC).
5 Northern 'spirits' cultures: Estonia, Finland, Latvia, Lithuania, Norway, Poland, Sweden.

Sources: Schmid and Gabhainn, 2004: Age at first drink, p. 81; 11-year-olds: weekly+ drinking: p. 75; age when first drunk: p. 81; Hibell et al., 2004: drunk 3+ times in life: pp. 346–7; drunk in last 30 days: pp. 352–53; 5+ drinks in last 30 days: pp. 355–6; total consumption, last occasion: pp. 340–41.

cultures are clearly differentiated, with the rates in all wine cultures below the rates in all other societies included.

In light of the wide publicity given to the ESPAD results, it is perhaps no surprise that on average the highest rates of reported drunkenness are actually in the beer cultures rather than in the former spirits cultures. Ireland stands out among both genders with particularly high rates (75 per cent and 74 per cent), while girls in the Netherlands and Estonia show relatively low rates (27 per cent and 28 per cent), though not as low as in the wine cultures. The gender difference in rates is somewhat greater in the wine cultures than elsewhere.

The pattern of results is rather similar for proportions reporting having been drunk 'during the last 30 days' (fifth column of figures in Table 2.1), although here the average proportions in the beer cultures more substantially exceed the proportions in the 'spirits' cultures. With this measure, the gender difference in absolute terms does not vary much between segments (in ratio terms, the differentiation is greater in the wine cultures).

So far the comparisons have been based on the respondent's self-definition of having been 'drunk' or an equivalent term in the local language. The sixth column of figures in Table 2.1 offers an alternative approach to measuring heavy drinking occasions, in terms of consuming 'five or more drinks in a row', with the 'drinks' defined for the respondent (the definitions imply that five drinks is equivalent to a full bottle of wine). Again, the time period covered is the 'last 30 days'.

With this measure, the results look rather different. In both genders, the proportions are considerably higher for respondents from beer cultures than for the other two segments. Among males, the proportions drinking 5+ drinks in the wine and spirits cultures are roughly equal, while for females they are lower for wine cultures. There is a considerable divergence within the wine culture category, with lower proportions in Portugal and France among both males and females. Conversely, the proportions for Malta are closer to the average for beer cultures, and those for Greece and Italy are close to the averages for the 'spirits' cultures.

The results for this hypothesis are thus mixed. For the difference between beer cultures and 'spirits' cultures, it is not supported: by whatever measure, beer cultures show higher rates of heavy drinking than 'spirits' cultures. In terms of self-described drunkenness, there is strong support for a lower rate in the wine cultures than elsewhere. In terms of a measure of heavy drinking in quantitative terms, the hypothesis in not supported for the wine culture vs. 'spirits' cultures comparison, but receives some support for the beer vs. wine cultures comparison. Rates of heavy drinking are particularly low in Portugal and France.

Hypothesis 4:

• Drunkenness will be least acceptable in wine cultures, and most acceptable in 'spirits' cultures.

There is a very large difference between the results for drunkenness and the results for drinking five or more drinks in the wine cultures. For both boys and girls in these cultures, over twice as many report drinking 5+ as report getting drunk in the last 30 days, while the ratios in the other groups are in the range 1.1–1.3. This might be a result of greater tolerance for alcohol, if wine culture respondents were drinking more frequently than others. However, the wine cultures do not stand out in the ESPAD data in terms of reported frequency of drinking. In terms of drinking 20 or more times in the last 12 months, Malta ranks seventh and Greece 12th among the ESPAD countries, while Italy (19th), France (26th) and Portugal (31st) are in the lower ranks of 33 sites (Hibell et al., 2004, p. 136). Or the difference might not reflect tolerance, but rather differences in drunken comportment (MacAndrew and Edgerton, 1969): in particular, that teenagers in wine cultures are less likely to expect to behave ostensively 'drunk' after, say, five drinks, and in fact less likely to behave so, than teenagers elsewhere in Europe after five drinks.

An alternative explanation is in terms of drunkenness being a more marginalised category, with respondents resisting application of the term to themselves, in wine cultures. A paper on earlier ESPAD data (Andersson et al., 1999) looked further into this question in eight cities, only one of which (Malta) is among the wine cultures in the present analysis. Boys and girls in Malta estimated that five drinks in a row would make them slightly less intoxicated (6.2 on a scale of 1–10) than boys and girls in other cities (roughly 6.7 for boys, 7.2 for girls). Respondents in Malta were considerably more likely than respondents elsewhere to report that they were taken by surprise when last intoxicated, rather than have expected to get drunk. Against this, two qualitative studies oriented to adult perceptions (Bennett et al., 1993; Cameron et al., 2000) did not find a clear-cut difference between wine and other cultures in any association of marginalisation with the concept of drunkenness. It is possible, but seems unlikely, that youth cultures vary on this from adult norms and conceptualisations. The issue deserves further study.

The results suggest some support for the idea that drunkenness as a status is less acceptable in wine cultures than elsewhere, but only marginal support for the potential corollary that respondents in wine cultures are less likely to drink five or more drinks at a time than those in 'spirits' cultures. There is strong support for the idea that both groups are less likely to do this, and also to report having being drunk, than those in beer cultures.

Hypothesis 5:

• There will be more gender differences in drinking, and particularly in heavy drinking, in wine cultures and less differences in the Nordic countries.

In terms of age at first drink or weekly drinking by 11-year-olds (first two columns of digits in Table 2.1), there is no evidence from the ESPAD data that gender differences vary between wine, beer and 'spirits' cultures. With respect to intoxication, there is a tendency toward a greater gender gap in wine cultures. In ratio terms, this applies for each of the last three columns of Table 2.1. In terms of differences in percentages, the results are more mixed.

The Nordic countries are clearly differentiated in this respect from other countries in the 'spirits' category. Female and male proportions are close on each of the three indicators for Finland, Norway and Sweden, and in Finland and Sweden the female rate is sometimes above the male rate. Elsewhere in Europe, the UK, Ireland and to some extent Denmark show few male/female differences. At the other end of the spectrum, the gender divergence is particularly strong in Estonia, with the male rates about twice as high as the female rates. Otherwise, only the Netherlands comes close to this divergence, for the two 'drunk' indicators but not the 5+ drinks indicator.

There is substantial evidence of gender equality in intoxication among 15–16-year-olds in the Nordic countries, but they are joined in this by the UK and Ireland. There is some evidence of a greater gender gap in heavy drinking or intoxication in the wine cultures, in part depending on how divergence is measured.

Hypothesis 6:

- In view of the strong traditions of drinking in 'pubs' and other drinking places, there will be more drinking in pubs and other public drinking venues in Central Europe than in northern or southern Europe.

This hypothesis reflects that Britain and Ireland both have strong 'pub cultures', with at least 70 per cent of alcohol consumed in public drinking places (Bridgeman, 2000, p. 27; Babor et al., 2003, p. 44), and there are relatively strong parallel traditions in a number of countries in the central European band. However, given the existence and apparent differential enforcement of minimum age limits on drinking, results may well vary in a study of 15–16-year olds. The indicator used here (Table 2.2, second row of figures) is the sum of the proportions reporting drinking in a bar or pub, in a disco, and in a restaurant on their most recent drinking day. Since multiple responses were allowed, the measure is an indicator rather than a percentage. In fact, the indicator is highest in the wine cultures, and lowest in the 'spirits' cultures. However, the divergence within categories is great. France shows a much lower score (20) than other wine cultures. The scores are low also for Denmark, Norway, Sweden and Finland (in the range 7–19), and fairly low for the UK (26), while the Czech Republic has an exceptionally high score (75). The scores seem to reflect not only the strength of the on-premise drinking tradition in the society, but also the extent to which a law like that on minimum drinking age is taken seriously in the culture. There is thus no support for the general hypothesis.

Hypothesis 7:

- To the extent that alcoholic beverages are regarded more as a food than as an intoxicant in southern Europe, expectancies of psychoactive effects of alcohol will be less common in southern Europe than elsewhere. In particular, drinking to forget problems, which tends to involve intoxication, will be more common in northern Europe.

The third, fourth and fifth rows of figures in Table 2.2 compare average proportions in the three European segments responding that it was 'very likely' or 'likely' that the item would 'happen to you personally, if you drank alcohol'. Each of the items reflects a somewhat different psychic effect of drinking which a drinker might be seeking. Respondents from wine cultures were least likely to expect to 'feel relaxed' or 'have a lot of fun', and less likely than those in 'spirits' cultures but more likely than those in beer cultures to expect to 'forget my problems' (which

Table 2.2   Contexts and expectations of drinking among teenagers, southern wine, central beer and northern 'spirits' cultures: percent giving answer. ESPAD 2003 study

	Wine cultures	Beer cultures	'Spirits' cultures
Drinking contexts on last drinking day:			
At home	21.8	22.8	23.7
	20–26	*13–30*	*22–27*
Bar, pub, disco, restaurant	49.6	39.7	21.9
	20–62	*19–75*	*7–38*
Expected consequences of alcohol consumption:			
Feel relaxed	38.0*	62.0	57.1
	32–48	*50–75*	*46–67*
Have a lot of fun	58.8*	82.2	66.1
	50–72	*78–92*	*22–84*
Forget my problems	42.3*	38.0	47.9
	39–45	*33–53*	*45–50*
Feel sick	37.8*	21.3	30.3
	28–52	*7–35*	*17–43*
Do something I would regret	38.8*	32.3	36.0
	34–41	*19–43*	*31–45*
Get into trouble with the police	14.8*	10.2	17.0
	6–19	*6–16*	*7–31*

Notes

*   Without Spain.
1   Figures in italics are the highest and lowest percents for the countries in the category.
2   Percentages for the three categories of bar and pub, disco, and restaurant are summed, though the respondent may have gone to more than one of these on the last drinking day.
3   Southern wine cultures: France, Greece, Italy, Malta, Portugal.
4   Central beer cultures: Czech Republic, Denmark, Germany, Ireland, Netherlands, United Kingdom.
5   Northern 'spirits' cultures: Estonia, Finland, Latvia, Lithuania, Norway, Poland, Sweden.

Source: Hibell et al., 2004: Drinking contexts: p. 361; Expected consequences: p. 364.

probably implies a larger amount of drinking than relaxing or having fun). There is thus moderate support for the hypothesis.

Interestingly, those from wine cultures were on average more likely than others to feel that drinking was likely to produce negative personal consequences (last three rows of Table 2.2), although on the specific item of the likelihood of getting in trouble with the police the highest proportion of positive responses came from those from 'spirits' cultures, reflecting particularly responses from the Baltic countries and Poland. There were other diverging results in specific countries. Lithuanian respondents were much less likely than others (22 per cent) to expect to have fun while drinking, while Dutch respondents reported less likelihood of forgetting problems as well as of each of the three negative consequences.

Hypothesis 8:

• Rates of problems from drinking will be higher in northern than in southern Europe. This will be particularly marked for rates of drinking-related violence and police trouble. Rates of problems for a given amount of drinking will also be higher in the north than in the south.

Table 2.3 shows results from a selection of items about problems the respondent had ever experienced 'because of my alcohol use'. Overall, the results are quite striking. For each type of problem, on average 3.1 per cent of wine culture respondents gave a positive response, 9.0 per cent of beer culture respondents, and 10.2 per cent of 'spirits' culture respondents. The percentage of wine culture respondents was lower for each of the six items, and particularly for the two sexuality items and trouble with the police. Beer culture respondents led on one item (sex with regrets), and 'spirits' culture respondents on four. Denmark, Ireland, and the UK stand out with especially high scores among the beer cultures, and Lithuania (except on sex) among the 'spirits' countries.

As a rough control in terms of trouble per drinking unit, an index was computed of the ratio of the average problem percentage to the average proportion reporting 5+ drinks in the last 30 days (averaging the genders). This index was three times as high for 'spirits' cultures (0.25) as for wine cultures (0.08), and twice as high for beer cultures (0.16). Just as with alcohol-related mortality among adults (Norström et al., 2001), on this measure northern Europeans appear to get in considerably more trouble than southern Europeans per unit of drinking.

An alternative measure would use 'drunk in the last 30 days' (fifth column of figures in Table 2.1) as the denominator of the ratio. In this case the index becomes much more even: 0.28 for the wine and 'spirits' cultures, and 0.21 for the beer cultures.

The hypothesis that rates of reported drinking problems will be higher in the north than in the south is thus strongly confirmed. Rates in the beer cultures, however, do not differ much from rates in the 'spirits' cultures. Results on the hypothesis that there will be more trouble for a given amount of drinking in the north than in the south are also confirmed if drinking over a named amount (5+ drinks in the last 30 days) is taken as the comparator. However, the hypothesis is not confirmed if reporting getting drunk in the same period is the comparator. Results in this case thus depend on the meaning of the north-south differences in the relation between reporting drunkenness and reporting drinking 5+ drinks that were discussed above.

Table 2.3 **Problems caused by own alcohol use among teenagers, southern wine, central beer and northern 'spirits' cultures: percent giving answer. ESPAD 2003 study**

	Wine cultures	Beer cultures	'Spirits' cultures
Problems in relationships with parents	4.0 *3–6*	8.5 *4–16*	13.3 *6–25*
Engaged in sex regretted the next day	2.6 *2–3*	8.0 *4–11*	6.0 *2–9*
Engaged in unprotected sex	1.6 *1–4*	8.7* *3–15*	9.6 *7–17*
Quarrel or argument	6.2 *4–9*	13.7* *6–28*	16.3 *12–28*
Scuffle or fight	3.0 *1–4*	8.7 *3–15*	9.6 *7–17*
Trouble with police	1.0 *1–1*	6.2 *3–12*	6.2 *4–9*

Notes

* without Ireland
1   Figures in italics are the highest and lowest percents for the countries in the category.
2   Southern wine cultures: France, Greece, Italy, Malta, Portugal.
3   Central beer cultures: Czech Republic, Denmark, Germany, Ireland, Netherlands, United Kingdom.
4   Northern 'spirits' cultures: Estonia, Finland, Latvia, Lithuania, Norway, Poland, Sweden.

Source: Hibell et al. 2004, pp. 369-370.

Conclusion

The scorecard on the hypotheses put forward in the light of the literature is mixed. The small differences in age at first drink make it unlikely that giving children wine at the family dinner-table is an important factor behind north-south differences in alcohol problems in Europe. North-south differences in the occurrence of relatively heavy drinking also seem relatively meagre – and the highest rates of such drinking among teenagers are actually in the central beer belt of Europe.

On the other hand, we found a strong differentiation between the wine cultures and the rest of Europe on reported problems from drinking, with rates in the south a fraction of rates elsewhere. Controlling roughly for drinking patterns did not change this, but opened up a differentiation between the beer and the 'spirits' cultures. Teenagers in the beer cultures appear to get drunk more often, but those in the 'spirits' cultures seem to get in more trouble per unit of drinking.

One possibility, in understanding this gradient, is that for teenagers in the 'spirits' cultures, a given level of drinking is taken as being more disinhibitory. As suggested above, teenage intoxication may indeed take a somewhat different form – more ostensive, more in the face of others, pushing further beyond bounds – in northern Europe than in southern. Certainly, we have found that teenagers in wine cultures expect somewhat less in the way of mind-bending effects from their drinking than teenagers in 'spirits' cultures.

Another possibility is that those around the drinker – police, family, age-mates – may set a lower threshold on what is allowable, so that the social controls are greater. There is some evidence in the data – for example from the index of on-premise drinking – of the clearly different attitude of authorities in northern Europe about selling alcohol to the underage drinker. Well-enforced policies on drinking-driving are another example of a panoply of alcohol control laws that affect the young at least as much as the general society, and which are generally more developed in northern than in southern Europe (Karlsson and Österberg, 2001).

These two elements very likely are related and interact. Nils Christie discussed this interplay some years ago, in discussing the experience in Nordic societies more generally:

> The causal chain probably goes like this: A drinking culture with a large degree of highly visible, non-beneficial effects of alcohol consumption leads to a strict system of control which somewhat reduces total consumption, which again influences and most often reduces the visible problems. But also, the system of control influences visible problems – sometimes probably in the direction of increasing them. (Christie, 1965)

What lessons can be drawn from these analyses and findings for policy and research? In the first place, the youth surveys underline that drinking is an important part of the life and culture of youth all over Europe. The drinking is intertwined with many of the important tasks of adolescence and young adulthood, but it also carries in its wake significant problems. Second, it is more than ever clear that, with respect to drinking cultures, problems and responses, the European Union encompasses enormous variety and complexity. A policy which is applicable and useful at one end of Europe may be irrelevant and even noxious at the other end. National and local solutions may often be best suited to the task, though they may well need support (rather than the undercutting which has been too common) from supranational institutions.

With respect to research, there is a need to extend our thinking and data collection and analysis beyond the existing base of cross-national research. This is not just a matter of doing for 20-year-olds what HBSC and ESPAD do for 15-year-olds. It involves also taking on the task of developing theories and study designs concerning youth drinking cultures and social responses to them, and developing them in a comparative perspective across the diverse societies of Europe. I would place a particular emphasis on measuring and understanding variations in drunken comportment in different youth cultures. We need to develop a better grasp on the norms concerning and functions of intoxication and its interpretation in different youth contexts, subcultures (Abel and Plumridge, 2004) and cultures. We also need some cogent thinking and study on the relationship between drinking in youth cultures and drinking cultures at large.

References

Abel, G.M. and Plumridge, E.W. (2004), 'Network "Norms" or "Styles" of "Drunken Comportment?"', *Health Education Research*, **19**, 492–500. [PubMed 15155589] [DOI: 10.1093/her%2Fcyg064].

Ahlström, S. et al. (2001), 'Gender Differences in Drinking Patterns in Nine European Countries: Descriptive Findings', *Substance Abuse*, **22**, 69–85. [DOI: 10.1023/A%3A1026475910263].

Ahlström-Laakso, S. (1976), 'European Drinking Habits: A Review of Research and some Suggestions for Conceptual Integration of Findings' in *Cross-Cultural Approaches to the Study of Alcohol: An Interdisciplinary Perspective*. Everett, M.W. et al. (eds) (The Hague and Paris: Mouton), 119–132.

Andersson, B. et al. (1999), 'The Concept of "Drunkenness" among Young People in Eight Major European Cities', *Presented at the 25th Annual Alcohol Epidemiology Symposium* Kettil Bruun Society for Social and Epidemiological Research on Alcohol, Montreal, Canada, 31 May–4 June.

Assailly, J.-P. (2004), 'The Prevention of Young Driver's DWI (Driving While Intoxicated) and RWDI (Riding with a Driver under Influence) in Europe: A Social Sequential Model', *Traffic Injury Prevention*, **5**, 237–240. [PubMed 15276924] [DOI: 10.1080/15389580490465283].

Babor, T. et al. (2003), *Alcohol: No Ordinary Commodity – Research and Public Policy* (Oxford: Oxford University Press).

Beccaria, F. and Guidoni, O.V. (2002), 'Young People in a Wet Culture: Functions and Patterns of Drinking', *Contemporary Drug Problems*, **29**, 305–334.

Beccaria, F. and Sande, A. (2003), 'Drinking Games and Rite of Life Projects: A Social Comparison of the Meaning and Functions of Young People's Use of Alcohol during the Rite of Passage to Adulthood in Italy and Norway', *Young: Nordic Journal of Youth Research*, **11**, 99–119.

Bennett, L.A. et al. (1993), 'Boundaries between Normal and Pathological Drinking: A Cross-Cultural Comparison', *Alcohol Health and Research World*, **17**, 190–195.

Bloomfield, K. et al. (2005), *Gender, Culture and Alcohol Problems: A Multinational Study* (Berlin: Institute for Medical Informatics, Biometrics and Epidemiology, Charité Universitätsmedizin). http://www.genacis.org/Divers/report_final_040205.zip.

Bridgeman, J. (2000), *The Supply of Beer* (London: Office of Fair Trading), December). http://www.oft.gov.uk, http://www.oft.gov.uk/nr/rdonlyres/34960586-5561-468f-adb7-1a0eb8a6f367/0/oft317.pdf.

Bullock, S. and Room, S. (2006), 'Drinking Behaviour, Coming of Age and Risk' in *Sex, Drugs and Young People: International Perspectives*. Aggleton, P. et al. (eds) (London: Routledge), 120–137.

Cameron, D. et al. (2000), 'Intoxicated across Europe: In Search of Meaning', *Addiction Research*, **8**, 233–242.

Christie, N. (1965), 'Scandinavian Experience in Legislation and Control', in *National Conference on Legal Issues in Alcoholism and Alcohol Usage*. (Boston: Boston University Law-Medicine Institute), 101–122.

Estrada, F. and Tryggvesson, K. (2001), '"Fotboll kräva dessa drycker": Alkohol, fotboll och manlig kamratskap', ['Soccer Demands these Drinks': Alcohol, Soccer and Manly Comradeship], '*Nordisk alkohol – och narkotikatidskrift*', 18, 245–260.

Freyssinet-Dominjon, J. and Wagner, A.-C. (2003), *L'Alcool en Fête: Manières de Boire de la Nouvelle Jeunesse Etudiante* (*Alcohol in Celebration: Ways of Drinking of the New Student Youth*) (Paris: L'Harmattan).

Gual, A. and Colom, J. (1997), 'Why has Alcohol Consumption Declined in Countries of Southern Europe?', *Addiction*, **92**, 21–32. [DOI: 10.1080/09652149738132].

Haavio-Mannila, E. (1958), *Kylätappelut: Sosiologinen tutkimus Suomen kylätappelu-instituutiosta* (*Sociological Study of Finnish Village Fights*) (Porvoo: WSOY).

Hibell, B. et al. (2004), *The ESPAD Report 2003: Alcohol and Other Drug Use among Students in 35 European Countries* (Stockholm: Swedish Council for Information on Alcohol and Other Drugs (CAN) and the Pompidou Group at the Council of Europe).

Hunt, G.P. and Laidler, K.J. (2001), 'Alcohol and Violence in the Lives of Gang Members', *Alcohol Research and Health*, **25**, 66–71. [PubMed 11496969].

Hupkens, C.L. et al. (1993), 'Alcohol Consumption in the European Community: Uniformity and Diversity in Drinking Patterns', *Addiction*, **88**, 1391–1404. [PubMed 8251877] [DOI: 10.1111/j.1360-0443.1993.tb02026.x].

Jernigan, D. (1997), *Thirsting for Markets: The Global Impact of Corporate Alcohol*. (San Rafael CA: Marin Institute for the Prevention of Alcohol and Other Drug Problems).

Karlsson, T. and Österberg, E. (2001), 'A Scale of Formal Alcohol Control Policy in 16 European Countries', *Nordisk Alcohol- och Narkotikatidskrift*, **18** (English supplement), 117–131.

Karlsson, T. and Simpura, J. (2001), 'Changes in Living Conditions and their Links to Alcohol Consumption and Drinking Patterns in 16 European Countries, 1950 to 2000', *Nordisk Alcohol- och Narkotikatidskrift*, **18** (English supplement), 82–99.

Knupfer, G. and Room, R. (1967), 'Drinking Patterns and Attitudes of Irish, Jewish and White Protestant American Men', *Quarterly Journal of Studies on Alcohol*, **28**, 676–699. [PubMed 6082195].

Leifman, H. (2001), 'Homogenization in Alcohol Consumption in the European Union', *Nordisk Alkohol- och Narkotikatidskrift*, **18** (English supplement), 54–70.

— (2002), 'A Comparative Analysis of Drinking Patterns in Six EU Countries in the Year 2000', *Contemporary Drug Problems*, **29**, 501–548.

Leonard, K. (2001), 'Domestic Violence and Alcohol: What is Known and What do we Need to Know to Encourage Environmental Interventions?', *Journal of Substance Use*, **6**, 235–247. [DOI: 10.1080/146598901753325075].

Levine, H.G. (1992), 'Temperance Cultures: Concern about Alcohol Problems in Nordic and English-Speaking Cultures,' in *The Nature of Alcohol and Drug Related Problems*. Lader, M. et al. (eds) (Oxford: Oxford University Press), 15–36.

Lindman, R.E. and Lang, A.R. (1994), 'The Alcohol-Aggression Stereotype: A Cross-Cultural Comparison of Beliefs', *The International Journal of the Addictions*, **29**, 1–13. [PubMed 8144263].

MacAndrew, C. and Edgerton, R. (1969), *Drunken Comportment* (Chicago: Aldine).

Marshall, M. (1979), 'Conclusions' in *Beliefs, Behaviors, and Alcoholic Beverages*. Marshall, M. (ed.) (Ann Arbor: University of Michigan Press), 451–457.

Norström, T. et al. (2001), 'Mortality and Population Drinking' in *Alcohol in Postwar Europe: Consumption, Drinking Patterns, Consequences and Policy Responses in 15 European Countries*. Norström, T. (ed.) (Stockholm: National Public Health Institute), 149–168.

Olsson, B. (1990), 'Alkoholpolitik och alkoholens fenomenologi: Uppfattningar som artikulerats i pressen' ('Alcohol Policy and Alcohol's Phenomenology: Opinions Expressed in the Press'), *Alkoholpolitik – Tidskrift för Nordisk Alkoholforskning*, **7**, 184–194.

Paglia, A. and Room, R. (1998), 'How Unthinkable and at what Age?' 'Adult Opinions about the 'Social Clock' for Contested Behaviour by Teenagers', *Journal of Youth Studies*, **1**, 295–314.

Pape, H. and Rossow, I. (2000), 'Challenges from a Quantitative and Epidemiological Research Perspective', *Nordisk Alkohol- och Narkotikatidskrift*, **17** (English supplement), 16–18.

Pyorälä, E. (1995), 'Comparing Drinking Cultures: Finnish and Spanish Drinking Stories in Interviews with Young Adults', *Acta Sociologica*, **38**, 217–229. [DOI: 10.1177/000169939503800301].

Ramstedt, M. and Hope, A. (2002), *The Irish Drinking Culture – Drinking and Drinking-Related Harm, a European Comparison* (Dublin: Health Promotion Unit, Department of Health and Children).. http://www.healthpromotion.ie/uploaded_docs/Irish_ Drinking_Culture.PDF.

Rehm, J. et al. (2001), 'Average Volume of Alcohol Consumption, Drinking Patterns and Related Burden of Mortality in Young People in Established Market Economies', *European Addiction Research*, **7**, 148–151. [PubMed 11509845] [DOI: 10.1159/000050732].

Room, R. (1984), 'A "Reverence for Strong Drink": the Lost Generation and the Elevation of Alcohol in American Culture', *Journal of Studies on Alcohol*, **45**, 540–546. http:// www.bks.no/reverenc.pdf. [PubMed 6521480].

— (1989), 'Responses to Alcohol-Related Problems in an International Perspective: Characterizing and Explaining Cultural Wetness and Dryness'. Presented at an international conference, San Stefano Belbo, Italy. (http://www.bks.no/response. htm).

— (1994), 'Adolescent Drinking as Collective Behaviour and Performance' in *The Development of Alcohol Problems: Exploring the Biopsychosocial Matrix of Risk*. Zucker, R. et al. (eds) (Md: Rockville): NIAAA Research Monograph No. 26), 205–208.

— (2004), 'Drinking and Coming of Age in a Cross-Cultural Perspective' in *Reducing Underage Drinking: A Collective Responsibility*. Bonnie, R.J. and O'Connor, M.E. (eds) (Washington, DC: National Academy Press), 654–677.

— (2005), 'Multicultural Contexts and Alcohol and Drug Use as Symbolic Behaviour', *Addiction Research and Theory*, **13**, 321–331. [DOI: 10.1080/16066350500136326].

Room, R. and Bullock, S. (2002), 'Can Alcohol Expectancies and Attributions Explain Western Europe's North-South Gradient in Alcohol's Role in Violence?', *Contemporary Drug Problems*, **21**, 619–648.

Room, R. and Mäkelä, K. (2000), 'Typologies of the Cultural Position of Drinking', *Journal of Studies on Alcohol*, **61**, 475–483.

Room, R. and Paglia, A. (2001), '"At What Age do you Think it's OK?": the Social Clock for Drinking and Drug use among Ontario Teenagers'. Presented at an International Research Conference, "Youth Cultures and Subcultures: Functions and Patterns of Drinking and Drug Use", Skarpö, Sweden, 23–26 April 2001.

Room, R. and Rossow, I. (2001), 'The Share of Violence Attributable to Drinking', *Journal of Substance Use*, **6**, 218–228. [DOI: 10.1080/146598901753325048].

Sande, A. (2002), 'Intoxication and Rite of Passage to Adulthood in Norway', *Contemporary Drug Problems*, **29**, 277–303.

Schmid, H. and Gabhainn, S.N. (2004), 'Alcohol Use' in *Young People's Health in Context: Health Behaviour in School-Aged Children (HBSC) Study, International Report from the 2001/2002 Survey*. Currie, C. et al. (eds), (Copenhagen: World Health Organization, European Office). http://www.euro.who.int/Document/e82923.pdf.

Schmid, H. et al. (2003), 'Drunkenness among Young People: a Cross-National Comparison', *Journal of Studies on Alcohol*, **64**, 650–661. [PubMed 14572187].

Simpura, J. (1998), 'Mediterranean Mysteries: Mechanisms of Declining Alcohol Consumption', *Addiction*, **93**, 1301–1304. [PubMed 9926536] [DOI: 10.1080/09652149834784].

— (2001), 'Trends in Alcohol Consumption and Drinking Patterns: Sociological and Economic Explanations and Alcohol Policies', *Nordisk Alkohol- och Narkotikatidskrift*, **18** (English supplement), 3–13.

Steptoe, A. and Wardle, J. (2001), 'Health Behaviour, Risk Awareness and Emotional Well-Being in Students from Eastern Europe and Western Europe', *Social Science and Medicine*, **53**, 1621–1630. http://www.who.int/substance_abuse/publications/alcohol/en/. [PubMed 11762888].

Steptoe, A. et al. (2004), 'Drinking and Driving in University Students: an International Study of 23 Countries', *Psychology and Health*, **19**, 527–540. [DOI: 10.1080/08870440310001616542].

Sulkunen, P. (1976), 'Drinking Patterns and the Level of Alcohol Consumption: an International Overview' in *Research Advances in Alcohol and Drug Problems*. Gibbins, R.J. et al. (eds) (New York: John Wiley and Sons), 223–281.

— (1979), 'Abstainers in Finland 1946-1976'. A Study in Social and Cultural Transition. Report No. 133 (Helsinki: Social Research Institute of Alcohol Studies).

— (1989), 'Drinking in France 1965-1979: an Analysis of Household Consumption Data', *British Journal of Addiction*, **84**, 61–72. [PubMed 2783870] [DOI: 10.1111/j.1360-0443.1989.tb00552.x].

Tryggvesson, K. (2004), 'The Ambiguous Excuse: Attributing Violence to Intoxication – Young Swedes about the Excuse Value of Alcohol', *Contemporary Drug Problems*, **31**, 231–261.

Turner, V. (1969), *The Ritual Process: Structure and Anti-Structure* (Chicago: Aldine).

Warner, H.S. (1970), 'Alcohol Trends in College Life: Historical Perspectives' in *The Domesticated Drug: Drinking among Collegians*. Maddox, G.L. (ed.) (New Haven: College and University Press). (article originally published in 1938).

WHO (2004), *Global Status Report on Alcohol 2004* (Geneva: Department of Mental Health and Substance Abuse, World Health Organization). http://www.who.int/substance_abuse/publications/alcohol/en/.

Zieliński, A. (1994), 'Polish Culture: Dry or Wet?', *Contemporary Drug Problems*, **21**, 329–340.

Chapter 3

Drunken Behaviour, Expectancies and Consequences among European Students

Barbro Andersson and Björn Hibell

Introduction

Young people, as well as adults, have different reasons for drinking and different relations to alcohol. How people view alcohol and what consequences or effects they expect from consumption depends on a variety of factors. The metabolic or chemical effects are mediated by expectancies, both in relation to what the subjects know, or think they know, about different beverages' intoxication potential, but also on what they believe they have consumed.

There is a rather large body of research literature on alcohol expectancies among young as well as older people, showing both sex and age differences as well as differences between light and heavy drinkers. However, some studies only include the positive expectancies towards alcohol consumption, that is questions about possible negative expectancies are not asked. In addition, as most studies in this area are done on limited populations or on samples from one single country only, little is known about how young people in various cultures differ in their expectancies towards alcohol consumption.

In an overview Windle and Windle (2005) state that drinking may have adverse effects in various 'domains of life such as academic and occupational achievement, family and peer relationships, and physical and mental health'. In line with this, we often assume that behavioural impairment is a negative outcome of alcohol consumption. However, in a study at the University of Washington, Fromme et al (1986) found in group discussions that it was obvious that some of the respondents considered behavioural impairment as a *desirable* effect from drinking. It should thus not be assumed that an expected effect, which an observer might view as a negative one, necessarily would be unwanted by the drinker.

Researchers, who have investigated different factors behind drinking behaviour and its negative consequences in student populations, point to the importance of norm perceptions, attitudes and beliefs about the effects of alcohol as explanations of the observed variance (Benton et al., 2006a; Benton et al., 2006b; Read and O'Connor, 2006).

Thus, anticipated effects of alcohol consumption may be moderated by the individual's attributed beliefs about the substance's effect. In a study, Finnigan et al. (1995) found that a non-alcoholic beverage can cause impairment in an individual's behaviour if he/she is made to believe that it contains alcohol. In an experimental setting it was demonstrated that subjects who incorrectly believed that they had consumed alcohol, performed with a slight impairment compared to base line, while those who knowingly consumed alcohol were able, to some degree, to compensate for the effects by reallocating efforts.

Brown et al. (1987) developed an 'Alcohol Expectancy Questionnaire' to measure the expectancies in relation to the effects of alcohol, both in an adult and an adolescent population. They stated that 'alcohol expectancies vary with such personal characteristics as age, sociodemographic background, personality characteristics and current drinking patterns'.

Marín (1996) reports about cultural differences in alcohol expectancies in a study focusing on prevention strategies. He concluded that 'abstainers and light drinkers tended to indicate more negative consequences' from a list of 35 expectations, while more frequent drinkers tended to expect more positive outcomes. According to Marín, 'the positive expectancies held by drinkers can be perceived as reinforcing psychological elements for the consumption of alcoholic beverages that maintain the behaviour'.

Similar observations of different functions for positive and negative expectancies have been noted earlier, for example by Whaley (1986) who in an overview concludes that there is a functional relationship between expectancies and alcohol use. He states in a note that 'alcohol-related expectancies play a significant role in the drinking behaviours of adolescents' but that 'expectations about the negative consequences of alcohol use seem to be unrelated to drinking behaviour'. In another project Werner et al. (1993), who studied 328 college freshmen, found that 'more heavily drinking students and those reporting more health problems expected more positive effects on their sociability and sexuality and were less concerned about cognitive and behavioural impairment as a result of drinking'. Werner et al. draw the conclusion that greater expectation of positive outcomes and fewer negative would be 'associated with heavier drinking and more alcohol-related health problems in a college population'.

Expectancies in relation to alcohol use seem to be highly related to both age and gender. Analysing a US sample aged 12 and over, Leigh and Stacy (2004) found that positive expectancies were positively related to alcohol use and negative expectancies were negatively related to alcohol use. However, positive expectancies about the effects of alcohol were stronger or equal predictors of drinking only among respondents under 35, while negative expectancies were the predominant predictors in most respondents over 35. They also found differences in the results if only current drinkers were analysed and they draw the conclusion that negative expectancies predicts abstention. Similar conclusions have been drawn by McNally and Palfai (2001). They reported from a study among college students that negative alcohol expectancies, and not positive, contributed significantly to the prediction of change in drinking behaviour.

Another study examining age and sex differences in expectancies and alcohol consumption reported a significant relationship between negative expectancies and lower alcohol consumption for older women, and that positive expectancies were related to increased consumption among younger women (Satre and Knight, 2001). Among older men the pattern was more mixed in that the negative expectancies were negatively related to consumption.

The European School Survey Project on Alcohol and Other Drugs (ESPAD) has been performed three times with four-year intervals in an increasing number of countries in Europe (26 in 1995, 30 in 1999 and 35 in 2003) (Hibell et al., 2004). The reports reveal that young people in Europe differ, not only in levels of consumption, but also in their views on alcohol and alcohol consumption. Although differences at the individual level should not be overlooked, the consumption pattern is to a large extent geographical, with different frequencies of consumption as well as different reported occasions of drunkenness in different parts of Europe. The ESPAD project also shows that expectancies towards alcohol consumption, as well as the consequences from it, are different in different parts of Europe.

Based on the ESPAD 2003 data, this chapter concentrates on the analyses of the relationship between a few crucial variables: drunkenness, alcohol intake on the last drinking occasion, positive and negative expectancies towards drinking and experienced negative consequences (problems) from drinking in different countries.

In addition it will investigate these relationships on the individual level in two countries with different alcohol traditions: Sweden as a 'dry' country with a long tradition of drunkenness, and Greece as a 'wet' country in which alcohol intake is not traditionally related to intoxication.

Method and Material

The 2003 ESPAD data were collected in 35 European countries.[1] Each country collected its own data as a separate study. The surveys were conducted on nationally representative samples of students using a common standardised methodology and a questionnaire that had been developed within the project. The target population of the ESPAD study is defined as the national population of students, whose 16th birthday is in the calendar year of the survey. In 2003, this meant students who were born in 1987. At the time of the data collections, mainly in March to May, the students' average age was 15.8 years (Hibell et al., 2004).

---

1   Austria, Belgium, Bulgaria, Croatia, Cyprus, the Czech Republic, Denmark, Estonia, Faroe Islands, Finland, France, Germany, Greece, Greenland, Hungary, Iceland, Ireland, the Isle of Man, Italy, Latvia, Lithuania, Malta, the Netherlands, Norway, Poland, Portugal, Romania, Russia (Moscow), the Slovak Republic, Slovenia, Sweden, Switzerland, Turkey, Ukraine and the UK.

The nationally representative samples of students in the ESPAD project are based on school classes as the final sampling unit. It was recommended that each national sample include at least 2,800 students. However, in small countries the total population was targeted (Greenland 555 students, Faroe Islands 640, the Isle of Man 721, Iceland 3,348 and Malta 3,500). In a few countries it was not possible to draw nationally representative samples. They include Russia (Moscow only), Germany (six Bundesländer) and Turkey (six cities in six major regions).

The main part of the ESPAD questionnaire consists of core questions to be used in all countries. In addition a number of module questions were included to be used at the option of each country. The original version of the ESPAD questionnaire is written in English and each country translated and back-translated it into English again to be able to detect misinterpretations. All variables in this chapter belong to the compulsory core questions section.

Data were collected by group-administered questionnaires in schools under the supervision of a teacher or a research assistant. The students answered the questionnaires anonymously in the classroom under conditions similar to a written test.

Data were analysed separately within each country using a common identical syntax. For the international report each country reported their findings in a standardised table format.

Every effort was made to standardise the methodology. The cultural contexts within which the students have answered the questions have, however, most probably differed somewhat between countries. On the other hand, when looking at each country's methodology, the main impression is that the validity and reliability were high in most ESPAD countries.

Data Used in this Chapter

Estimated *alcohol volumes* on the last drinking occasion refer to five questions formulated in the following way: 'The last time you had an alcoholic drink, did you drink any beer/cider/alcopops/wine/spirits? If so, how much?' The calculations of volume are based on the alcohol content of each type of beverage, with the amount reported recalculated into pure alcohol. The alcohol content for alcopops was assumed to be 4.5 per cent, beer and cider 5 per cent, wine 11 per cent and spirits 40 per cent. Average volumes are given in centilitres of pure (100 per cent) alcohol.[2]

The *binge drinking* and *drunkenness* variables are based on the following questions: 'Think back over the last 30 days. How many times (if any) have you had five or more drinks in a row?' and: 'On how many occasions (if any) have

---

2   There is a risk that some students may have misunderstood the questions about volumes consumed and described the consumption at last time they had any of the beverages, instead of how much they had of each on the last drinking occasion, which would result in an overestimation. However, there is reason to believe that the influence of this possible misunderstanding does not differ systematically between countries.

you been drunk from drinking alcoholic beverages?' The variable 'expected personal consequences' derives from the question: 'How likely is it that each of the following things would happen to you personally, if you drink alcohol?' Eleven statements followed, five presumed to be positive and six negative.[3] The variable 'experienced problems' derives from the question: 'Have you ever had any of the following problems?' The 14 items listed[4] have been collapsed into four problem categories: Individual (5 items), Relationship (4), Sexual (2) and Delinquency (3). Four response categories were provided: 'never', 'yes, because of my alcohol use', 'yes, because of my drug use' and 'yes, for reasons other than alcohol or drug use'. For the purposes of this chapter, only the proportions indicating that the problem was related to alcohol were used.

The analyses are mainly based on table data (Hibell et al, 2004). Relevant table data have been transferred into Excel-tables and into an SPSS data set. The variables used are: country, sex, estimated alcohol volumes on the last drinking occasion, frequent binge drinking (5+ drinks in a row), frequent drunkenness, expected consequences from drinking alcohol and experienced problems in relation to alcohol consumption. Pearson's product-moment correlation, and Spearman's rank correlation coefficients have been calculated on country level data for some variables. In addition, a few individual data analyses have been done using the Greek and Swedish data sets.

For some variables data are missing for a few countries, due to deviations in the national questionnaires from the official ESPAD version. These countries include Austria, France, Germany and Switzerland. In addition, the Netherlands' results on the binge-drinking variable have been left out, due to recently discovered discrepancies in the question format.

Results

Drunkenness, Binge Drinking and Consumption on Last Drinking Occasion

The proportions of students in the ESPAD countries who have been drunk three times or more during the last 30 days, who have been binge drinking equally often, and the reported average consumption in centilitres of pure alcohol on the last drinking occasion in each country are presented in Figure 3.1. When reading

---

3   Feel relaxed, get into trouble with police, harm my health, feel happy, forget my problems, not be able to stop drinking, get a hangover, feel more friendly and outgoing, do something I would regret, have a lot of fun, and feel sick.

4   Quarrel or argument, scuffle or fight, accident or injury, loss of money or other valuable items, damage to objects or clothing you owned, problems in your relationship with your parents, problems in your relationship with your friends, problems in your relationship with your teachers, performed poorly at school or work, victimised by robbery or theft, trouble with police, hospitalised or admitted to an emergency room, engaged in sexual intercourse you regretted the next day, and engaged in sexual intercourse without a condom.

the figure it should be noted that the results on drunkenness and binge drinking are given as percentages of all students (left y-axis), while the last consumption variable represents average centilitres in pure alcohol (100 per cent) consumed on last drinking occasion (right y-axis).

Alcohol consumption among 15–16-year-old European students seem to a large extent to be geographically oriented (Figure 3.1). About one-fourth of the students in the high prevalence countries indicate that they have been drunk three times or more during the last 30 days. These countries are all found in the western parts of Europe, including Denmark and Ireland (both 26 per cent), the Isle of Man and the UK (both 23 per cent). The countries that reported the lowest proportions, 5 per cent or less, are mainly found in the Mediterranean area and include Malta (5 per cent), Greece, Portugal, Romania (3 per cent each), Cyprus and Turkey (both 1 per cent).

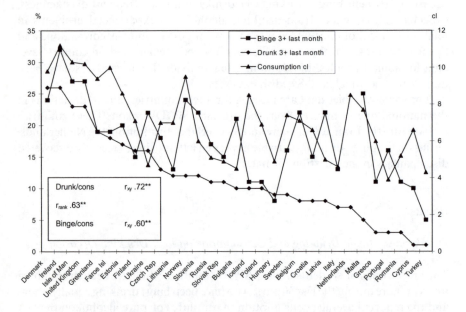

Figure 3.1   Proportion of students (%) who were drunk 3 times or more during the last 30 days, estimated average consumption in cl. 100% alcohol on the last drinking occasion and proportion of binge drinkers by country

Data missing for Austria, France, Germany and Switzerland.
Data on binge drinking are missing for the Netherlands. See Method.
Data sorted by the drunkenness variable.

Source: Hibell et al., 2004.

The proportions of students that reported binge drinking three times or more during the last 30 days are not exactly congruent with the frequent drunkenness prevalence on country level. The top countries with around 25 per cent or more include the Isle of Man (37 per cent), Ireland (32 per cent), the UK (27 per cent), Malta (25 per cent), Denmark and Norway (both 24 per cent). Countries reporting low proportions on this variable (around 10 per cent or lower) include Greece, Iceland, Poland, Romania (11 per cent each), Cyprus (10 per cent), Hungary (8 per cent) and Turkey (5 per cent). Although the geographical pattern is similar, the north/west and south/east orientation that was emerging from the frequent drunkenness variable is less visible in relation to frequent binge drinking.

The estimated consumption levels on the last drinking occasion show a geographical pattern similar to the one concerning frequent drunkenness. The highest average consumption (more than 9 cl of 100 per cent alcohol) was observed in the northern/western parts of Europe, including Denmark, the Faroe Islands, Greenland, Ireland, the Isle of Man, Norway and the UK. At the opposite end, reporting an average consumption of 5 cl. or less, are found countries from the southern/eastern parts of Europe, including Bulgaria, Hungary, Italy, Portugal, the Slovak Republic, Turkey and Ukraine. Corresponding data for Greece and Sweden were 6.0 and 7.4 cl of pure alcohol.

It is obvious that some countries with very low prevalence rates on frequent drunkenness, reported high or relatively high prevalence rates on frequent binge drinking, and relatively large amounts consumed on the last drinking occasion. Thus, among the countries with the lowest rates of frequent drunkenness we find a few with relatively high intake on the last drinking occasion. They include the Netherlands, Malta, Cyprus and Greece.

The frequent drunkenness rate correlates quite strongly with the average intake on the last consumption occasion (r_{xy} 0.72**, r_{rank} 0.63**). As expected, the coefficients for frequent binge drinking and average consumption are somewhat weaker (r_{xy} 0.60**, r_{rank} 0.56**), as well as for frequent drunkenness and binge drinking (r_{xy} 0.65**, r_{rank} 0.56**), but still significant and clearly positive.

Since binge drinking has the weakest relation with the other two consumption variables the analyses in this chapter will focus on the frequent drunkenness and last alcohol consumption variables in relation to positive and negative expectancies as well as experienced problems. In the last section individual data from Greek and Swedish students will be analysed separately on these variables.

Expected Personal Consequences

There is a very strong positive relationship on the country level between the proportions reporting drunkenness three times or more during the last 30 days and the average proportions reporting positive expectancies related to one's own alcohol consumption (feel relaxed, feel happy, feel more friendly and outgoing, have a lot of fun and forget my problems) (all students r_{xy} 0.76**, r_{rank} 0.68**). There is also a positive, but somewhat weaker, relationship between positive expectancies and the amount of alcohol consumed on the last drinking occasion (all students r_{xy} 0.61**, r_{rank} 0.51**).

Controlling for gender reveals that the strength of the relationships between frequent drunkenness and positive expectancies does not differ much between boys and girls, while the relationship is slightly stronger among girls than among boys when it comes to amount consumed on the last drinking occasion and positive expectancies.

The relationships between the prevalence rates of frequent drunkenness and negative expectancies towards alcohol consumption are negative but not significant. The same is true in relation to amounts consumed on the last drinking occasion. Thus, the non-significant tendency is that the higher the proportion of students in different countries expecting alcohol consumption to lead to negative consequences, the lower the prevalence rates of drunkenness (r_{xy} – 0.24, r_{rank} – 0.31, both non-significant). The relations with the consumed quantities on the last drinking occasion and negative expectancies are also non-significantly negative; r_{xy} – 19, r_{rank} – 22.

Figures 3.2 and 3.3 show the correlations as distributions of ESPAD countries in scatterplots. The strong positive relationship for positive expectancies and drunkenness shows clearly in the grouping of countries near the diagonal from the lower-left to the higher-right corners of the figure (Figure 3.2). Interestingly, those countries which are about in the middle on the expectancy variable are spread from left to right on the drunkenness axis, with mainly Mediterranean countries far left and mainly eastern European countries to the right, that is the drunkenness prevalence varies geographically despite the expectancies. Countries where many students have been frequently drunk *and* expect positive outcomes from drinking are geographically to the west, including Denmark, the Faroe Islands, Ireland, the Isle of Man and the UK.

Negative expectancies (Figure 3.3) are, as already mentioned, not significantly correlated with frequent drunkenness, and the weak correlation is negative on the country level. This means that several countries reporting low prevalence rates on frequent drunkenness are scoring high on negative expectations. They include Romania, Croatia, Italy, Latvia and Portugal.

On the other hand, very few expected negative consequences are found in certain countries where many students have been drunk very often. These countries are about the same that scored high on positive expectations: Denmark, Ireland, the Isle of Man and the UK.

Experienced Problems in Relation to Frequent Drunkenness and Alcohol Consumption

The variable 'experienced problems' refers to the question 'Have you ever had any of the following problems?' (cf. Method and Material). The various items were grouped together into four problem categories: Individual, Relational, Sexual and Delinquency problems. In Figure 3.4 the number of variables within each 'problem group' for which a country's percentage exceeds the average of all countries is presented. Countries with the highest number of experienced problems

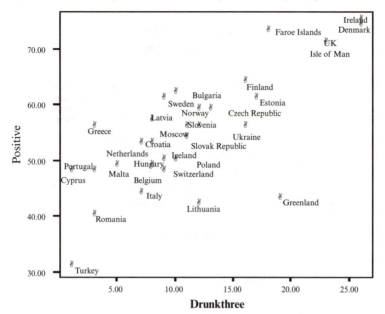

Figure 3.2   Correlation between positive expectancies (positive) of own alcohol consumption and having been drunk 3 times or more during the last 30 days

Note: Austria, France and Germany are missing—see Method and Material.

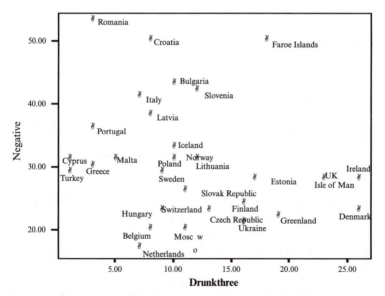

Figure 3.3   Correlation between negative expectancies (negative) of own alcohol consumption and having been drunk 3 times or more during the last 30 days

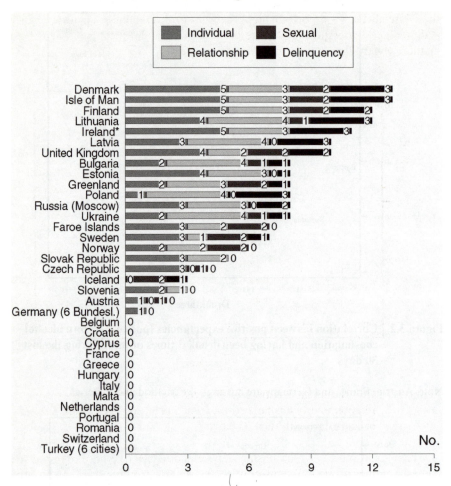

Figure 3.4   Experienced problems caused by alcohol. All students

The number of variables within each 'problem group' for which a country's percentage exceeds the average of all countries.

*   Ireland did not include sexual problems in their questionnaire.

Source: Hibell et al., 2004.

are mainly found in the north, while countries around the Mediterranean Sea and surroundings all reported lower percentages than average.

There is a strong relationship between the proportion of students in different countries that have experienced any of the problems listed in the questionnaire (all prob) and drunkenness (Figure 3.5). Students in countries with the highest proportions of frequent drunkenness (three times or more during past month) experience a significantly higher frequency of problems (r_{xy} 0.85**, r_{rank} 0.87**). The only country that deviates from this pattern is Lithuania, where a high proportion of the students had experienced alcohol-related problems even though relatively few reported a high frequency of drunkenness. This discrepancy is difficult to understand and there is reason to assume that there might be a methodological flaw behind this extreme position.

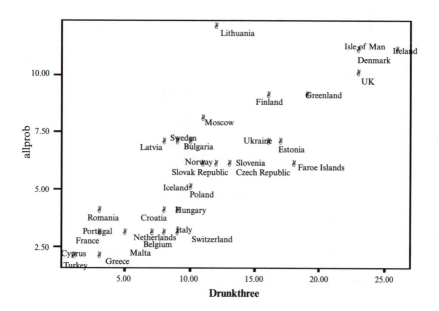

Figure 3.5   Correlation on country level between any experienced problems in relation to own alcohol consumption and having been drunk 3 times or more during the last 30 days

There is also a clear relationship between countries that have reported the highest volumes of alcohol consumption on the last drinking occasion and the proportions of students with any of those problems (r_{xy} 0.52**, r_{rank} 0.46**).

The relationships between these variables and experienced problems are stronger among girls than among boys. For experienced problems and drunkenness the correlations were r_{xy} 0.94** and r_{rank} 0.94** among girls, versus r_{xy} 0.80** and r_{rank} 0.89** for boys. The corresponding values for experienced problems and consumption on the last drinking occasion were r_{xy} 0.74** and r_{rank} 0.67** for girls, while they were r_{xy} 0.34 and r_{rank} 0.37* for boys.

The relationship between frequent drunkenness and each of the four problem groups vary but is strong for all of them. Experienced individual problems (performed poorly at school or work, loss of money and other valuable items, and so on) and frequent drunkenness are highly associated (r_{xy} 0.83**, r_{rank}. 86**) (Figure 3.6). Countries clearly deviating from this pattern are Greenland and Lithuania, but in different directions. Again, the correlation coefficients are somewhat stronger for girls (r_{xy} 0.89**, r_{rank}. 89**) than for boys (r_{xy} 0.79**, r_{rank}. 85**).

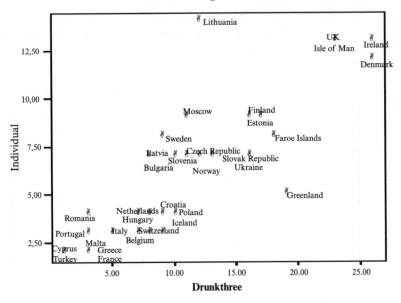

Figure 3.6   **Correlation on country level between experienced individual problems in relation to own alcohol consumption and having been drunk 3 times or more during the last 30 days**

Figure 3.7 shows the scatterplot for relational problems (problems with parents, friends, teachers, and so on) and frequent drunkenness. The correlation is strong (r_{xy} 0.71**, r_{rank}. 85**), but again Lithuania is an outlier. Also for this variable the associations are stronger for girls (r_{xy} 0.79**, r_{rank}. 87**) than for boys (r_{xy} 0.59**, r_{rank}. 73**).

The sexual variable includes two items; regretted sex and unprotected sex. The correlations are very strong also for this variable and frequent drunkenness (r_{xy} 0.81**, r_{rank}. 89**) (Figure 3.8). An interesting observation in the figure is that the Greenlandic students reported sexual problems to a higher degree than students in other countries. Also for this variable the correlations are stronger among girls (r_{xy} 0.89**, r_{rank} 97**) than among boys (r_{xy} 0.71**, r_{rank} 79**).

The delinquency variable is a little less associated with frequent drunkenness than the other problem variables, but still very strong (r_{xy} 0.76**, r_{rank} 78**) (Figure 3.9). Countries falling outside the pattern are Lithuania, Greenland and the Faroe Islands. The association with alcohol intoxication and this variable is again much stronger for girls (r_{xy} 0.91**, r_{rank} 87**) than for boys (r_{xy} 0.70**, r_{rank} 76**).

To sum up, there are strong relationships with frequent drunkenness and each of the four problem groups on the macro level. The group of countries that are low on both variables are about the same in each problem category, and nearly all of them are found in the Mediterranean area (Cyprus, Greece, France, Italy, Malta, Portugal, Romania and Turkey).

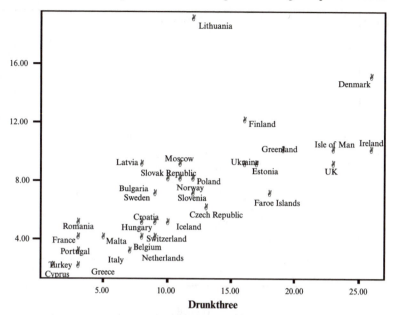

Figure 3.7 **Correlation on country level between experienced relational problems in relation to own alcohol consumption and having been drunk 3 times or more during the last 30 days**

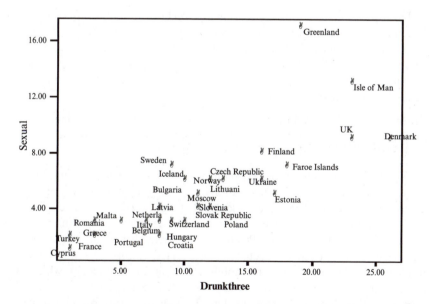

Figure 3.8 **Correlation on country level between experienced sexual problems in relation to own alcohol consumption and having been drunk 3 times or more during the last 30 days**

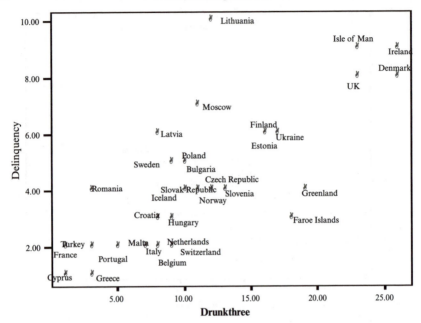

Figure 3.9 **Correlation on country level between experienced delinquency problems in relation to own alcohol consumption and having been drunk 3 times or more during the last 30 days**

The top group, those who are scoring high on both variables, differ somewhat in their positions. The four countries scoring high include Denmark, Ireland, the Isle of Man and the United Kingdom. This is especially true in relation to the three variables 'individual', 'relationship' and 'delinquency' problems. The relationship with the problem variables is stronger for drunkenness than for consumption on the last drinking occasion and it is stronger for girls than for boys.

Analysis of Individual Data in Two Alcohol Cultures

To explore the outcome on the expectancies and consequence variables in two different drinking cultures, in this section individual data have been analysed for Greece and Sweden.[5] The same variables that were used at the macro level in previous sections of this article have been used in their original form directly in the two data sets. The category 'Positive expectancies' is now broken down into five variables and 'Negative expectancies' into six (cf. Method and Material). The problem variables (individual, relational, sexual and delinquency), which also are summary variables, are however kept as such also in these analyses. For the purpose of this chapter, the students have been divided into four consumption

---

5   The Greek researchers have generously shared their data with the authors.

groups in relation to their alcohol consumption on the last drinking occasion: < 2 cl, 2–3.99 cl, 4–8.49 cl and ≥ 8.5 cl of 100 per cent alcohol. Furthermore, the drunkenness variable (last 30 days) has been collapsed into three prevalence groups: those who have not been drunk during the past 30 days, those who were drunk 1–2 times and those who had been drunk three times or more.

Table 3.1 shows the proportions of students in the three groups of drunkenness prevalence (see above) that answered 'very likely' or 'likely' on the separate items of the question: 'How likely is it that each of the following things would happen to you personally, if you drink alcohol?' There is a strong positive relationship between drunkenness and all positive expectancies, among both Greek and Swedish students, even though the Greek figures generally are lower. However, it should be noted that most of the differences between the three groups are found between those that have not been drunk during the last 30 days and those who have.

The results related to negative expectancies show a more mixed pattern, although for the majority of the variables the relations are positive, that is the more often you get intoxicated the larger is the proportion of students who report negative expectancies from drinking. Exceptions are the variables 'feel sick' and 'harm my health'. Among the Swedish students there is hardly any difference between the three prevalence groups in relation to the 'feel sick' variable, and for the Greek students this is true for the last two categories. For the variable 'harm my health' there are no differences between the groups either among Greek or Swedish students. Thus, these expected consequences do not seem to be more relevant to the students who get drunk often than to those who get drunk only seldom or not at all.

The variable 'get into trouble with the police' gives a very interesting picture. Both in Sweden and Greece there is practically no difference at all between those who got drunk once or twice and those who did not get drunk, but among those who get drunk three times or more in the last 30 days one-fifth of the Swedish and one-fourth of the Greek students expected trouble with the police.

Table 3.2 shows the proportions of the Greek and the Swedish ESPAD students in different alcohol consumption groups who expect the various outcomes from alcohol consumption. In both countries, there is a strong relationship between positive expectancies and consumption on the last drinking occasion. Again, the proportions in each consumption group are generally somewhat higher among the Swedish students than among the Greeks. The proportions, who indicated that they would 'feel relaxed' if they drank alcohol range in the Swedish sample from 39 per cent in the lowest consumption group to 74 per cent in the highest, while corresponding figures for Greece are 33 and 57 per cent. Similarly, the proportion of students indicating they would 'feel happy' increases by consumption group from 61 to 95 per cent among the Swedish vs. 42–70 per cent among the Greek students.

Again, the relation between own alcohol consumption and expected negative consequences is different from what was observed in relation to the expected positive consequences. As was observed in relation to drunkenness, there is no

Table 3.1　Expected personal consequences of alcohol consumption and the 30 days drunkenness prevalence rates among Swedish and Greek students

	Not drunk last 30 days		Drunk 1–2 times		Drunk 3 times or more	
	Sweden n=2045	Greece n=1559	Sweden n=728	Greece n=237	Sweden n=313	Greece n=65
Positive expectancies						
Feel relaxed	41	45	73	58	76	52
Feel happy	61	53	96	76	95	68
More friendly and outgoing	48	58	82	77	80	74
Have fun	60	67	98	86	96	78
Forget my problems	40	34	64	51	71	60
Negative expectancies						
Feel sick	35	25	32	37	31	35
Get a hangover	36	52	56	70	63	60
Not be able to stop drinking	10	13	15	26	29	31
Harm my health	36	38	34	44	37	37
Do something I would regret	32	33	44	49	57	46
Get into trouble with police	5	5	5	5	19	26

Table 3.2 Expected personal consequences of alcohol consumption by alcohol consumption group on the last drinking occasion. Proportion of Greek and Swedish students

| | Alcohol consumption groups | | | | | | | |
| | < 2 | | 2.00 – 3.99 | | 4.00 – 8.49 | | 8.5 + | |
	Sweden n=537	Greece n=356	Sweden n=468	Greece n=484	Sweden n=527	Greece n=536	Sweden n=982	Greece n=405
Positive expectancies								
Feel relaxed	39	33	54	47	66	52	74	57
Feel happy	61	42	79	53	88	63	95	70
More friendly and outgoing	48	49	65	59	73	68	80	71
Have fun	59	52	78	68	90	76	97	85
Forget my problems	39	26	45	35	58	39	65	50
Negative expectancies								
Feel sick	36	27	30	21	35	23	32	32
Get a hangover	32	49	37	53	47	55	59	59
Not be able to stop drinking	8	8	8	11	10	15	22	24
Harm my health	35	36	31	35	35	38	37	38
Do something I would regret	30	31	34	31	40	35	48	41
Get into trouble with police	5	4	5	4	5	4	10	9

relationship between the consumption groups and the variables 'feel sick' and 'harm my health'. This is true in both the Greek and the Swedish samples.

A positive, but not very strong, relationship is found in both countries for the variables 'get a hangover' and 'do something I would regret'. The two remaining variables 'not be able to stop drinking' and 'get into trouble with the police' are both slightly positively related to the consumption variable in both Greece and Sweden, but mainly for the two highest consumption groups.

A clear difference between the countries appears when it comes to drunkenness and experienced problems (Table 3.3). Although the relationships between the variables are positive in both countries, the magnitude of the relationship is much stronger in Sweden for all four variables.

In Sweden the proportion of students in the category that had not been drunk during the past 30 days and who reported experience of 'individual problems' is 8 per cent, compared to 64 per cent in the group that had been intoxicated three times or more. In Greece these figures are 4 and 17 per cent respectively. Corresponding figures for the 'relationship' variable are 8 and 55 per cent in Sweden and 3 and 20 per cent in Greece, for the 'sexual' variable 3 and 37 per cent vs. 1 and 17 per cent and, finally, the 'delinquency' variable 4 and 45 per cent vs. 1 and 8 per cent. Thus, among those who had been drunk several times, more students had experience of problems compared to the group with less frequent intoxication behaviour, but the proportions were much higher among Swedish than among Greek students.

Table 3.4 presents the comparison between the countries on the experienced problem variable in relation to the different alcohol consumption groups (last occasion). The differences between the countries are again very obvious. Although there is a clear relationship between experienced problems and consumption only for the highest consumption group in Greece, the Swedish figures reveal a strong relationship through all four consumption categories.

To sum up, there are important similarities between the two countries representing two different alcohol cultures in Europe, but also differences. The positive expectancies towards alcohol consumption are associated with both frequency of intoxication and amounts of alcohol consumed on the last drinking occasion in both countries, but the relationship is stronger in Sweden.

There is also a clear relation between consumption and adverse consequences in the two cultures, but the proportions getting into different problems are higher in the Swedish than in the Greek culture.

Discussion

Data reported here show that there is a significant positive relationship at the macro (country) level between level of alcohol consumption and drunkenness frequency on one hand and positive expectancies towards alcohol on the other among European teenage students in 35 countries. There is also a significant positive relationship between consumption and experienced problems. It is obvious that students in many countries in *northern/western Europe* hold a strong positive view on alcohol despite a wide range of problems caused by this consumption. In

Table 3.3 Experienced problems due to alcohol consumption and the 30 days drunkenness prevalence rates among Swedish and Greek students

	Not drunk last 30 days		Drunk 1–2 times		Drunk 3 times or more	
	Sweden n=2045	Greece n=1559	Sweden n=728	Greece n=237	Sweden n=313	Greece n=65
Experienced problems						
Individual problems	8	4	47	12	64	17
Relational problems	8	3	33	8	55	20
Sexual problems	3	1	15	6	37	17
Delinquency problems	4	1	20	4	45	8

Table 3.4 Experienced problems due to alcohol consumption by alcohol consumption group on the last drinking occasion. Proportion of Greek and Swedish students

	Alcohol consumption groups							
	< 2		2.00–3.99		4.00–8.49		8.5+	
	Sweden n=537	Greece n=356	Sweden n=468	Greece n=484	Sweden n=527	Greece n=536	Sweden N=982	Greece n=405
Experienced problems								
Individual problems	3	1	13	4	29	4	51	13
Relational problems	4	2	11	4	23	4	39	9
Sexual problems	1	0	5	2	10	1	21	6
Delinquency problems	0	0	5	1	11	1	28	4

many countries in *southern/eastern Europe*, however, where the students did not experience so many problems, the view on alcohol is less positive.

The 'drunkenness' variable was found to be a better risk indicator for getting into trouble than the variable '5+ drinks in a row' (binge drinking), at least for the present analyses. It might be that many young people, and probably especially girls, do not need to drink large amounts of alcohol to feel the effects or to get drunk. Drunken comportment is probably the factor contributing to certain behaviours, no matter how much (or little) alcohol has been indulged. The high correlations for the drunkenness variable indicate that this might be the most reliable measure of harmful drinking in the ESPAD study.

As mentioned above, there is a clear geographical pattern evolving—students in many (but not all) countries around the Mediterranean Sea report lower alcohol consumption, and especially a low drunkenness frequency. This is often related to low proportions expecting positive consequences but at the same time few reported experienced problems related to alcohol consumption.

ESPAD countries with high drunkenness figures, large proportions expecting positive consequences and large proportions that have experienced alcohol-related problems, are mainly found in the north-west of Europe (including Denmark, Ireland, the Isle of Man and the UK). This has been observed earlier, for example by Room (1989; see also Room, 2001) who, in a paper on cultural 'wetness' and 'dryness', points out that disorderly public drunkenness appears to be more common in 'dryer' societies than at least in European wine cultures. Room also comments that 'there has not been much apparent convergence in the cultural positioning of alcohol [in Europe], though southern European cultures seem to worry these days about youthful beer-drinking in cafes in terms that resemble the concerns about drunken comportment of 'dryer' societies'.

However, there is reason to believe that the traditional drinking pattern in different parts of Europe is subject to change. Many young people adopt new drinking styles. Beccaria and Guidoni (2002) discuss the functions and patterns of drinking among students in Italy, defined by the authors as a 'wet culture'. They conclude that the new drinking culture emerging among young Italians (more beer and spirits, less wine) mixes the traditional Italian model with a North-European drinking style, for example the wine drinking culture vs. the beer and spirits drinking one.

Data presented here suggest that whatever the factors are behind different levels of alcohol consumption in different countries, the expectancies towards alcohol consumption tend to be more positive the higher the consumption is. The same is true for the number of experienced problems related to the consumption of alcohol.

As noted earlier in this chapter, even very young people and people without their own experience of alcohol consumption have expectancies concerning the effects (Oei and Angel, 2005). Oei and Angel reported from their study that less experienced drinkers tended to hold global and general expectancies while experienced drinkers had more refined and specific expectancies. Also noted earlier, adult abstainers and light drinkers tend to expect more negative consequences than frequent drinkers (Marín, 1996). The tendency is the same in the ESPAD material – however not significantly so.

The gender differences on the macro level are interesting. The positive relationship between expectancies and drunkenness as well as between expectancies and consumption on the last drinking occasion are about the same for both boys and girls, and so is the non-significant negative relationship with the negative expectancies. There is reason to believe, however, that further analyses might reveal a more complex pattern. Rosenthal et al. (1998), for example, have found gender differences in alcohol expectancies in a teenage population. They report strong expectancies concerning sex for boys but not for girls, while the opposite was true in relation to cognitive change.

However, the relationship between experienced problems and alcohol consumption is stronger for girls than for boys. One contributing factor to this might be that girls are more vulnerable to high alcohol blood concentrations due to physiological characteristics such as body fat concentration, and so on. Another aspect might be that girls are more likely to get into troublesome situations because of gender roles and societal expectations. A third aspect could be that a girl who gets drunk as often as a boy, or drinks the same large quantity as a boy, has a more extreme consumption pattern compared to the female norms than a boy compared to the male norms.

The strong relationship on the country level between drunkenness/high alcohol consumption and expected positive consequences also appears on the individual level, which is in line with data on college freshmen reported by Werner et al. (1993).

Results from the ESPAD material show that among Swedish students (living in a 'dry' culture with positive attitudes towards drunkenness), the higher their consumption on the last drinking occasion, the more likely they were to anticipate positive consequences. Interestingly, the same pattern also appeared among Greek students (living in a 'wet' culture with negative attitudes towards drunkenness), only with somewhat lower proportions.

Also the consumption pattern in relation to negative expectations was very similar in the two countries. In no country were the relations entirely positive or negative. This seems to contradict the findings on the macro level described earlier, where the relations between drunkenness and consumption variables and negative expectations were negative. It should be observed, however, that this negative tendency was not significant and that, although the main direction of the relationship on macro level was negative, the scatterplot pointed in the direction of important variations at the country level. The clear differences in the relationships between drunkenness/high alcohol consumption and positive and negative expectancies indicate that they represent different universes of meanings.

At the individual level, both in the Mediterranean country Greece and in the northern country Sweden, heavy drinkers anticipate more positive outcome from alcohol consumption than those who drink less. However, there are clear cultural differences when the different alcohol consumption levels are related to experienced problems. While a strong positive relationship between level of consumption and experienced problems was observed in the Swedish sample, the relationship among the Greek students was much weaker, almost non-existent, except for students in the highest consumption group.

The relationship between drunkenness and experienced problems was stronger in both countries than the relationship between amounts consumed on the last drinking occasion and experienced problems, especially in Greece. A contributing factor to this is probably that drunkenness is a more 'extreme' behaviour than the consumption of a relatively large quantity on the last drinking occasion.

Students in high prevalence countries demonstrate a positive view upon alcohol consumption despite the negative outcomes they have experienced. It is obvious, however, that for most people the engagement in alcohol consumption is a process—from the (possible) euphoria after the first drink(s), through feeling the effects more substantially, toward sheer drunkenness. The negative consequences at the end of this process might well be overlooked or neglected when looking back at the event because of the fun at the beginning of the evening.

In line with Fromme et al.'s (1986) remarks, we don't know for sure whether all the problems included in the ESPAD problem questions really are seen as negative consequences by all students. It cannot be excluded that some/many students in a drunkenness culture might find it positive to have had a quarrel or to have been in a fight.

The difference in anticipated consequences between students in northern and southern Europe is challenging. It would be most interesting to discover the cultural pattern that makes young people in some countries in southern Europe report a relatively high consumption on the last drinking occasion, but at the same time a very low drunkenness prevalence. The stronger relationship for girls than for boys between drunkenness/high alcohol consumption and experienced problems needs also to be explored further to see what the factors are behind this and how this is related to different alcohol cultures in Europe. The individual-level cross-country database under construction within the ESPAD project will be a useful source for a better understanding of cultural differences and changing behaviours among younger generations.

Note

The authors wish to thank Assistant Prof. Anna Kokkevi and Anastasios Fotiou at the University Mental Health Research Institute in Athens, Greece, for their generosity in sharing their national data with us.

References

Beccaria, F. and Guidoni, O.V. (2002), 'Young People in a Wet Culture: Functions and Patterns of Drinking', *Contemporary Drug Problems*, **29**, 305–334.

Benton, S.L. et al. (2006a), 'College Student Drinking, Attitudes Toward Risks, and Drinking Consequences', *Journal of Studies on Alcohol*, **67**, 543–551.

— (2006b), 'Predicting Negative Drinking Consequences: Examining Descriptive Norm Perception', *Journal of Studies on Alcohol*, **67**, 399–405.

Brown, S.A. et al. (1987), 'The Alcohol Expectancy Questionnaire: An Instrument for the Assessment of Adolescent and Adult Alchol Expectancies', *Journal of Studies on Alcohol*, **48**(5), 483–491. [PubMed 3669677].

Finnigan, F. et al. (1995), 'The Effects of Expectancy and Alcohol on Cognitive-Motor Performance', *Addiction*, **90**, 661–672. [PubMed 7795502] [DOI: 10.1046/j.1360-0443.1995.9056617.x].

Fromme, K. et al. (1986), 'Alcohol Expectancies, Risk Identification, and Secondary Prevention with Problem Drinkers' in *Advances in Behaviour Research and Therapy: an International Review Journal*, 237–251 (Oxford: Pergamon).

Goldman, M.S. et al. (1999), 'Alcohol Expectancy Theory: The Application of Cognitive Neuroscience' in *Psychological Theories of Drinking and Alcoholism*. Leonard, K.E. and Blame, H.T. (eds) (New York: Guilford Publications), 203–246.

Hibell, B. et al. (2004), *The ESPAD Report 2003. Alcohol and other Drug Use among Students in 35 European Countries* (Stockholm: Swedish Council for Information on Alcohol and Other Drugs (CAN) and the Pompidou Group at the Council of Europe).

Leigh, B.C. and Stacy, A.W. (2004), 'Alcohol Expectancies and Drinking in Different Age Groups', *Addiction*, **99**, 215–227. [PubMed 14756714] [DOI: 10.1111/j.1360-0443.2003.00641.x].

Long, F.K. et al. (2004), 'Adults' Approval and Adolescents' Alcohol Use', *Journal of Adolescent Health*, **34**(5), 17–26.

Marín, G. (1996), 'Expectancies for Drinking and Excessive Drinking among Mexican Americans and Non-hispanic Whites', *Addicitve Behaviors*, **21**(4), 491–507. [DOI: 10.1016/0306-4603%2896%2985558-4].

McNally, A.M. and Palfai, T.P. (2001), 'Negative Emotional Expectancies and Readiness to Change among College Student Binge Drinkers', *Addictive Behaviors*, **26**, 721–734. [DOI: 10.1016/S0306-4603%2800%2900157-X].

Oei, T.P.S. and Angel, S. (2005), 'Alcohol Expectancies and Drinking Refusal Self-efficacy in Children: Development and Family Influences', *Alcohol Research*, **10**(3), 97–103.

Read, J.P. and O'Connor, R.M. (2006), 'High- and Low-Dose Expectancies as Mediators of Personality Dimensions and Alcohol Involvement', *Journal of Studies on Alcohol*, **67**, 204–214.

Room, R. (1989), 'Responses to Alcohol-Related Problems in an International Perspective: Characterizing and Explaining Cultural Wetness and Dryness', paper presented at 'La ricerca Italiana sulle bevande alcoliche nel confronto internazionale', Santo Stefano Belbo (CN), Italy, 22-23 September 1989. http://www.bks.no/response.htm.

— (2001), 'Intoxication and Bad Behaviour: Understanding Cultural Differences in the Link', *Social Science and Medicine*, **53**, 189–198. [DOI: 10.1016/S0277-9536%2800%2900330-0].

Rosenthal, G.L. et al. (1998), 'Social Skills, Expectancies, and Drinking in Adolescents', *Addictive Behaviors*, **23**(5), 587–599. [DOI: 10.1016/S0306-4603%2898%2900025-2]

Satre, D.D. and Knight, B.G. (2001), 'Alcohol Expectancies and their Relationship to Alcohol Use: Age and Sex Differences', *Ageing and Mental Health*, **5**(1), 73–83. [DOI: 10.1080/13607860020020672].

Werner, M.J. et al. (1993), 'Alcohol Expectancies, Problem Drinking, and Adverse Health Consequences', *Journal of Adolescent Health*, **14**(6), 446–452. [PubMed 8241201] [DOI: 10.1016/1054-139X%2893%2990116-7].

Whaley, A.L. (1986), 'Cognitive Processes in Adolescent Drug Use: The Role of Positivity Bias and Implications for Prevention Policy', *The International Journal of the Addictions*, **21**(3), 393–398. [PubMed 3721644]

Windle, M. and Windle, R.C. (2005), *Alcohol Consumption and its Consequences among Adolescents and Young Adults,'*, in *Recent Developments in Alcoholism,'*. Galanter, M. (ed.) (New York: Kluwer Academic/Plenum Publishers).

Chapter 4

Gender Differences in Youth Drinking Cultures

Salme Ahlström

*With Barbro Andersson, Marie Choquet, Zsuzsanna Elekes,
Fernanda Feijao, Anastasios Fotiou, Björn Hibell, Anna Kokkevi,
Martin Plant, Svend Sabroe*

Introduction

The cultural position of drinking has been previously characterised under different typologies as reviewed by Room and Mäkelä (2000) – see also Chapter 2 in this volume. The concept of integrated drinking was first used by Ullman (1958), and Ahlström-Laakso (1976) has also used the integration-segregation concept, illustrating it by data on drinking as an accompaniment to meals and the setting selected for drinking in various European countries. The integration of alcohol with everyday activities was understood in part by describing how alcoholic beverages were consumed with meals and in part by describing what place was selected as the proper place to drink. On the other hand, a traditionally dominant beverage type was the basis of Sulkunen's (1976, 1983) typology of drinking cultures in Europe. He used alcohol consumption statistics as the basis of his typology and named the countries in relation to beverage preferences 'beer, wine, and spirits countries'. Mäkelä's (1983) starting point was the use-value of alcohol. He differentiated three main uses: nutritional use, medical use and use as an intoxicant, although he noted that, in consuming alcohol, the three effects are always simultaneously present. When classifying alcohol cultures, he proposed that the historically dominant use should be adopted as a primary criterion. Reflecting the different dominant use values, in Mediterranean countries heavy intoxication is culturally condemned, while in the northern countries intoxication is sought as an end in itself. Also, the cultural dynamics of controlling excessive drinking vary according to the dominant use. Partanen proposed that the key aspects of drinking were its inherent sociability, and the altered individual state of consciousness, alcohol intoxication (1991). While sociability is the basic impulse bringing people together to drink, it can easily turn to its opposite. Therefore, social controls are necessary parts of drinking, in one form or another and more or less thoroughly interiorised by individuals. In addition, European societies have also been characterised as wet or dry (Room and Mitchell, 1972). Traditionally, 'wet' meant a high integration of alcohol in the society's everyday activities (low prevalence of abstainers, high prevalence of chronic alcohol-related problems), whereas 'dry' meant low integration of alcohol in the social life (a high prevalence of abstainers, a low prevalence of chronic alcohol-related problems). Wine-producing countries were seen as wet and the Nordic countries as dry.

To the extent that they were based on or referenced Europe, these typologies tended to refer to a Europe of the 1970s or earlier. However, the European Comparative Alcohol Study (ECAS) indicated that an increase in alcohol consumption among central and northern European countries during the first three decades after the Second World War provided the basis for reporting a homogenisation of alcohol consumption in Europe (Norström, 2002). During the period after the mid-1970s, homogenisation occurred due to a decline in total alcohol consumption in the Mediterranean countries. This fall was a result of a substantial decrease in wine consumption. Secondly, beverage preferences also showed a trend towards homogenisation for the entire study period. Former spirits-drinking countries shifted to beer as the dominant beverage and, along with the traditionally beer-drinking countries, they now represent most of the EU member states. Wine continues to dominate the traditionally wine-drinking countries (Hope and Byrne, 2002). Therefore, due to the convergence in drinking habits in Europe, the traditional wet/dry typology is of uncertain value today, as is the typology based on the dominant beverage type.

Room and Mäkelä (2000) end their review by suggesting two dimensions for a typology of drinking cultures: regularity of drinking and extent of intoxication. Most young people do not drink regularly. Therefore, for a comparative analysis where the focus is on young people, the regularity of drinking is not as important as the extent of intoxication, which is of great importance.

The aim of this chapter is to compare gender differences in young people's drinking habits in different European countries. For the analysis we have chosen four countries where the prevalence of intoxication among young people is high: the UK, Denmark, Sweden and Finland, and four countries where the prevalence of intoxication is low: France, Portugal, Hungary and Greece. In choosing the countries for analysis two other criteria were used: the accessibility of data for the chosen study variables and for three study years (1995, 1999 and 2003). In the rest of the chapter we call the first four 'intoxication countries' and the second four 'non-intoxication countries'.

Gender and age are important factors affecting drinking behaviour. In almost every society, young adult males drink more often than young adult females (Ahlström et al., 2001; Mäkelä et al., 2005). In addition, previous research has shown that in every culture women consume smaller amounts of alcohol than men (Wilsnack et al., 2000; Ahlström et al., 2001; Mäkelä et al., 2005). During adolescence, drinking patterns are less differentiated by gender, and at the onset of young adulthood females may even drink more frequently than males, partly because females typically mature earlier than males and partly because they do not yet have family bonds and responsibility – factors limiting women's drinking later. Once they reach and pass through young adulthood, however, young women tend to consume less alcohol, drink less frequently, and get drunk less often than young men (Ahlström et al., 2001).

On the basis of previous findings among the adult population we expect there to be less gender differences in young people's drinking habits in the intoxication countries than in the non-intoxication countries (Ahlström et al., 2001; Mäkelä et al., 2005). Our second hypothesis is that girls consume on average smaller quantities of alcohol per drinking occasion in every country.

Ahlström et al. (2001) have shown that gender differences among the adult population in nine European countries were greatest for beer consumption, followed by spirits consumption, while the differences were smallest for wine consumption. The results of Mäkelä et al. (2005) for beer and spirits drinking were consistent with these findings. Thus, men reported drinking beer and spirits much more often than women. The situation was different for wine: men and women reported drinking wine equally often in the Nordic countries, but in France and Switzerland men were drinking wine more often than women. Therefore, our hypothesis is that boys drink beer and spirits more often than girls in every country, but boys drink wine more often than girls only in the non-intoxication countries.

Hupkens and her colleagues (1993) studied uniformity and diversity in drinking patterns in the European Community and found that gender differences in the consumption of a beverage type which was not traditionally dominant in a society were smaller than in the frequency of a traditional beverage type. It might be that, compared with the norms regarding the drinking of the traditional beverage type, the norms concerning the drinking of the new beverage type differ less between the genders. Therefore, it is expected that gender differences in the frequency of drinking will be smaller when the beverage type is new in the drinking culture than when the beverage type is traditional.

Bloomfield et al. (2001) have studied gender convergence among the adult population (21–70 years) in alcohol consumption in Finland, Germany, the Netherlands and Switzerland. A closing of the gender gap in current drinking and mean consumption could be found only in Finland. Some of the country reports of GENACIS (Gender, Culture and Alcohol Problems: A Multi-national Study) indicated a convergence in the alcohol consumption of adult men and women (Eisenbach-Stangl, 2005). The convergence seems to have started several decades ago. The process of convergence differs greatly between the countries (Austria, Finland, France, Germany, Italy, Israel and the UK) concerning onset and intensity, and it also differs with respect to the segments of the population carrying it. In Finland, as partly in Austria, it was especially rural women who were no longer abstaining and who were increasing consumption. In France and Finland, it seems to be women from higher strata who are at present drinking the most. In Finland it seems to be mostly a matter that women's drinking approached the level of men's, while in Austria both men's and women's drinking contributed to the convergence of drinking habits. Based on earlier research showing that convergence is not a new phenomenon, our hypothesis is that among young people there has been no closing-in of female and male drinking patterns since the mid-1990s.

It is interesting to see if the patterns found among the adult population will be the same among young people, and if there is a uniform pattern across study countries in the gender differences.

The present analysis is part of the European School Survey Project on Alcohol and Other Drugs (ESPAD) – for a presentation of the ESPAD-project see Chapter 3 and Hibell et al. (2004).

Data and Methods

Data

The data to be analysed come from the latest ESPAD-study (2003). The data concern 15–16 year olds from the UK, Denmark, Sweden, Finland, France, Portugal, Hungary and Greece, with response rates of 84, 89, 87, 91, 96, 91, 82 and 83 per cent respectively. Table 4.1 describes the samples used in the comparison.

Table 4.1   Survey characteristics

Country	Number of participating students			Response rates, %		
	Boys	**Girls**	**Total**	**Boys**	**Girls**	**Total**
United Kingdom	1.083	985	2.068			84*
Denmark	1.504	1.474	2.978	90	88	89
Finland	1.739	1.804	3.543	92	91	91
Sweden	1.592	1.640	3.232	87	87	87
Portugal	1.389	1.557	2.946	97	96	96
France	1.087	1.112	2.199			91
Hungary	1.398	1.279	2.677			82
Greece	886	1.020	1.906			83

*   Calculated on all students in participating classes

Measurements

The measurements used were the prevalence of drinking at least 10 times during the previous 30 days, prevalence of intoxication at least 10 times during the previous 12 months, estimated average consumption of beer, wine, spirits, alcopops and cider in centilitres of 100 per cent alcohol on the last drinking occasion, and the prevalence of drinking beer, wine and spirits at least three times during the previous 30 days. Because we are especially interested in gender comparisons, we devote special attention to gender ratios – that is, the percentage/mean of boys' drinking against that of girls.

Results

Prevalence of Frequent Drinking

There are enormous differences between the countries in the prevalence of frequent drinking during the previous 30 days. Among both boys and girls the prevalence of frequent drinking was highest in the UK, Denmark and Greece, quite high in Portugal, France and Hungary, and very low in Sweden and Finland (Figure 4.1). Hence, frequent drinking is common both in the non-intoxication countries of southern Europe and in some intoxication countries (the UK and Denmark).

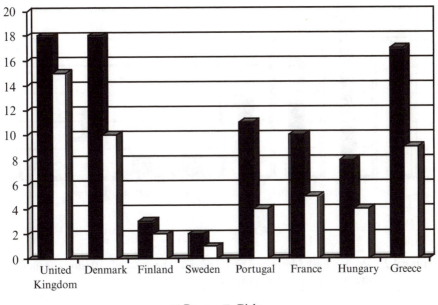

Figure 4.1   Use of any alcoholic beverage 10 times or more during the last 30 days. Percentages among boys and girls, 2003

The gender ratio was highest in Portugal, quite high in France, Hungary, Greece, and Denmark and low in the UK (Table 4.2.). The prevalence in Finland and Sweden are too low for meaningful gender ratios.

There is no clear association between the prevalence of frequent drinking and the gender ratio. For instance, in Sweden the prevalence of frequent drinking is very low, in Greece high, but the gender ratio is the same.

Prevalence of Intoxication

Figure 4.2 illustrates the main difference between intoxication countries and non-intoxication countries, showing huge geographical variation. Among both boys and girls the prevalence of intoxication was highest in Denmark, the UK, and Finland, quite high in Sweden and low in Portugal, France and Greece.

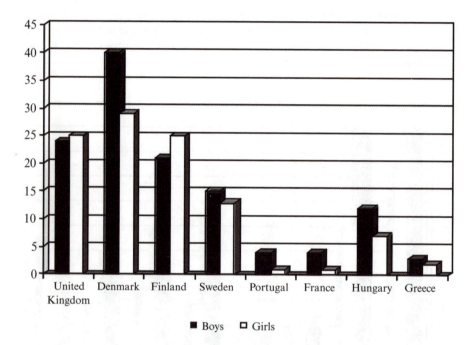

Figure 4.2   Proportion of boys and girls who have been drunk 10 times or more during the last 12 months, 2003

The gender ratio in intoxication was highest in France and Portugal, quite high in Hungary, Greece, Denmark and low in the rest of the countries (Table 4.2). In the UK and Finland, the prevalence of intoxication among girls was higher than that of boys. In Finland, this reversed gender difference among adolescents has been documented since 1995, but in the UK it first appeared in the data in 1999 (Hibell et al., 2004). In two of the three countries where the prevalence of intoxication was very low (Portugal and France), the gender ratio was exceptionally high.

Although there is a pattern with smaller gender differences in some intoxication countries, the relationship is not unambiguous. Denmark and Greece break the pattern: in Denmark the gender difference is larger than expected; in Greece it is smaller.

Average Consumption of Alcohol

There are large differences between the countries in the average consumption of alcohol on the previous drinking occasion (Figure 4.3). Among both boys and girls, the estimated average consumption was highest in the UK and Denmark, quite high in Sweden, Finland, Greece, Hungary and Portugal and lowest in France.

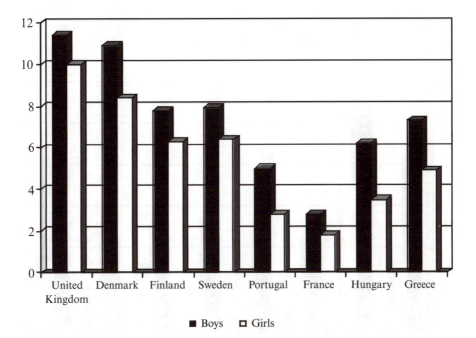

Figure 4.3   Estimated average consumption of alcohol in cl 100%, on the last drinking occasion

There are also differences in the gender ratios of average consumption between the countries. The gender ratio was highest in Portugal and Hungary, quite high in France and Greece and low in the UK, Sweden, Finland and Denmark (Table 4.2).

There is a clear association between the estimated average consumption of alcohol and the gender ratio. The gender ratio was lower in intoxication countries than in non-intoxication countries.

Frequency of Drinking by Beverage Type

Beer   Among boys, the frequency of beer consumption during the previous
30 days was highest in Denmark, the UK and Greece; in the other study countries
it was at a much lower level (Figure 4.4). It is interesting that beer drinking is
an important part of male drinking both in the intoxication countries of north-
western Europe and in a wine-producing country like Greece. ESPAD-data show
that this is not an entirely new phenomenon; the prevalence of drinking beer has
not increased among boys in these countries between 1995 and 2003 (Hibell et
al., 2004).

Among girls the frequency of beer consumption during the previous 30 days
was highest in Denmark and was at a lower level in other study countries. For girls
as well, there is no systematic difference in beer consumption between intoxication
countries and non-intoxication countries.

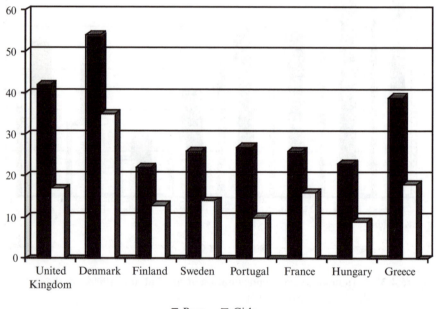

**Figure 4.4   Beer consumption 3 times or more during the last 30 days.
Percentages among boys and girls**

The gender ratio was highest in the UK, Portugal, Hungary and Greece
(Table 4.2).

Wine   Among boys the frequency of wine consumption during the previous
30 days was especially high in Greece, quite high in Hungary and the UK, and
lowest in Finland (Figure 4.5).

Among girls the frequency of wine consumption during the last 30 days was especially high in the UK, quite high in Hungary and Greece, and lowest in Portugal. The frequency of wine consumption was greater among girls in Sweden and Finland than in France and Portugal. According to other ESPAD-data (Hibell et al., 2004) girls' typical drinking places varied between countries. In Greece, Hungary and Portugal, girls' drinking place on the last drinking day was often a bar, pub or disco. In Finland, Sweden and the UK, the most popular drinking place on the last drinking day was at someone else's home. It is very possible that wine drinking among girls does not take place at meals in a family setting in any of the study countries, but is part of spending time with friends in a 'Dionysian' wine drinking style. In other words, adolescent wine drinking is not necessarily as 'integrated' (cf. the discussion of drinking cultures above) as often supposed in the classifications of European countries according to beverage type.

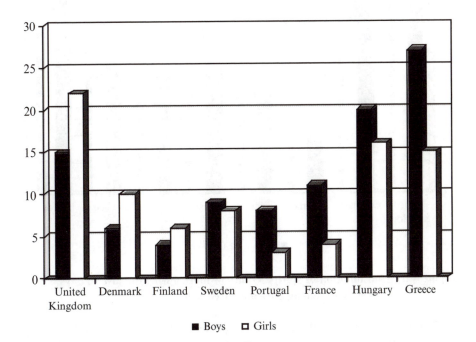

Figure 4.5   Wine consumption 3 times or more during the last 30 days. Percentages among boys and girls, 2003

The gender ratio in wine drinking was highest in France, Portugal and Greece. In Hungary and Sweden it was nearly non-existent. In the UK, Denmark and Finland, the frequency of wine consumption among girls was higher than among boys (Table 4.2).

Spirits   Among both boys and girls the frequency of spirits consumption during the previous 30 days was highest in Greece, Denmark and the UK and lowest in Finland (Figure 4.6). Of the countries included in the present analysis, only Finland has age limits discriminating between purchase of spirits (20 years) and purchase of beer and wine (18 years). The restricted availability of spirits as compared to other alcohol beverages may be part of the explanation of Finnish youth's low spirits consumption. Whatever the reason, this pattern again challenges the traditional European classifications of drinking cultures. Although growing up in an alcohol culture that used to be dominated by spirits, young Finns drink less spirits than adolescents in wine-producing countries.

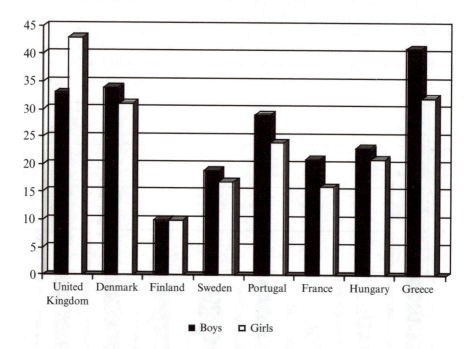

Figure 4.6   Consumption of spirits 3 times or more during the last 30 days. Percentages among boys and girls, 2003

The gender ratio in spirits drinking was quite low or reversed in the intoxication countries (Table 4.2). Also in the non-intoxication countries the rate was low. In Finland, there was no gender difference, while in the UK the prevalence of girls drinking spirits was higher than that of boys. As noted, in Finland spirits are not really part of young people's drinking culture. On the contrary, in the UK girls like to drink spirits-based drinks, which have the symbolic value of being feminine and sexy.

Convergence in Drinking Habits

The gender ratios in drinking variables in 1995, 1999 and 2003 are shown in Table 4.2. In general the ratios are relatively stable for this period. Hungary is the only

Table 4.2 Gender ratios in drinking variables

		UK	Denmark	Finland	Sweden	Portugal	France	Hungary	Greece
Use of any alcohol beverage 10 times or more during the last 30 days. Percentages among boys and girls	1995	1.4	1.9	1	1	4	(-)	6	(-)
	1999	1.3	1.8	2	2	2.5	2.4	3	1.9
	2003	1.2	1.8	1.5	2	3.7	2	2	2
Proportion of boys and girls who have been drunk 10 times or more during last 12 months	1995	1.1	1.1	0.8	1	2	(-)	3	(-)
	1999	1.2	1.2	1	1.3	6	6	4.5	2
	2003	1	1.4	0.8	1.2	3	4	2.4	1.5
Estimated average consumption of alcohol in cl. 100%, on the last drinking occasion	1995	(-)	(-)	(-)	(-)	(-)	(-)	(-)	(-)
	1999	1.2	1.3	1.6	1.5	1.6	1.4	1.7	1.5
	2003	1.1	1.3	1.2	1.2	1.8	1.6	1.8	1.5
Beer consumption 3 times or more during the last 30 days. Percentages among boys and girls	1995	2.2	1.3	1.4	1.8	2.1	(-)	3.8	(-)
	1999	1.8	1.5	2	1.9	2.3	2	3.6	1.8
	2003	2.5	1.5	1.7	1.9	2.7	1.6	2.6	2.2
Wine consumption 3 times or more during the last 30 days. Percentages among boys and girls	1995	0.6	0.9	1	0.7	3	1.8	2.2	(-)
	1999	0.6	0.8	0.8	1	2	2.8	2	2.1
	2003	0.7	0.6	0.7	1.1	2.7	2.8	1.2	1.8
Consumption of spirits 3 times or more during the last 30 days. Percentages among boys and girls	1995	0.6	1.1	0.9	1.1	1.6	(-)	1.3	(-)
	1999	0.6	1	1.2	1.2	1.4	1.4	1	1.4
	2003	0.8	1.1	1	1.1	1.3	1.3	1.1	1.3

country where the gender ratio has decreased for many of the analysed variables: the prevalence of frequent drinking, the prevalence of beer consumption and wine consumption. In addition, the gender ratio of frequent drinking in France decreased from 1999 to 2003 because the prevalence among boys decreased.

Conclusion and Discussion

This chapter has mainly been based on a distinction between intoxication countries and non-intoxication countries. If we, as suggested by Room and Mäkelä (2000), take into consideration not only intoxication but also regularity of drinking, the countries included in the analysis gather in three groups. In the UK and Denmark young people drink often and also report high frequencies of intoxication. In Finland and Sweden, young people drink seldom, but when they do, they very often drink to the point of intoxication. And in the third group of countries (Portugal, France and Greece) young people drink often but very seldom experience intoxication. However, Hungary remains somewhere in between.

Our first hypothesis was that gender differences in young people's drinking are smaller in the intoxication countries than in the non-intoxication countries. The hypothesis was tested in three ways. First, an analysis of gender differences in frequent drinking showed no clear distinction between intoxication countries and the rest. Although the gender differences were small in the UK and Finland, they were considerable in Denmark and Sweden. Second, an analysis of the gender differences in intoxication showed a pattern that was more consistent with the hypothesis. The gender ratio was smaller in the northern countries (except Denmark) and the UK than in the South-European countries. However, there were differences between the South-European countries as well: the gender difference in intoxication was much bigger in France and Portugal than in Hungary and Greece. Third, there was a clear association between the estimated average consumption of alcohol and the gender ratio. The gender ratio was lower in the intoxication countries than in the non-intoxication countries.

Our second hypothesis was that girls in all countries consume less alcohol than boys. This hypothesis was confirmed: despite considerable variation between the studied countries, girls across Europe still consume lesser amounts of alcohol than boys.

The difference in gender ratios between northern and southern Europe and, for some variables between France and Portugal vs, Greece and Hungary may have something to do with the level of informal control in these countries. In a comparative study of young people's drinking in France and the Netherlands it was found that acceptance of drinking was as important as sheer availability of alcohol for explaining adolescent drinking (Knibbe et al., 2005). The proportion of adolescents drinking frequently and drinking five or more units of alcohol at least once a month was higher in the Netherlands than in France. The authors' interpretation was that in France the informal control and especially parental control (rules about adolescent drinking and the enforcement of these rules) was a stronger determinator of how adolescents perceive availability than in the

Netherlands. As regards the results of our analysis, it is possible that informal control of adolescent drinking in Portugal is similar to that of France while the informal control in Hungary and Greece is weaker. Strong informal control may prevent especially girls from drinking heavily in Portugal and France. In the intoxication countries, the informal control of adolescent drinking seems to be very weak for both boys and girls. In some intoxication countries (Sweden, Finland) this may be because there has been a long tradition of formal alcohol control. In other countries (UK, Denmark) where there is neither a strong formal alcohol policy nor strong informal alcohol control, the prevalence of intoxication among young people is extremely high.

Our third hypothesis was that boys drink more beer and spirits than girls in all countries, but that boys drink more wine than girls only in the wine-producing countries. The analyses showed that boys do drink more beer than girls across the study countries and that wine-drinking is dominated by boys only in southern Europe. As regards spirits, the hypothesis was confirmed for all countries except the UK and Finland. Obviously, girls in the UK are especially fond of spirits-based drinks. Their alcohol consumption has risen markedly in recent years (Plant and Plant, 2006). In Finland, the level of spirits consumption was the lowest and there was no gender difference, probably due to control of spirits availability in the monopoly shops and gender equality in the drinking behaviour in this age group.

Our hypothesis that gender differences in the frequency of drinking are smaller when the beverage type is new in the drinking culture than when the beverage type is traditional was partly confirmed. In the intoxication countries the gender ratio was high in the frequency of beer drinking, a traditional male beverage. In the non-intoxication countries where wine is the traditional beverage, the gender ratio in wine-drinking was high in Portugal and France and of medium size in Greece and Hungary.

Finally, our hypothesis that among young people there has been no convergence in drinking patterns since the mid-1990s was confirmed for all countries except Hungary. It is possible that this reflects that the level of drinking among girls in Hungary was very low in 1995 and that informal social control of girls' drinking has lessened, so that girls there have had an opportunity to increase their drinking.

The gendered drinking patterns found among young people resemble those of the adult population. In every country, girls consume less per drinking occasion than boys, as do women in comparison with men (Leifman, 2002; Mäkelä et al., 2005). This is a uniform pattern across study countries. In general, gender differences in intoxication countries are smaller than in the other countries. However, there are differences among the non-intoxication countries as well. In Portugal and France the informal social control seems to prevent girls from imitating the drinking behaviour of boys better than in Greece and Hungary. In the intoxication countries, and especially the UK and Finland the restrictions on girls' drinking seem to have diminished dramatically or disappeared altogether.

References

Ahlström, S. et al. (2001), 'Gender Differences in Drinking Patterns in Nine European Countries: Descriptive Findings', *Substance Abuse*, **22**(1), 69–85. [DOI: 10.1023/A%3A1026475910263].

Ahlström-Laakso, S. (1976), 'European Drinking Habits: A Review of Research and some Suggestions for Conceptual Integration of Findings' in *Cross-cultural Approaches to the Study of Alcohol: An Interdisciplinary Perspective*. Everett, M.V. et al. (eds) (The Hague and Paris: Mouton), 119–132 (distributed in the US by Aldine, Chicago, IL)).

Bloomfield, K. et al. (2001), 'Investigating Gender Convergence in Alcohol Consumption in Finland, Germany, The Netherlands and Switzerland: A Repeated Survey Analysis', *Substance Abuse*, **22**(1), 39–53. [PubMed 12466668] [DOI: 10.1023/A%3A1026471809354].

Eisenbach-Stangl, E. (2005), 'Country Reports' in *Gender, Culture and Alcohol Problems: A Multi-national Study*. Bloomfield, K. et al. (eds) (Berlin: Charité Campus Benjamin Franklin), 189–217.

Hibell, B. et al. (2000), *The 1999 ESPAD Report: Alcohol and Other Drug Use among Students in 30 European Countries* (Stockholm: Swedish Council for Information on Alcohol and Other Drugs (CAN) and the Pompidou Group at the Council of Europe).

— (2004), *The ESPAD Report 2003. Alcohol and Other Drug Use among Students in 35 European Countries* (Stockholm: Swedish Council for Information on Alcohol and Other Drugs (CAN) and the Pompidou Group at the Council of Europe).

Hope, A. and Byrne, S. (2002), 'ECAS Findings: Policy Implications from an EU Perspective' in *Alcohol in Postwar Europe. Consumption, Drinking Patterns, Consequences and Policy Responses in 15 European Countries*. Norström, T. (ed.) (Stockholm: Almqvist and Wiksell International), 206–212.

Hupkens, C.L. et al. (1993), 'Alcohol Consumption in the European Community: Uniformity and Diversity in Drinking Patterns', *Addiction*, **88**(10), 1391–1404. [PubMed 8251877] [DOI: 10.1111/j.1360-0443.1993.tb02026.x].

Knibbe, R.A. et al. (1996), 'Modernization and Geographical Diffusion as Explanations for Regional Differences in the Consumption of Wine and Beer in the European Community', *Substance Use and Misuse*, **31**(11–12), 1639–55.

— (2005), 'Perceived Availability of Substances, Substance Use and Substance-Related Problems: a Cross National Study among French and Dutch Adolescents', *Journal of Substance Use*, **10**(2–3), 151–163.

Leifman, H. (2002), 'A comparative analysis of drinking patterns in six EU countries in the year 2000', *Contemporary Drug Problems*, **29**, 501–48.

Mäkelä, K. (1983), 'The Uses of Alcohol and their Cultural Regulation', *Acta Sociologica*, **26**, 21–31.

— (2005), 'Drinking and Gender Differences in Drinking in Europe: A Comparison of Drinking Patterns in European Countries' in *Gender, Culture and Alcohol Problems: A Multi-national Study*, pp. 49–65. Bloomfield, K. et al. (eds) (Berlin: Charité Campus Benjamin Franklin).

Norström, T., ed. (2002), *Alcohol in Postwar Europe. Consumption, Drinking Patterns, Consequences and Policy Responses in 15 European Countries* (Stockholm: Almqvist and Wiksell International).

Partanen, J. (1991), *Sociability and Intoxication: Alcohol and Drinking in Kenya, Africa and the Modern World* (Helsinki: The Finnish Foundation for Alcohol Studies), vol.

39 (Distributed by Rutgers University Center of Alcohol Studies, New Brunswick, NJ)).

Plant, M.A. and Plant, M.L. (2006), *Binge Britain: Alcohol and the National Response* (Oxford: Oxford University Press).

Room, R. and Mäkelä, K. (2000), 'Typologies of the Cultural Position on Drinking', *Journal of Studies on Alcohol*, **61**(3), 475–483.

Room, R. and Mitchell, A. (1972), 'Notes on Cross-national and Cross-cultural Studies', *Drinking and Drug Practices Surveyor*, **5**(14), 16–20.

Sulkunen, P. (1976), 'Drinking Patterns and the Level of Alcohol Consumption: An International Overview' in *Research Advances in Alcohol and Drug Problems*. Gibbins, R.J. et al. (eds) (New York: John Wiley & Sons), 223–281.

— (1983), 'Alcohol Consumption and the Transformation of Living Conditions. A Comparative Study', in *Research Advances in Alcohol and Drug Problems*. Gibbins, R.J. et al. (eds) (New York: Plenum), 247–297.

Ullman, A.D. (1958), 'Sociocultural Backgrounds of Alcoholism', *Annals of the American Academy of Political and Social Science*, **315**, 48–54. [DOI: 10.1177/000271625831500107].

Wilsnack, R. et al. (2000), 'Gender Differences in Alcohol Consumption and Adverse Drinking Consequences: Cross-Cultural Patterns', *Addiction*, **95**(2), 251–265. [PubMed 10723854] [DOI: 10.1046/j.1360-0443.2000.95225112.x].

Chapter 5

The Impact of Socio-Economic Status on Adolescent Drinking Behaviour

Matthias Richter, Anja Leppin, Saoirse Nic Gabhainn
and Klaus Hurrelmann

Introduction

Several contributions in this volume have shown that alcohol use among young people is associated with a wide range of social, psychological and cultural factors (adult drinking patterns and attitudes towards drinking in a country, adolescents' own expectancies regarding alcohol use and intoxication, gender roles, and so on). The main focus of the present chapter is on the relationship between adolescent drinking behaviour and parental occupational and family affluence. Numerous public health studies have shown that these determinants, which compose the individual socio-economic status (SES) within a society, have a profound influence on mortality and morbidity in adulthood (Macintyre, 1997; Adler and Ostrove, 1999; Mackenbach et al., 2002). Those with lower socio-economic status are consistently found to be more likely to be ill, to require medical attention, to suffer more severe and chronic illness and to die from a range of causes at a younger age. While these patterns are well established, our understanding of the underlying mechanisms are less clear. One approach to explaining social class effects has been to focus on health-related behaviours and how they vary across socio-economic groups. Several researchers have indeed found a steep social gradient in adult lifestyle patterns: the lower the socio-economic status, the higher the risk for health-damaging behaviours and their associated biomedical risk factors (Crum et al., 1993; Cavelaars et al., 1997; Droomers et al., 1999; Tyroler, 1999). Thus, it is argued that behavioural factors such as smoking, malnutrition, excessive consumption of alcohol and lack of physical activity play a major role in the explanation of these social inequalities in health (Stronks et al., 1996; Denton and Walters, 1999; Richter and Mielck, 2000).

Many health-damaging behaviours are established before or during adolescence. As such, their emergence is influenced by a range of social factors, such as modelling within the family, access (as determined by location and familial or societal resources and structures), peer relations and life goals, as well as attitudes and perceived social norms. Experimenting with substance use can to some degree be seen as a normal experiential stage of adolescent development, and has even been associated with positive psychosocial adjustment (Engels, 1998).

However, very early as well as habitual or excessive substance use in adolescence can be considered a risk factor for developmental problems and has been linked to health and social consequences such as accidents, aggressive behaviour or academic problems (Wechsler et al., 1994; Windle et al., 1996; Hoel et al., 2004; Richter and Hurrelmann, 2006). Above and beyond these adolescence-specific problems, established health behaviours tend to continue to exist throughout adulthood and become determining factors for future health (Davey Smith, 2003; Wardle et al., 2003).

Although the importance of individual lifestyle patterns for current and future health has long been accepted, little is known about the development of socio-economic differences in behavioural patterns over the life course. Despite the relative consistency in socio-economic differences in health risk behaviour in adulthood, it is less clear at which stage in life the differences are established (Lenthe et al., 2001). In addition, the existing evidence about the relationship between socio-economic status and health risk behaviours in adolescence is inconsistent and even contradictory. This is especially true for alcohol use. While some studies have identified an unequal distribution of adolescent drinking behaviour among social groups, others found no or only slight socio-economic differences. For example, Donato et al. (1995) showed that educational and occupational status of the parents had no significant influence on the (daily) alcohol consumption of 14–15 and 18–19-year-old Italian adolescents. For repeated drunkenness during the past 12 months a significant but weak effect of parental education for 18–19-year-old adolescents was found, with an increasing risk of drunkenness with increasing educational level of the parents. Goodman and Huang (2002) also found an inverse social gradient of alcohol consumption among US adolescents, based on the income of their parents. For parents' educational level, no significant effect was found. Similar weak associations between parental SES and various alcohol measures have been reported for Dutch (Tuinstra et al., 1998), French (Challier et al., 2000), Belgian (Vereecken et al., 2003) as well as English (Botting and Bunting, 1997) and Scottish (Shucksmith et al., 1997) adolescents.

On the other hand, episodic heavy drinking was inversely related to parental education and family income among 12–17-year-old US adolescents (Lowry et al., 1996). Another US study on 1,242 6-year-olds who were followed until age 32 reported an inverse relationship between family social status and adolescent problem drinking in boys as well as girls (Fothergill and Ensminger, 2006). Tur et al. (2003) reported a negative relationship between mother's educational level and adolescent drinking for boys and girls in Mallorca (Spain), but also the opposite finding for parents' occupational status, that is children of parents with high occupational status were more likely to consume alcohol. Geckova et al. (2002) found an increasing risk of drinking at all and frequency of alcohol consumption with decreasing parental occupation and education among Slovakian girls, but no consistent relation for boys. A similar gender-specific pattern was also found for Finnish adolescents (Lintonen et al., 2000).

In general, it is difficult to evaluate findings from so many different studies, as they were conducted in different socio-cultural contexts, with different methods and at different times. It may be that the lack of clarity apparent in the literature is at least partially due to the lack of comparability between studies. To our knowledge, the present study is the first to examine the influence of socio-economic status on alcohol use and drunkenness among adolescents in a wide range of European and North American countries, using directly comparable time frames, sampling and measurement techniques and identical questions. The inclusion here of two different measures of socio-economic status may also assist interpretation. Occupational status is included, as the most widely agreed and employed measure of socio-economic status in Europe. But there are difficulties in collecting valid data from children on the occupational status of their parents, as evidenced by high rates of missing data, and such an indicator also in fact assesses a country-specific status, while the social meaning of different types of employment may vary with urbanisation, ethnicity or other social group characteristics. A second indicator of socioeconomic status, also employed here, is the family affluence scale (FAS), an assessment of a related but more specific set of familial attributes, reflecting not just the financial resources within a family, but how those resources are deployed in acquiring material goods or experiences (for example on holidays). Material wealth is therefore a requirement for a high score on FAS, but not all affluent families have a high score. Thus, these are distinct measures of socio-economic status and may be differentially related to both the resources available to and the expectations of adolescents within families.

Children from families with higher occupational status may reasonably be operating with the expectation that they themselves are expected to 'succeed' in a similar way, and thus may experience and respond to a greater degree of pressure and support to perform academically, and may concurrently have fewer opportunities to engage in heavy or frequent substance use. Thus, we hypothesise that children from high occupational status parents will report lower frequency of both alcohol consumption and drunkenness. The role of family affluence may be slightly different, as not only are financial resources a key prerequisite of consumption, but as the FAS is also an assessment of the degree to which such resources are being allocated. So we tentatively hypothesise that higher FAS scores will be associated with higher frequencies of alcohol consumption and drunkenness. In addition, we hypothesise that family affluence will be a stronger predictor for boys than for girls, because boys typically consume more alcohol per drinking episode than girls and thus require greater financial resources to sustain their consumption.

Material and Methods

Data were obtained from the Health Behaviour in School-aged Children (HBSC) study 2001/02, a cross-national survey supported by the World Health Organization (Currie et al., 2004). The aim of the HBSC study is to describe young people's health and health behaviour and to analyse how these outcomes are related to the social context. Cross-sectional surveys of 11-, 13- and 15-year-old children and adolescents are carried out every four years in a growing number of countries based on an internationally agreed protocol (Currie et al., 2001). The latest survey, in 2001/02, included a total of 35 countries from Europe and North America. A detailed description of the aims and theoretical framework of the study, as well as the research protocol and sampling procedures, can be found elsewhere (Currie et al., 2001, 2004).

Sample

Students are selected using a clustered sampling design, where the initial sampling unit is the school class. However, due to differences in the school systems across countries, national adaptations in sampling had to be made. In some countries the school was sampled instead of the class, when lists of classes were not available. Approximately 1500 respondents in each of the three age groups (that is 11-, 13- and 15-year-olds) were targeted in every country. The minimum recommended sample size was met by the majority of countries. A regional sample was selected in Germany (Nordrhein-Westfalen, Berlin, Hessen and Sachsen). Separate studies cover the Flemish- and French-speaking populations in Belgium, and separate studies were also undertaken for England, Scotland and Wales in the UK. Data collection took place between the autumn of 2001 and the spring of 2002 in all countries.

The present analysis is based on 69,249 male and 73,619 female students from 29 countries. Countries excluded were Austria, Belgium (Wallonia), England, Greenland, Lithuania and Macedonia because of high rates of missing values for occupational status (above 15 per cent).

Instrument and Variables

The data were collected by collaboratively designed, standardised questionnaires, administered in school classrooms according to specific instructions. The questionnaire consisted of a number of mandatory questions, which were similar in all participating countries, and several optional items, which allowed participating countries to include additional questions of national or local interest.

Adolescent Drinking Behaviour

We included two indicators of adolescent drinking behaviour in this study, (1) frequency of alcohol consumption and (2) frequency of drunkenness. For each, a dichotomous variable was constructed.

Frequency of alcohol use was addressed by three separate questions about the frequency of the consumption of beer, wine, and spirits: 'At present, how often do you drink anything alcoholic, such as beer, wine or spirits? Try to include even those times when you only drink a small amount'. Possible responses were: 'every day', 'every week', 'every month', 'rarely' and 'never'. Responses indicating daily or weekly consumption of either beer, wine or spirits were recoded into a new category 'regular alcohol consumption' (coded as 1).

Frequency of drunkenness was assessed by asking whether the adolescents had ever had so much alcohol that they were really drunk. Possible answers were: 'no, never', 'yes, once', 'yes, two to three times', 'yes, four to ten times' and 'yes, more than ten times'. Response options were recoded into a dichotomous outcome variable (1 = two to three times or more, 0 = less than two to three times). This cut off point has been suggested in recent studies. It marks an established consumption pattern that moves beyond purely sporadic consumption. Indicating a more established rather than experimental pattern of drunkenness, it is thus more likely to measure a potentially health-damaging alcohol consumption pattern (Schmid and Gabhainn, 2004).

Socioeconomic Status

The first SES indicator was based on father's and mother's occupational class (OCC). Two open-ended questions have been asked to assess the parents' occupational status. Students were asked to indicate separately where their father and mother worked (for example in a hospital, factory, garage) and to describe as well as possible what kind of job they did (for example a hairdresser, a dentist, teacher in primary school). Those students whose parents did not work were asked to indicate what they were doing instead: 'is sick, or retired or a student', 'is looking for a job', 'takes care of others, or is full-time in the home'. For those who really had no idea, there was also a response option 'I don't know'. Countries were required to condense the answers into six categories labelled from 1 (high SES) to 5 (low SES) and 6 (economically inactive). Since many women were economically inactive and many responses on parental occupation were missing, information on the occupational status of the father and mother was combined, using the highest occupational status of each couple. For children living with single parents, the occupational status of that parent was used for classification purposes. Finally, the six categories were recoded into three categories of high (1 and 2), middle (3) and low (4, 5 and 6) occupational status.

Taking into account the known difficulties adolescents have when reporting their parents' occupation, another measure, the 'Family Affluence Scale (FAS)' has been developed within the HBSC study as an alternative measurement of socio-economic status (Currie et al., 1997; Boyce and Dallago, 2004; Torsheim et al., 2004). This scale consists of four different items: does your family own a car (0, 1, 2 or more); how many times did you travel away on holiday with your family during the past 12 months? (0, 1, 2, 3 or more); do you have your own bedroom for yourself? (0, 1); and how many computers does your family own (0, 1, 2, 3 or more). A composite FAS score is calculated by summing the responses to these four items, ranging from 0 to 9. The FAS scores were subsequently recoded into tertiles within each country (high, middle, low).

Analysis

The analyses were conducted using SPSS version 12.0.1. Prevalences for the different categories of alcohol and drunkenness were computed for each country.

Logistic regression analyses including both SES indicators simultaneously were used to investigate the independent effect of both indicators on adolescent drinking behaviour (Spearman's rho values between family affluence and parental occupation varied from 0.18 in the Ukraine to 0.38 in Germany). All models were adjusted for age (dummy variable with three categories: 11-, 13- and 15-year-olds), because of its major relevance for occurrence of these lifestyle behaviours in adolescence. Results are presented as odds ratios with 95 per cent confidence intervals. The highest group of family affluence and parental occupation served as the reference category, with odds ratios being computed for the other two groups in comparison. All analyses were conducted separately for each country and gender.

Results

Prevalences

Table 5.1 shows the frequency of alcohol use and repeated episodes of drunkenness by country and gender. On average across countries, 12.3 per cent of all 11–15 year olds reported regular alcohol use (boys 15.6 per cent, girls 9.3 per cent). Nevertheless, these findings mask large differences between countries. Regular alcohol use varied from 5.7 per cent in Ireland to 31.9 per cent in Malta for boys and 3.8 per cent in Finland and 20.8 per cent in Malta for girls. The highest rates of regular alcohol consumption were found in Italy, Malta and Wales, with rates of above 20 per cent. In almost all countries boys reported more frequent alcohol consumption than girls, and this gender gap tended to widen with age (results not shown). The only exceptions to this pattern appeared in Norway, Ireland and Scotland.

Regarding drunkenness, 15.9 per cent of all 11–15 year olds reported having been drunk two or more times in their life. As Table 5.1 illustrates, the highest rates of drunkenness among 11–15 year olds were observed in Wales, Denmark and Ukraine. In these countries, approximately every fourth student had been drunk at least two times during their life span. The lowest rates for repeated drunkenness were found for the southern European countries. For example, in France only 10 per cent of the boys and 6 per cent of the girls reported repeated drunkenness. Across all countries, boys were more likely than girls to report having been drunk twice or more (18.2 per cent of boys vs. 13.7 per cent of girls). This pattern was observed for many countries. Exceptions were Canada, Ireland, Norway, Scotland, Sweden, USA, Spain, Finland and Wales. The largest gender differences were found in the Eastern European countries.

Socio-economic Differences in Adolescent Alcohol Use

Occupational status   Tables 5.2 and 5.3 show the relationships between regular alcohol use, drunkenness and parental occupation for 11–15-year-olds across countries for boys and girls separately, adjusting for age and SES indicators. We

Table 5.1   **Regular alcohol use and repeated drunkenness among 11- to 15-year-olds, by country and gender (%)**

	Weekly alcohol consumption					Have been drunk at least twice				
	N	Total	Boys	Girls	P[1]	N	Total	Boys	Girls	p
Belgium (Flanders)	5720	13.6	18.0	9.7	***	5806	14.3	17.9	11.0	***
Canada	3651	10.2	11.8	9.0	**	3671	17.6	17.7	17.6	ns
Croatia	4168	13.3	16.4	10.1	***	4177	13.2	16.4	10.0	***
Czech Republic	4776	19.3	24.5	14.5	***	4789	14.6	17.3	12.2	***
Denmark	3936	17.6	20.2	15.2	***	3953	28.4	30.4	26.6	**
Estonia	3870	9.5	13.4	5.6	***	3869	23.4	27.8	19.0	***
Finland	4605	4.9	6.0	3.8	***	4677	24.3	23.7	24.8	ns
France	7392	7.4	9.5	5.3	***	7536	7.9	9.7	6.1	***
Germany	4941	13.1	15.6	10.7	***	5032	17.0	18.9	15.2	***
Greece	3667	16.4	22.1	10.9	***	3698	10.3	12.6	8.1	***
Hungary	3753	15.1	21.1	10.5	***	3781	15.8	19.9	12.5	***
Ireland	2531	5.3	5.7	5.0	ns	2648	13.3	12.8	13.7	ns
Israel	4616	14.4	19.9	9.9	***	4769	8.2	11.9	5.1	***
Italy	4166	22.8	30.2	16.1	***	4167	8.5	10.3	6.9	***
Latvia	2927	7.7	9.6	6.1	***	2960	15.6	20.9	11.2	***
Malta	1742	25.8	31.9	20.8	***	1744	10.4	13.0	8.3	**
Norway	4236	6.6	6.5	6.7	ns	4302	15.1	14.4	15.9	ns
Poland	5829	7.3	10.1	4.6	***	5836	15.1	19.1	11.1	***
Portugal	2680	7.7	10.0	5.6	***	2673	10.8	13.7	8.2	***
Russia	6970	13.8	17.4	10.7	***	6994	18.8	22.1	16.0	***
Scotland	3532	18.3	18.8	17.8	ns	3516	22.3	22.1	22.4	ns
Slovenia	3608	10.9	14.6	7.3	***	3603	16.2	20.2	12.2	***
Spain	5576	8.1	9.7	6.6	***	5580	9.3	9.3	9.3	ns
Sweden	3272	6.7	8.2	5.3	***	3330	14.8	15.1	14.5	ns
Switzerland	3968	10.6	15.0	6.3	***	4029	13.6	17.1	10.2	***
Ukraine	3575	18.8	25.0	13.6	***	3613	28.5	34.1	23.8	***
USA	4168	7.6	9.6	5.9	***	4223	11.5	12.7	10.5	ns
Wales	3100	20.6	25.0	16.1	***	3120	31.2	32.4	30.0	ns

[1]   test for gender difference.

*   p< .05, ** p< .01, *** p< .001, ns = non significant.

Youth Drinking Cultures

Table 5.2 **The relationship between alcohol use (at least once a week) and parental occupation by country, percentages and odds ratios,[1] girls and boys**

	Boys					Girls				
	Parental occupation (OCC)			Parental occupation (OCC)		Parental occupation (OCC)			Parental occupation (OCC)	
	% high	% mid	% low	OR mid	OR low	% high	% mid	% low	OR mid	OR low
Belgium (Flanders)	18	18	18	1.28	1.04	10	10	9	0.99	0.79
Canada	12	11	11	1.06	1.01	9	9	8	1.11	0.98
Croatia	14	17	17	1.39	**1.44**	10	12	9	1.12	0.84
Czech Republic	26	21	26	0.91	1.16	14	14	17	1.10	1.26
Denmark	23	23	18	1.06	0.91	19	16	13	0.87	0.73
Estonia	15	13	13	0.91	0.98	5	6	6	1.16	1.12
Finland	5	7	5	1.72	1.25	3	4	5	1.47	**2.05**
France	10	11	9	1.17	0.95	5	5	5	1.00	0.96
Germany	17	17	13	1.17	1.00	11	13	9	1.33	0.84
Hungary	23	23	15	0.98	0.94	10	11	9	1.03	1.12
Ireland	4	8	8	**2.25**	2.31	5	6	4	1.05	0.85
Israel	18	23	19	**1.41**	1.17	11	10	8	1.00	0.80
Italy	31	29	32	1.05	0.94	20	13	20	0.83	1.03
Greece	24	22	21	1.03	1.15	11	10	11	0.86	0.94
Latvia	13	7	9	**0.55**	0.75	8	5	6	0.61	0.82
Malta	35	26	33	0.80	1.37	22	20	21	1.02	1.16
Norway	7	6	8	1.10	1.61	9	5	7	0.76	1.10
Poland	9	10	11	1.20	1.41	6	4	4	0.78	0.74
Portugal	12	11	9	1.20	1.19	5	5	6	0.88	1.24
Russia	18	18	15	1.08	0.96	12	11	10	0.89	0.85
Scotland	22	15	17	0.71	0.98	20	20	15	1.08	0.98
Slovenia	14	16	14	1.19	1.21	7	9	6	1.33	0.99
Spain	9	10	10	1.35	**1.61**	8	6	6	0.75	0.80
Sweden	10	7	7	0.85	0.84	5	5	6	1.13	1.57
Switzerland	17	13	16	0.69	0.84	8	7	6	0.92	0.81
Ukraine	25	21	26	0.84	1.14	13	15	14	1.17	1.23
USA	10	11	9	1.17	0.92	6	6	6	0.99	1.01
Wales	26	22	25	0.93	1.11	17	16	15	0.93	1.00

1 logistic regression models, adjusted for age.
Bold = OR does not include 1.

Table 5.3 The relationship between drunkenness (2 to 3 times or more) and parental occupation by country, percentages and odds ratios,[1] girls and boys

	Boys					Girls				
	Parental occupation (OCC)			Parental occupation (OCC)		Parental occupation (OCC)			Parental occupation (OCC)	
	% high	% mid	% low	OR mid	OR low	% high	% mid	% low	OR mid	OR low
Belgium (Flanders)	17	17	21	1.24	**1.40**	9	11	14	**1.35**	**1.69**
Canada	18	18	17	1.18	1.09	17	18	18	1.30	1.16
Croatia	15	16	17	1.24	1.44	11	11	9	1.06	0.84
Czech Republic	17	14	22	0.95	1.60	12	11	15	1.18	1.36
Denmark	30	34	29	1.35	1.28	28	28	25	1.21	1.05
Estonia	31	25	27	0.88	1.09	20	19	19	0.85	1.00
Finland	22	25	24	**1.33**	1.24	22	26	27	**1.34**	**1.37**
France	11	9	9	0.73	0.76	8	4	7	**0.44**	0.76
Germany	21	20	17	1.11	0.90	15	16	14	1.29	1.07
Hungary	19	23	15	**1.41**	1.57	11	14	11	1.11	1.06
Ireland	13	11	16	1.03	1.63	12	18	15	**1.61**	1.45
Israel	13	12	11	1.02	0.88	6	4	4	0.75	0.67
Italy	10	9	13	1.36	1.16	8	5	11	0.83	1.09
Greece	14	13	12	1.02	1.04	8	9	7	1.04	0.83
Latvia	25	20	18	0.79	0.82	12	12	10	1.12	1.16
Malta	17	10	12	0.67	0.90	10	10	7	1.23	0.84
Norway	16	13	15	1.05	1.29	17	13	19	0.92	**1.51**
Poland	18	20	19	1.42	1.28	13	13	9	1.03	0.69
Portugal	15	13	13	1.11	1.44	7	9	8	1.49	1.60
Russia	20	22	23	1.23	**1.46**	17	15	17	0.93	1.27
Scotland	23	22	21	1.15	1.15	23	22	23	0.94	1.34
Slovenia	16	21	21	1.39	**1.58**	12	15	11	1.42	1.12
Spain	9	9	9	1.16	1.31	11	10	8	0.98	0.75
Sweden	15	18	15	**1.88**	**1.58**	14	13	15	1.02	1.22
Switzerland	17	16	18	0.95	1.05	10	12	9	1.26	0.90
Ukraine	34	34	35	1.12	1.05	25	24	23	0.84	0.88
USA	13	14	12	1.22	1.25	11	10	11	0.91	1.00
Wales	32	35	32	1.45	1.24	29	31	31	1.09	1.21

1 logistic regression models, adjusted for age.
Bold = OR does not include 1.

hypothesised that children from families with a higher occupational status will report lower frequencies of both alcohol consumption and drunkenness.

In general, the results give very little support for our hypothesis as the analyses indicate an increasing risk of regular alcohol use with decreasing parental status only for boys in Ireland, Croatia and Spain (Table 5.2). In Finland and Israel the highest risk of regular alcohol consumption was observed in boys from families with a medium occupational status. An opposite effect was found for Latvian boys who had a significantly lower odds ratio for regular alcohol use in the middle category of parental occupation. For girls, the only significant effect of parental occupational status appeared for Finnish girls. For this group the odds ratio of drinking alcohol at least once a week increased from the reference category of high occupational status up to 2.05 in the lowest category.

In drunkenness among boys, of the nine countries that showed significant effects between parental occupation and repeated drunkenness, the risk of drunkenness increased with decreasing occupational status in six countries (Croatia, Czech Republic, Hungary, Belgium, Russia and Slovenia). For girls, a significant effect of parental occupation was observed in six countries (Finland, France, Ireland, Belgium, Norway and Poland). For Finland, Belgium and Norway the risk of repeated drunkenness increased with decreasing occupational status, while for Ireland the highest odds ratio was found in the middle occupational status category. For French girls the direction of the effect was reversed, indicating a significantly lower odds ratio for repeated drunkenness for girls with a medium as compared to a high occupational status of their parents. A lower risk of being drunk 2–3 times in life was also found for girls from Poland, but this time the effect was observed in the lowest occupational status category.

Family affluence   In contrast to parental occupation, we hypothesised that higher FAS scores would be associated with higher frequencies of alcohol consumption and drunkenness, and that this effect would be greater for boys than for girls. Significant effects of family affluence on regular alcohol use for boys were observed in 15 countries without any geographical or socio-cultural pattern emerging (Table 5.4). In addition, the direction of the effect of SES differed between countries. For boys a decreasing risk of drinking alcohol at least once a week with decreasing family affluence was found in 11 out of the 15 countries. The remaining four countries (Hungary, Poland, Portugal and Sweden) had the lowest risk of regular alcohol use in the medium-affluent group, followed by the lowest FAS category. In only 5 out of the 29 countries is a significant relationship between family affluence and regular alcohol consumption among girls apparent. The risk of regular alcohol use decreased with decreasing family affluence in Denmark, Italy and Wales. In Spain and Hungary a significantly lower OR for drinking at least weekly was observed in the middle category of family affluence.

For repeated drunkenness, a significant effect for boys was found in nine countries for family affluence (Table 5.5). Regarding family affluence for boys in Croatia, Portugal, Russia and Sweden, the risk of repeated episodes of drunkenness decreased with decreasing family affluence. In Scotland, Latvia,

Table 5.4 **The relationship between alcohol use (at least once a week) and family affluence by country, percentages and odds ratios,[1] girls and boys**

	Boys					Girls				
	Family affluence (OCC)			Family affluence (OCC)		Family affluence (OCC)			Family affluence (OCC)	
	% high	% mid	% low	OR mid	OR low	% high	% mid	% low	OR mid	OR low
Belgium (Flanders)	19	19	16	0.91	**0.77**	10	9	10	0.78	0.92
Canada	13	10	12	0.66	0.81	10	9	9	0.89	0.81
Croatia	18	16	15	0.73	**0.66**	10	7	12	0.66	1.07
Czech Republic	25	28	21	1.06	**0.73**	14	13	16	0.83	0.92
Denmark	22	21	17	0.81	0.74	16	17	12	1.04	**0.56**
Estonia	14	14	13	0.94	0.74	4	6	7	1.22	1.32
Finland	8	6	4	0.67	**0.47**	4	3	5	0.57	0.70
France	10	10	9	0.83	0.75	5	5	6	0.89	0.98
Germany	18	16	12	0.85	**0.59**	11	11	11	1.07	1.02
Hungary	23	19	22	**0.71**	0.72	12	9	11	**0.58**	**0.63**
Ireland	6	8	4	1.23	0.61	6	4	5	0.65	0.77
Israel	21	19	18	0.80	**0.77**	11	9	9	0.84	0.83
Italy	31	29	31	0.86	1.13	21	14	12	**0.59**	**0.55**
Greece	27	20	18	**0.64**	**0.49**	10	11	12	1.06	1.20
Latvia	10	9	10	0.98	1.02	6	6	7	0.87	1.08
Malta	38	33	26	0.82	**0.62**	21	22	20	0.87	0.82
Norway	9	6	5	0.66	0.62	9	6	7	0.64	0.73
Poland	11	9	11	**0.71**	0.79	6	4	4	0.69	0.75
Portugal	12	9	8	**0.63**	0.68	5	5	6	0.93	1.13
Russia	20	18	14	**0.76**	**0.57**	12	10	11	0.79	0.80
Scotland	21	19	17	0.75	**0.67**	17	20	16	0.99	0.76
Slovenia	15	15	13	0.89	**0.65**	8	7	7	0.83	0.81
Spain	9	10	10	0.84	0.77	5	4	9	**0.57**	1.29
Sweden	10	7	8	**0.56**	0.69	5	5	6	0.85	0.98
Switzerland	14	15	18	1.03	1.21	7	6	6	0.73	0.61
Ukraine	27	24	23	0.87	0.79	14	15	13	0.99	0.78
USA	9	10	10	1.10	1.20	6	6	6	1.14	0.98
Wales	24	27	23	1.06	0.85	18	16	15	0.73	**0.65**

1 logistic regression models, adjusted for age.
Bold = OR does not include 1.

Table 5.5   **The relationship between drunkenness (2 to 3 times or more) and family affluence by country, percentages and odds ratios,[1] girls and boys**

	Boys					Girls				
	Family affluence (OCC)			Family affluence (OCC)		Family affluence (OCC)			Family affluence (OCC)	
	% high	% mid	% low	OR mid	OR low	% high	% mid	% low	OR mid	OR low
Belgium (Flanders)	19	17	17	0.76	0.78	10	11	12	0.94	1.00
Canada	18	17	18	0.75	0.78	16	17	19	1.09	1.02
Croatia	17	17	16	0.80	**0.73**	10	9	10	0.92	0.88
Czech Republic	17	18	17	0.92	0.87	11	11	14	0.84	0.99
Denmark	31	30	30	0.81	0.95	25	28	26	1.08	0.79
Estonia	29	26	29	**0.75**	0.77	16	19	22	1.08	1.16
Finland	24	22	25	0.80	0.96	22	22	31	0.79	1.19
France	10	9	11	0.84	1.08	5	6	7	1.13	1.07
Germany	22	17	18	**0.71**	0.78	15	15	15	0.99	0.94
Hungary	20	18	21	**0.62**	**0.62**	12	10	16	0.70	0.97
Ireland	14	13	11	0.74	0.67	13	13	15	0.75	0.82
Israel	13	10	11	0.74	0.80	5	5	5	0.80	0.86
Italy	11	10	9	0.76	0.90	8	6	7	0.73	1.00
Greece	13	13	10	0.95	0.69	8	8	8	1.07	1.12
Latvia	24	18	20	**0.68**	0.70	13	11	10	0.72	**0.65**
Malta	16	13	10	0.82	0.73	9	10	7	1.04	0.82
Norway	18	13	13	0.76	0.84	15	15	19	1.06	1.13
Poland	20	18	20	0.81	0.79	12	9	12	0.77	1.05
Portugal	17	13	10	**0.63**	**0.49**	9	8	8	0.70	0.76
Russia	24	22	20	**0.78**	**0.64**	24	22	20	1.05	0.84
Scotland	23	19	25	**0.64**	0.90	18	24	24	1.13	1.11
Slovenia	20	18	22	0.73	0.80	13	13	11	1.05	0.71
Spain	8	10	10	0.90	0.87	8	9	11	0.88	0.97
Sweden	19	13	13	**0.46**	**0.44**	12	14	17	1.10	1.23
Switzerland	16	17	20	1.01	1.13	9	10	12	0.88	1.01
Ukraine	34	35	35	1.11	1.08	24	23	24	0.86	0.91
USA	14	12	12	0.81	0.78	9	11	11	1.24	1.22
Wales	30	35	31	1.10	0.91	27	32	29	1.10	0.88

1   logistic regression models, adjusted for age.
Bold = OR does not include 1.

Estonia, Germany and Hungary the lowest risk of repeated drunkenness was observed for boys from medium-affluent families. However, in most of these countries the risk of repeated drunkenness for the medium-affluent category was only slightly lower than for the lowest category. For girls, repeated drunkenness was found to be largely unrelated to family affluence. In only one out of the 29 countries, Latvia, a significant effect of family affluence was found for female students.

Discussion

Little is known about the relationship between parental socio-economic status and adolescent drinking behaviour. Previous studies analysing the relationships between social inequality and various measures of drinking behaviour in youth have shown very different results. However, the comparability of these findings across countries is questionable, in view of the differences in sampling, methodology and measurement instruments used. The HBSC study provides a unique opportunity for more systematic between-country comparisons.

Overall, we found very limited evidence for a close relationship between SES and adolescent drinking behaviour, with little support especially for our first hypothesis. Instead our results support the assertion that socio-economic differences in adolescent drinking behaviour are not as pronounced as for adults. It needs to be acknowledged, though, that the picture for adults is also rather complicated and distinct socio-economic differences are mainly found for rather 'extreme' measures of excessive alcohol use. This suggests that the determining role of socio-economic background for patterns of alcohol consumption might emerge only later in life (Droomers et al., 2003). These findings thus underline previous studies, which identified only weak or even no relationship between parental SES and alcohol use in adolescence (Shucksmith et al., 1997; Tuinstra et al., 1998; Challier et al., 2000; Vereecken et al., 2003).

Instead, during adolescence, there might be other factors which may have a greater impact on substance use than SES. For instance, the specific character of adolescence as a stage of experimenting with 'new' behaviours identified with adult status might also create generalised developmental stage-related demands and temptations beyond the boundaries of family class background (Shucksmith et al., 1997) and these again might culturally differ across countries. More important yet might be the consideration that while health behaviour in childhood is strongly determined by parents, with the onset of adolescence the influence of peers and youth culture increases, which in turn is closely related to adolescent risk behaviour (Maggs and Hurrelmann, 1998; Simons-Morton et al., 2000; Richter, 2005). This process may lead to a decreasing influence of family background and increasing importance of peers and peer-determined social norms and values on health risk behaviours during adolescence (West, 1997; Chen et al., 2002). This might apply especially for those behaviours, which do not usually start until adolescence, such as alcohol and tobacco consumption. Moreover, while parents' influence might decrease in the course of adolescence, the influence, which remains may be mediated through more qualitative aspects of family climate and family support rather than through structural dimensions such as SES (Dodge et al., 1994; Radziszweska et al., 1996; Shucksmith et al., 1997).

The finding of a non-effect of SES, however, has to be qualified to some degree. Detailed analyses showed that for girls, indeed, almost no significant effects of either SES-indicator were observed. But for boys there was some evidence for socio-economic differences, particularly in relation to family affluence, thus providing limited support for our hypotheses. Boys from low and/or medium affluent background showed lower risks of regular drinking or frequent drunkenness than boys from high-affluent families. While significant effects of this type occurred in less than half of the countries, it might be noted that a majority of countries, that is 24 for regular alcohol consumption and 20 for drunkenness, showed tendencies for low-affluent boys to be less at risk for regular alcohol consumption than high-affluent boys, even if these trends did – sometimes barely – fail to attain significance. These results thus support the findings of Botting and Bunting (1997); Donato et al. (1995) and Goodman and Huang (2002), who also found a decreasing risk of alcohol use with decreasing SES.

For boys as well as for girls, the effects of parental occupation were few – with the exception of drunkenness for boys, where the numbers of significant relations were similar for FAS and for parental occupation – and these effects most often indicated a higher risk in adolescents with parents of low or medium occupational status. Thus, while for FAS the risk of alcohol use and drunkenness decreased with decreasing family affluence, for parental occupation – in those few cases were an effect was found – the risk tended to increase with decreasing status. This was even true for countries that showed significant effects on both indicators. These findings strongly suggest that different dimensions of SES have different effects on alcohol use in adolescence – in terms both of strength of effects and of direction.

The most plausible explanation for these differences might be found when the specific consequences deriving from these two SES dimensions are considered. Parental occupation to some extent might reflect parents' educational status. Educational strategies, values, norms and model behaviour of parents from a higher educational background might be somewhat more likely to curb substance use in adolescence because these parents might be more aware of the health-damaging effects of alcohol and try more to protect adolescents, thus explaining the congruence of parental educational background and adolescents' alcohol consumption patterns. However, as reasoned above, the overall influence of parents on adolescents' health risk behaviour might be limited, thus allowing for few significant effects. Family affluence, on the other hand, seems much more related to income and/or spending patterns, and therefore also to the availability of adolescents' resources to indulge in the relatively costly consumption of alcohol in the first place. This might also explain at least part of the gender differences found in the relationship between FAS and drinking behaviour. Our results show that the overall level of alcohol consumption is much higher in boys than in girls in most countries. Therefore, the relevance of resources, such as pocket money to buy alcohol, might also be considerably higher for boys, thus increasing the role of family affluence.

Within this explanatory framework, it would be expected that family affluence might have been a particularly influential factor in the economically less developed European countries. A closer look at the data for regular alcohol consumption showed that indeed there were significant effects for FAS in Croatia, the Czech Republic, Slovenia, Russia and Greece. However, contrary to this assumption, significant effects also occurred in Belgium, Germany, Finland, Scotland and Israel, thus rendering an exclusively economic explanation less likely. It seems therefore that further, more specific cultural factors such as social norms concerning alcohol consumption as well as national policies on taxation of alcohol might play a decisive role. On the other hand, if only frequent drunkenness is taken into account – which can be considered a more financially expensive behaviour – the pattern becomes clearer, with Croatia, Estonia, Hungary, Latvia, Portugal and Russia showing significant differences, and only Germany, Scotland and Sweden – where such effects also occurred – not fitting this pattern. Additionally, Sweden might be considered a special case due to the extremely high alcohol prices, which might make affordability issues more prevalent for adolescents.

Limitations

Several methodological aspects restrict the explanatory power of these findings. The veracity of self-reported data on parental occupation can be questioned. Even though several studies indicate that the classifiable answers of adolescents (even at the age of 11–13) can be considered as good proxy reports of parental occupation (Lien et al., 2001; et al., 2001; Vereecken and Vandegehuchte, 2003), it remains problematic that a relatively large number of adolescents (up to 15 per cent) do not seem to be able to report their parents' occupation at all. If missing or unclassifiable responses are unequally distributed among social groups, which might be expected, this is likely to effect results. Therefore, the results on occupational differences should be interpreted cautiously.

Similarly, there are questions of validity about self-reports of adolescent drinking behaviour. Such self-reports may involve an element of social desirability, and may be differentially valid according to the reference group or gender. However, it has been repeatedly shown that these self-reports usually can claim a rather high degree of validity (Lintonen and Rimpelä, 2001; Lintonen et al., 2004). Moreover, the students were assured of the confidentiality of the study, and that neither their parents nor teachers were informed about the individual results, in order to underline the importance of giving honest responses. Another source of self-reporting bias would emerge if under-reporting is associated with parental SES. Unfortunately, not much is known about these mechanisms in adolescence. Nevertheless, while dichotomous classifications of alcohol use and drunkenness are crude, they are probably less vulnerable to reporting errors.

The generalisability of the current findings could be limited by the fact that only two rather global indicators of alcohol consumption have been used. Thus, it is possible that looking at other indicators such as amount of alcohol consumed or taking into account the specific types of alcohol such as beer, wine or spirits might have produced results that have been obscured by the more general measures employed here.

Conclusions

In spite of the limitations mentioned above, the present study clearly indicates that SES seems to be of limited importance for the development of drinking behaviour in early adolescence, and that this very limited role seems to apply for girls more than for boys and for the SES dimension of parental occupation more than for family affluence. However, it might be interesting for future studies to look at the effects of socio-economic status within the context of other – possibly more relevant – actors, such as peer or school influence on the one hand, or other parental factors such as social support on the other, in order to assess to what extent such factors might strengthen or weaken the effects of socio-economic background.

Acknowledgment

HBSC is an international study conducted in collaboration with the WHO Regional Office for Europe. The current International Coordinator is Professor Candace Currie, University of Edinburgh and the Data Bank Manager is Dr Oddrun Samdal, University of Bergen. We acknowledge the help and support of all researchers, teachers, students, parents and funders across Europe and North America that make HBSC possible.

References

Adler, N.E. and Ostrove, J.M. (1999), 'Socioeconomic Status and Health: What we Know and what we Don't', *Annals of the New York Academy of Sciences*, **896**, 3–15. [PubMed 10681884] [DOI: 10.1111/j.1749-6632.1999.tb08101.x].

Botting, B. and Bunting, J. (1997), 'Children's Health and Lifestyle – a Review' in *Health Inequalities – Decennial Supplement*. Drever, F. and Whitehead, M. (eds) (London: The Stationery Office), 186–197.

Boyce, W. and Dallago, L. (2004), 'Socio-economic Inequalities' in *Young People's Health in Context– Health Behaviour in School-aged Children (HBSC) Study: International Report from the 2001/02 Survey*. Currie, C. et al. (eds) (Copenhagen: WHO-Europe), 13–25.

Cavelaars, A.E. et al. (1997), 'Socio-economic Differences in Risk Factors for Morbidity and Mortality in the European Community', *Journal of Health Psychology*, **3**, 353–372. [DOI: 10.1177/135910539700200306].

Challier, B. et al. (2000), 'Associations of Family Environment and Individual Factors with Tobacco, Alcohol and Illicit Drug Use in Adolescents', *European Journal of Epidemiology*, **16**, 33–42. [PubMed 10780340] [DOI: 10.1023/A%3A1007644331197].

Chen, E. et al. (2002), 'Socioeconomic Differences in Children's Health: How and Why do These Relationships Change with Age?', *Psychological Bulletin*, **2**, 295–329. [DOI: 10.1037/0033-2909.128.2.295].

Crum, R.M. et al. (1993), 'Level of Education and Alcohol: Abuse and Dependence in Adulthood: a Further Inquiry', *American Journal of Public Health*, **6**, 830–837.

Currie, C. et al. (1997), 'Indicators of Socio-Economic Status for Adolescents: the WHO Health Behaviour in School-aged Children Survey', *Health Education Research*, **12**, 385–397. [PubMed 10174221] [DOI: 10.1093/her%2F12.3.385].

—, eds (2001), *Health Behaviour in School-aged Children: a WHO Cross-National Study (HBSC), Research Protocol for the 2001/2002 Survey* (Edinburgh: University of Edinburgh, Child and Adolescent Health Research Unit (CAHRU)).

—, eds (2004), *Young People's Health in Context – Health Behaviour in School-aged Children (HBSC) Study: International Report from the 2001/02 Survey* (Copenhagen: WHO-Europe).

Davey Smith, G. (2003), *Health Inequalities: Lifecourse Approaches* (Bristol: Policy Press).

De Vries, H. (1995), 'Socio-economic Differences in Smoking: Dutch Adolescents' Beliefs and Behaviour', *Social Science and Medicine*, **41**(3), 419–424. [PubMed 7481935].

Denton, M. and Walters, V. (1999), 'Gender Differences in Structural and Behavioral Determinants of Health: an Analysis of the Social Production of Health', *Social Science and Medicine*, **48**, 1221–1235. [PubMed 10220021].

Dodge, K.A. et al. (1994), 'Socialization Mediators of the Relation between Socioeconomic Status and Child Conduct Problems', *Child Development*, **65**, 649–665. [PubMed 8013245] [DOI: 10.2307/1131407].

Donato, F. et al. (1995), 'Patterns and Covariates of Alcohol Drinking among High School Students in 10 Towns in Italy: a Cross-Sectional Study', *Drug and Alcohol Dependence*, **37**, 59–69. [PubMed 7882874] [DOI: 10.1016/0376-8716%2894%2901053-N].

Droomers, M. et al. (1999), 'Educational Differences in Excessive Alcohol Consumption: the Role of Psychosocial and Material Stressors', *Preventive Medicine*, **29**, 1–10. [PubMed 10419792] [DOI: 10.1006/pmed.1999.0496].

— (2003), 'Occupational Level of the Father and Alcohol Consumption During Adolescence; Patterns and Predictors', *Journal of Epidemiology and Community Health*, **57**, 702–710. [DOI: 10.1136/jech.57.9.704].

Engels, R.C.M.E. (1998), *Forbidden Fruits: Social Dynamics in Smoking and Drinking Behavior of Adolescents* (Maastricht: University of Maastricht).

Fothergill, K.E. and Ensminger, M.E. (2006), 'Childhood and Adolescent Antecedents of Drug and Alcohol Problems: a Longitudinal Study', *Drug and Alcohol Dependence*, **82**, 61–76. [PubMed 16150555] [DOI: 10.1016/j.drugalcdep.2005.08.009].

Geckova, A. et al. (2002), 'Socio-economic Differences in Health Risk Behaviour and Attitudes towards Health Risk Behaviour among Slovak Adolescents', *Sozial- und Praventivmedizin*, **47**, 233–239. [DOI: 10.1007/BF01326404].

Goodman, E. and Huang, B. (2002), 'Socio-economic Status, Depressive Symptoms, and Adolescent Substance Use', *Archives of Pediatrics and Adolescent Medicine*, **156**, 448–453. [PubMed 11980549].

Hoel, S. et al. (2004), 'Adolescent Alcohol Use, Psychological Health, and Social Integration', *Scandinavian Journal of Public Health*, **5**, 361–367. [DOI: 10.1080/14034940410027894].

Holmen, T.L. et al. (2000), 'Health Problems in Teenage Daily Smokers versus Nonsmokers, Norway, 1995-1997 – The Nord-Trondelang Health Study', *American Journal of Epidemiology*, **2**, 148–155.

Lenthe, van F.J. et al. (2001), 'Socioeconomic Position and Coronary Heart Disease Risk Factors in Youth: Findings from the Young Heart Project in Northern Ireland', *European Journal of Public Health*, **11**, 43–50. [DOI: 10.1093/eurpub%2F11.1.43].

Lien, N. et al. (2001), 'Adolescents' Proxy Reports of Parents' socioeconomic Status: How Valid are They?', *Journal of Epidemiology and Community Health*, **55**, 731–737. [PubMed 11553657] [DOI: 10.1136/jech.55.10.731].

Lintonen, T. and Rimpelä, M. (2001), 'The Validity of the Concept of 'Self-perceived Drunkenness' in Adolescent Health Surveys', *Journal of Substance Use*, **3**, 145–150. [DOI: 10.1080/14659890152558750].

Lintonen, T. et al. (2000), 'The Effect of Societal Changes on Drunkenness Trends in Early Adolescence', *Health Education Research*, **3**, 261–269. [DOI: 10.1093/her%2F15.3.261].

Lintonen, T. et al. (2004), 'The Reliability of Self-reported Drinking in Adolescence', *Alcohol and Alcoholism*, **4**, 362–368.

Lowry, R. et al. (1996), 'The Effects of Socio-Economic Status on Chronic Disease Risk Behaviors among US Adolescents', *Journal of the American Medical Association*, **276**, 792–797. [PubMed 8769588] [DOI: 10.1001/jama.276.10.792].

Macintyre, S. (1997), 'The Black Report and Beyond – What are the Issues?', *Social Science and Medicine*, **6**, 723–745.

Mackenbach, J.P. et al. (2002), 'Socioeconomic Inequalities in Health in Europe – An Overview' in *Reducing Inequalities in Health: a European Perspective*. Mackenbach, J.P. and Bakker, M.J. (eds) (London: Routledge), 3–24.

Maggs, J.L. and Hurrelmann, K. (1998), 'Do Substance Use and Delinquency Have Differential Associations with Adolescents' Peer Relations?', *International Journal of Behavioral Development*, **2**, 367–388.

Radziszewska, B. et al. (1996), 'Parenting Style and Adolescent Depressive Symptoms, Smoking, and Academic Achievement: Ethnic, Gender, and Sex Differences', *Journal of Behavioral Medicine*, **3**, 289–305. [DOI: 10.1007/BF01857770].

Richter, M. (2005), 'Health and Health Behaviour in Adolescence: the Influence of Social Inequality'(in German). (Wiesbaden: VS-Verlag).

Richter, M. and Hurrelmann, K. (2006), 'Risk Behaviour in Adolescence – The Relationship between Developmental and Health Problems', *Journal of Public Health*, **14**, 20–28. [DOI: 10.1007/s10389-005-0005-5].

Richter, M. and Mielck, A. (2000), 'Structural and Behavioural Determinants of Socio-economic Inequalities in Health' (in German), *Zeitschrift für Gesundheitswissenschaften*, **3**, 198–215.

Schmid, H. and Gabhainn, S.N. (2004), 'Alcohol Use' in *Young People's Health in Context – Health Behaviour in School-aged Children (HBSC) Study*. Currie, C. et al. (eds), 73–83. *International Report from the 2001/02 Survey* (Copenhagen: WHO-Europe).

Shucksmith, J. et al. (1997), 'Adolescent Drinking Behavior and the Role of Family Life: a Scottish Perspective', *Journal of Adolescence*, **10**, 85–101. [DOI: 10.1006/jado.1996.0066].

Simons-Morton, B. et al. (2000), 'Peer and Parent Influences on Smoking and Drinking among Early Adolescents', *Health Education and Behavior*, **1**, 95–107.

Stronks, K. et al. (1996), 'Behavioural and Structural Factors in the Explanation of Socio-economic Inequalities in Health: an Empirical Analysis', *Sociology of Health and Illness*, **5**, 653–674. [DOI: 10.1111/1467-9566.ep10934524].

— (2004), 'Material Deprivation and Self-rated Health: a Multilevel Study of Adolescents from 22 European and North American Countries', *Social Science and Medicine*, **1**, 1–12.

Tuinstra, J. et al. (1998), 'Socio-economic Differences in Health Risk Behavior in Adolescence: do they Exist', *Social Science and Medicine*, **1**, 67–74.

Tur, J.A. et al. (2003), 'Alcohol Consumption among School Adolescents in Palma de Mallorca', *Alcohol and Alcoholism*, **38**, 243–248. [PubMed 12711659] [DOI: 10.1093/alcalc%2Fagg061].

Tyroler, H.A. (1999), 'The Influence of Socioeconomic Factors on Cardiovascular Disease Risk Factor Development', *Preventive Medicine*, **29**, 36–40. [DOI: 10.1006/pmed.1998.0441].

Vereecken, C.A. and Vandegehuchte, A. (2003), 'Measurement of Parental Occupation'. 'Agreement between Parents and their Children', *Archives of Public Health*, **61**, 141–149.

Vereecken, C.A. et al. (2003), 'The Influence of Parental Occupation and the Pupils' Educational Level on Lifestyle Behaviours among Adolescents in Belgium', *Journal of Adolescent Health*, **4**, 330–338.

Wardle, J. et al. (2003), 'Socioeconomic Disparities in Cancer-risk Behaviors in Adolescence: Baseline Results from the Health and Behaviour in Teenagers Study (HABITS)', *Preventive Medicine*, **6**, 721–730. [DOI: 10.1016/S0091-7435%2803%2900047-1].

Wechsler, H. et al. (1994), 'Health and Behavioral Consequences of Binge Drinking in College: A National Survey of Students at 140 Campuses', *Journal of the American Medical Association*, **272**, 1672–1677. [PubMed 7966895] [DOI: 10.1001/jama.272.21.1672].

West, P. et al. (2001), 'We Really do Know what You do: a Comparison of Reports from 11 Year Olds and Their Parents in Respect of Parental Economic Activity and Occupation', *Sociology*, **2**, 539–559. [DOI: 10.1177/S0038038501000268].

— (1997), 'Health Inequalities in the Early Years: is there Equalisation in Youth?', *Social Science and Medicine*, **44**, 833–858. [PubMed 9080566] [DOI: 10.1016/S0277-9536%2896%2900188-8].

— (1999), 'Youth' in *Inequalities in Health – the Evidence*. Gordon, D. et al. (eds) (Bristol: Policy Press), 12–22.

Windle, M. et al. (1996), 'Alcohol Use' in *Handbook of Adolescent Health Risk Behavior*. DiClemente, R.J. et al. (eds) (New York: Plenum Publishing), 115–159.

Chapter 6

The Impact of Parents on Adolescent Drinking and Friendship Selection Processes

Rutger C.M.E. Engels, Rebecca N.H. de Leeuw, Evelien A.P. Poelen,
Haske Van Der Vorst, Carmen S. Van Der Zwaluw
and Jan F.J. Van Leeuwe

Introduction

Reviews of theories on adolescents' substance use state that peer influences are the most consistent and strongest factor in the initiation and maintenance of substance use (Petraitis et al., 1995). The period of adolescence is characterised by an increase in time spent with peers, and young people have a strong need for social approval, group membership, and close friends (for example Hartup, 1996). Therefore, persons seem to be more susceptible to conforming to norms in their peer environment in the teenage years than in any other period (Finkenauer et al., 2002), which makes them vulnerable to initiate or maintain risky habits when they are in a context with substance using peers.

There is a debate in the literature on the magnitude of peer influences. Longitudinal studies have shown that alcohol consumption of best friends and members of the immediate peer group does not do much to explain changes in juvenile drinking over time (for example Urberg et al., 1997, 2003; Sieving et al., 2000; Andrews et al., 2002; Jaccard et al., 2005; Poelen et al., 2005). For example, in a longitudinal study on the effects of best friend's alcohol use on changes in drinking in a sample of 13–17-year-olds, Jaccard et al. (2005) conclude that close friends and other peers are less relevant in affecting adolescent risk behaviours than is often assumed. This is also reported by other scholars (see Bauman and Ennett, 1996; Engels et al., 1999a; Bot et al., 2005a).

On the other hand, some decades ago a small set of experimental observational studies on imitation and alcohol use were carried out (see review by Quigley and Collins, 1999). It was shown that when people are in the company of a drinker (a confederate of the experimenter), the drinking pace of this person affects individual drinking rates and consumption levels. The fact that in most of these experimental studies the participants (mostly college and university students) did not even know the confederate underscores the persuasive effect of peer drinking, as one might assume stronger modelling effects (in terms of reinforcing features) in social interactions of people who know each other well.

Strong support for peer influence processes can also be seen in observational research on drinking in peer groups. In our bar laboratory, we found strong modelling effects of peer drinking on individual drinking (Bot et al., 2005b). The picture that arises from our observational findings is that once people are in a drinking context, processes of imitation play a strong role, and these processes unfold rather independently of specific social relationships people have with others in the peer group or the social status they have in the group. The way some (heavy drinking) people synchronise their drinking pace (in terms of ordering rates as well as sipping frequency) (see Gollancz, 1943) over the course of a session led us to believe that in some cases this behaviour is almost automatic, and difficult for people to control deliberately.

It is important to stress that the assumed relevance of peers in steering youth drinking has strongly affected the focus of mass media campaigns and school-based prevention in the past decades. If research would show that peer influences on drinking are overstated, this will have consequences on the theoretical background of many prevention programmes. Further, empirical evidence of the extent to which peer selection processes play a large role in explaining homogeneity in drinking in peer groups and friendships: people who drink are more likely to affiliate with drinking peers (Bauman and Ennett, 1996), can also be valuable input for prevention.

All in all, the empirical evidence for existence of peer influence processes is straightforward. The magnitude to which individual behaviour is affected by peer drinking is however a matter of debate. Although some longitudinal surveys suggest that peer influences might be overestimated in terms of driving major changes (for instance from regular to problematic drinking) in alcohol use, observational research strongly points to processes of norm-setting and imitation in social interactions within specific drinking contexts.

Parents as Socialising Agents

Although the role of general parenting dimensions like emotional availability, monitoring and supervision, psychological and manipulative control, and support, have been explored (for example Van Der Vorst et al., 2005), the attention on alcohol-specific parenting has been limited (for exceptions see Jackson et al., 1999; Yu, 2003; Wood et al., 2004). In the past decade only a few (prospective) studies have been conducted – and almost exclusively in North-American samples – demonstrating that parents' own alcohol use as well as concrete parenting practices like setting alcohol-specific norms and rules, frequency of communication about drinking issues, and availability of alcohol in the household are associated with adolescent drinking.

First, there is substantial evidence for the direct effects of parents' own substance use on adolescent use (Engels et al., 1999a). To give an example, in prospective analyses predicting adolescent and young adult alcohol use over periods of two and seven years, we found small consistent effects of parental use on adolescent use over time, even after controlling for sibling and peer group drinking (Poelen et al., 2005). It should be stressed that, because of the strong association between parental drinking and some parenting practices (like setting rules), the direct effect of parental drinking on adolescent drinking sometimes vanishes when other explanatory alcohol-specific parental factors are considered.

Second, one of the most important alcohol-specific socialisation practices seems to be imposing strict rules on adolescents' alcohol use. In cross-sectional analyses, Van Der Vorst et al. (2005) found a strong negative association between imposing strict rules and adolescent drinking. This association was found on the basis of separate reports of different family members (father, mother, and adolescents themselves), and in older (on average 14.3 years old) as well as younger (on average 12.5 years old) adolescents in one family, demonstrating the robustness of the findings. Further, the results clearly demonstrate that parents treated their adolescents differently concerning rule-setting. Parents imposed stricter rules on younger adolescents than on the older ones. This might be explained that many parents adhere to a kind of 'social clock'; social norms on appropriate and inappropriate behaviours are dependent on the age and developmental phase people (for example children) are in. So parents become more permissive as soon as children start to drink frequently, although interestingly parents are also more strict towards the first born than toward the later born. In the Netherlands, there is a sharp increase in prevalence of alcohol use between the ages of 12 and 16 (Hibell et al., 2004). One possible explanation might be that, instead of parents continuing to be restrictive concerning alcohol, they loosen the ties. We also found this effect in a sample of adolescents enrolled in special education, underlining the robustness of the impact of rule-setting (Van Zundert et al. 2006). In longitudinal analyses on this dataset, we found that enforcement of rules in particular prevents adolescents starting to drink. So alcohol-specific rules seem to postpone the age of onset (Van Der Vorst et al., 2006a). As soon as adolescents have developed a regular drinking pattern, enforcing rules appears to be less effective.

Third, parents vary in the extent to which they have alcohol available at home. Although parents who drink substantially themselves of course have more alcohol at home, even drinking parents differ in how easily they distribute alcohol to their kids, or the extent to which they set boundaries on obtaining alcoholic drinks at home. Van Zundert et al. (2006) demonstrated that having alcohol available at home is related to higher drinking levels in adolescents.

Fourth, another strategy parents might have to handle adolescents' alcohol consumption is communication about alcohol. According to Ennett et al. (2001), parents talk more often with their offspring about alcohol use if both parents are non-users than if one of the parents or both drink. However, in both using and non-using parents, frequency of communication on alcohol matters was not related to adolescents' alcohol use. In our analyses, we found that parents who talk frequently about alcohol issues with their kids are more likely to have drinking adolescents. This might be explained by a) parents discussing these issues way too late, so their child is already experimenting, and b) parents discussing these issues rather poorly and not in a constructive manner, leading to contrary responses. Another explanation is more methodological; cross-sectional associations between parenting and adolescent behaviour can also be interpreted as parents responding to children's actions instead of children acting upon parental behaviours. In other words, perhaps parents start to instigate a discussion *after* their child has started to drink.

Parents and Friendships of their Offspring

The influence of parents may be underestimated in that most studies concentrated exclusively on the direct impact of parental alcohol use and parenting on adolescent alcohol consumption, but parents also play a role in affecting the peer environment of adolescents. In that sense, part of the peer influences may be attributed to indirect parental influences. Parents may affect the selection of potential peers by making explicit or implicit 'choices' concerning neighbourhood and school, and providing rules about leisure time activities. Further, parents may try to direct children to affiliate with specific peers or try to obstruct affiliation with what parents consider unsuitable peers (Mounts, 2000). In other areas of problem behaviour it has been shown that: (a) high parental supervision prevents adolescents from affiliating with deviant peers, and (b) parents' negative reactions to friendships may affect the continuation of those friendships. Related to this issue, parents may affect adolescent's feelings of self-efficacy. For example, when parents provide children with confidence and knowledge on how to resist peer pressure, this may strengthen their offspring's self-efficacy. Finally, intergenerational transference of parental norms to offspring may affect young people's affiliations with peers.

Only a few empirical studies have concentrated on the link between parent and adolescent's peer contexts in relation to substance use. In one of these studies, we tested the effect of parental smoking on selective peer associations. Our findings showed that the selection of new friends in late adolescence could be predicted by parental smoking, after controlling for the effects of the adolescent's own smoking (Engels and Willemsen, 2004). When parents smoked, children were more likely to affiliate with a smoker when establishing a new friendship. In other analyses we found that parental communication and setting rules were related to higher levels of self-efficacy to resist (peer) pressure to smoke (see Engels and Willemsen, 2004; Huver et al., 2006). More recently, we tested in longitudinal analyses whether parental smoking-specific communication affects selective peer affiliation, and it appeared that constructive, satisfactory discussions of parents with their offspring was related to a lower likelihood of affiliation with smoking peers (in new friendships), whereas frequent discussions are related to a higher likelihood of affiliation with smoking peers (De Leeuw et al., 2006). Explanations for these latter unexpected findings are that a) many parents do not talk constructively and positively and their kids react by acting deviant, or b) that the causality is the other way around; when parents find out that their kid is drinking, they start to increase conversations about it.

It is rather essential in our opinion to carry out these types of longitudinal analyses, as they not only provide further insight into the complex mechanisms underlying parental behaviours and adolescent substance use, but they also provide a better understanding of the relative roles of friends and parents in adolescent (and young adult) alcohol use.

The Present Study

We had three main aims in this study; 1) to test the extent to which adolescent alcohol use affects subsequent peer affiliations, 2) to examine the role of best friends in the development of alcohol use in adolescents, and 3) to test the role of parenting practices and parental drinking in friendship selection processes. Data from a two-wave prospective study, with a family design including two parents and two adolescents, were used.

Methods

Procedure

For the present study we used data from the Family and Health Project (Harakeh et al., 2005; Van Der Vorst et al., 2005). The participating families, with at least two adolescents (aged 13–16 years), were obtained from the records of 22 municipalities in the Netherlands and were recruited by means of a letter. A total of 428 families (a father, a mother and two adolescent children) participated. Data collection for the first wave (T1) took place between November 2002 and April 2003. The second wave (T2) took place 1 year later. The families were visited by a trained interviewer. To maintain confidentiality the interviewers asked the participants to sit apart from each other and not to discuss the questions while completing the questionnaires. A total of 416 families participated at T2. Attrition analyses revealed no differences between the families that participated both times and those that dropped from the study.

Sample Characteristics

The majority of the participating adolescents were of Dutch origin (> 95 per cent). At T1 the age of the older siblings ranged from 14 to 17 years, with a mean age of 15.2 ($SD = 0.60$) years. The age of the younger siblings ranged from 13 to 15 years, with a mean age of 13.4 ($SD = 0.50$) years. There was almost an equal distribution of boys and girls: 52.8 per cent of the older siblings and 47.7 per cent of the younger siblings were boys at T1. Furthermore, approximately one-third of all adolescents followed special or low education, one-third followed intermediate general education, and the remaining adolescents followed the highest level of secondary school, namely preparatory college and university education.

Measures

Alcohol consumption Both siblings were asked how often they had consumed alcohol in the previous four weeks. Quantity of drinking was assessed by the number of alcoholic beverages the siblings had consumed in the previous week during weekdays and in weekends, separately for the contexts at home and outside the home (Engels et al., 1999). By asking about these four specific situations, respondents are forced to actively recall episodes in their memory, which is supposed to increase the reliability of response (Bot et al., 2005a). The scores on these four questions were summed to obtain the total number of glasses of alcohol each sibling consumed in the previous week before administration of the questionnaires. Because of the skewness of these scores, we divided the quantity of drinking into seven categories: (0) no alcohol, (1) one or two glasses, (2) three to five glasses, (3) six to ten glasses, (4) 11–20 glasses, (5) 21–30 glasses, and (6) more then 31 glasses.

Parents were also asked how often they consumed alcohol in the previous 4 weeks. Scores were dichotomised between (1) regular drinker: drinking at least 5 days in a week, or (2) drinking less than 5 days a week or not at all. Using the responses of both parents we calculated a new score which we called 'parental drinking', with the categories: (1) both parents are not regular drinkers, (2) one of the parents is a regular drinker, and (3) both parents are regular drinkers.

Best friend's alcohol use Adolescents were asked to write down the full first name and the first letter of the last name of their best friend. We explicitly asked them not to give the name of a sibling or an intimate partner. They were then asked to fill out similar items for their friends concerning the frequency and quantity of alcohol use as for themselves.

To establish whether the adolescents were relatively accurate in their reports about their friends' drinking habits, we gathered data among the adolescent friends in a sub-sample. At the second wave, 301 of the mentioned friends filled out a questionnaire on their own drinking. Comparison of the scores on best friend's drinking reported by the participant and best friend's self-reports revealed relatively high agreement (Poelen et al., 2005).

Frequency of communication Frequency of communication was assessed by eight items referring to how often in the past 12 months each parent talked with their child about alcohol-related issues (for example 'During the last 12 months, how many times did your father/mother talk to you about how to resist peer pressure to use alcohol?') on a 5-point scale ranging from 1 = 'never' to 5 = 'very often' (Ennett et al., 2001; see for a Dutch adaptation, Van Der Vorst et al., 2005).

Rules about alcohol We developed a 10-item scale to measure the degree to which parents permit their children to consume alcohol in various situations, such as 'in the absence of parents at home' or 'at a friends' party' (Van Der Vorst et al., 2005). Thus, we asked both adolescents interviewed in the family what rules the parents had or what they prohibited concerning alcohol. Respondents had to answer to what degree these rules were applicable at their home. Response categories ranged from 1 = 'completely applicable' to 5 'not applicable at all'. Higher scores indicate having strict rules about alcohol consumption.

Alcohol availability   An instrument of five items assessed how often parents had beer, wine, strong liquor, and mixed drinks available at home (Van Der Vorst et al., 2005). Response choices ranged from 1 = 'never' to 4 = 'always', and mean scores were used in the analyses.

Strategy for Analysis

Data on alcohol use were available for 620 adolescents and their best friends on both occasions in time. First, correlations were computed between model variables. To investigate whether the independent variables – frequency of communication about alcohol use, availability of alcohol, rules about alcohol use, and parental drinking – were related to adolescent alcohol use and their best friend's alcohol use, Structural Equation Models were tested with the software package Mplus (Muthén and Muthén, 2006). In the models (see Figure 6.1-6.3) frequency of communication with the father and the mother were combined into one latent variable. Alcohol uses of adolescents and of best friends were treated as ordered categorical variables. For this reason, missing variables were not allowed in the data and we had to restrict the analysis to 608 kids for whom the data were complete. Mplus provides the opportunity to compute standard errors and a χ^2-test of model fit taking into account the non-independence of observations due to cluster sampling – as the older and younger children belong to the same family (Muthén and Muthén, 2006; see also Kuntsche and Jordan, 2006). The parameters in the models were therefore estimated using the Mean- and Variance-adjusted Weighted Least Square (WLMSV). The fit of the model was assessed by the following global fit indexes: χ^2, the CFI (Comparative Fit Index, with > 0.90 considered an acceptable fit) and the RMSEA (Root Mean Square Error of Approximation), which is satisfactory with p < 0.08).

The model will be tested for three groups of adolescents. Besides for the total group, the analysis will be performed for the group of adolescents with stable friendships, that is where the data of the best friend refers to the same friend on the two occasions (n = 178), and for the group of adolescents with changing friendships (n = 439). Thus, to disentangle friendship-selection processes from peer influences, we divided the sample into two groups: one group of adolescents with a stable friendship during the three measurements (that is adolescents who reported the same friend at each wave) and one group of adolescents with changing friendships during the three measurements (that is adolescents who reported a different friend at two or three waves). The group with changing friendships between T1 and T2 was utilised to determine whether parenting practices and parental drinking affect adolescents' friendship selection processes. To examine whether the best friend influences the adolescent over time and vice versa, we tested the model on the group of adolescents with a stable friendship. In addition, we were able to determine whether parental behaviours affect adolescent drinking when the impact of the best friend's alcohol use was taken into account.

Since samples are not independent, no χ^2 difference test is available to test differences between groups.

Results

Similarities in Drinking between Adolescents, Parents and Friends

Concerning the relative similarity in drinking among friends, the data showed high cross-sectional correlations (0.60 (T1), 0.68 (T2), p < 0.001) between weekly drinking of friends and adolescents. Thus, it seems that, according to the adolescents themselves, best friends and adolescents were similar in their drinking patterns. Further, drinking by parents and adolescents were positively associated, with Pearson correlations 0.12 (T1) and 0.12 (T2), p < 0.002. Parental drinking was also partly linked to friend's drinking, with Pearson correlations ranging from r = 0.07 (T1, non-significant) and r = 0.12 (T2), p < 0.004.

Total Model

To determine whether parental communication about alcohol-related issues, availability, rules and parental drinking are related to adolescent alcohol use and their best friend's alcohol use, we tested the two-wave model as depicted in Figure 6.1. The fit of the model was good (χ^2 (6) = 10.036, p = 0.123; CFI = 0.997; RMSEA = 0.033). Factor loadings were also satisfactory. For information on explained variances see Table 6.1.

Table 6.1   Proportions explained variance for alcohol use of adolescent and best friend at two time points

	Total group	Stable friends	Changing friends
Adolescent T1	0.38	0.40	0.38
Adolescent T2	0.37	0.58	0.31
Best friend T1	0.29	0.32	0.27
Best friend T2	0.36	0.57	0.29

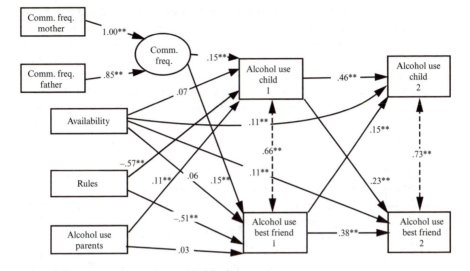

Figure 6.1   Parental behaviour, adolescent drinking and friends' drinking. Structural model, total group

Note: * p < .05, ** p. < .01.

First, drinking was relatively stable for adolescents (T1 → T2: β = 0.46, p < 0.01) as well as for their friends (T1 → T2: β = 0.38, p < 0.01), implying that those who drink at the first measurement are more likely to drink later on in their teenage years. Second, cross-sectionally, positive associations were found between drinking of adolescents and friends at the two waves. Furthermore, we found that parental drinking was neither related to the adolescent's nor to the friend's drinking, in a multi-variate analysis. Frequent communication was positively linked to adolescent's (γ = 0.16, p < 0.01) and friend's alcohol use (γ = 0.15, p < 0.01), suggesting that frequently raising the issue of drinking is not really preventing adolescents from drinking. Setting rules was strongly linked to less alcohol use in adolescents (γ = –0.57, p < 0.01) as well as their friends (γ = –0.51, p < 0.01). This is a multivariate analysis which implies that there is a link between parental rules and friend's drinking, after controlling for the effect of parental rules on the adolescent's own drinking as well as the association between the adolescent's and the best friend's drinking at T1. This could imply that there is a direct effect of rule enforcement by the parents on their child's best friend.

Finally, we found positive cross-lagged associations from the adolescent's alcohol use on the best friend's use over time (T1 → T2: β = 0.23, p < 0.01), and from the best friend's alcohol use on the adolescent's use (T1 → T2: β = 0.15, p < 0.01). The effects of the best friend's use can be interpreted as peer influence where the friend remains unchanged, whereas in the group of target adolescents with changing friendships this path can be interpreted both in terms of influence and selection. Therefore, we need to conduct the analyses separately

for adolescents who report having the same best friend over time, and those who
have a new best friend.

Group of adolescents with changing friendships   To examine whether alcohol-
specific parenting and parental alcohol use were related to adolescents' drinking
and friendship selection processes, we tested the theoretical model for the group
of adolescents with changing friendships (Figure 6.2). The model showed a
satisfactory fit to the data; χ^2 (*d.f.* = 5) = 6.635, p = 0.249, CFI = 0.998 and the
RMSEA = 0.028.[1]

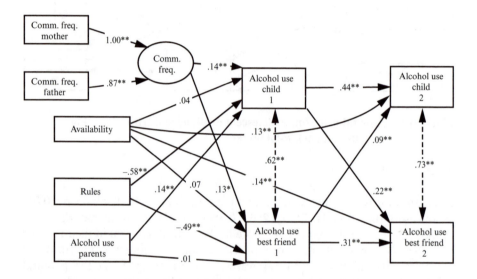

**Figure 6.2   Parental behaviour, adolescent drinking and friends' drinking.
             Structural model, changing friends**

Note: * p < .05, ** p. < .01.

We found that in the sample with changing friendships, best friend's use hardly
affected the adolescent's drinking over time, whereas the cross-lagged paths showed
a significant association between the adolescent's alcohol use and the best friend's
drinking (β = 0.22, p < 0.01). These findings indicate that adolescents selected
new friends partly on the basis of their (comparable) alcohol use.

  In these analyses we found stronger effects of alcohol availability (linked to peer
drinking (selection) at T2, and adolescent drinking at T2) and parental drinking
(direct association with adolescent drinking at T1) as compared to analyses in
the total sample, whereas all other links between parental behaviours and the
adolescent's and the best friend's drinking were similar to those in the analyses

---

1   We will primarily discuss the findings that differ from those in the total sample

for the total sample. Standardised estimates of these analyses are presented in Figure 6.2.

Group of adolescents with stable friendships   To examine whether adolescents and their best friends influence each other over time, and what role parents play in this process, we tested the model for the group of adolescents who had a stable friendship during the measurement period. The model showed a good fit to the data; χ^2 (*d.f.* = 9) = 10.524, p = 0.161, CFI = 0.993 and the RMSEA = 0.053.

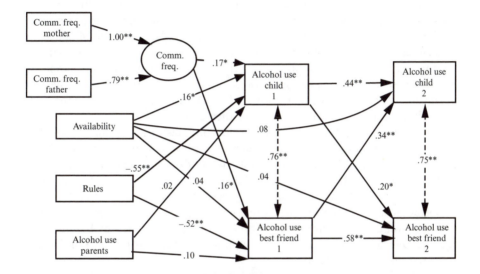

Figure 6.3   Parental behaviour, adolescent drinking and friends' drinking. Structural model, stable friends

Note: * p < .05, ** p. < .01.

We found that in the sample with stable friendships, the best friend's use at T1 robustly affected the adolescent's drinking at T2 (β = 0.34, p < 0.01), whereas the findings showed that adolescents also affected the best friend's drinking over time (β = 0.20, p < 0.01). Concerning parental influences, it appeared that alcohol availability was longitudinally related to both the adolescent's and the best friend's drinking. Standardised estimates of these analyses are presented in Figure 6.3.

Discussion

To investigate the impact of alcohol-specific parenting and parental drinking on adolescents' friendship selection processes over time, we differentiated two groups in our sample: one group of adolescents who reported having the same best friend over a period of a year (that is the group in which no selection processes occurred) and the group of adolescents with changing friendships over this period. In line with previous findings, we found evidence for friendship selection based on alcohol consumption, as the adolescent's drinking affected the best friend's drinking over time (Bauman and Ennett, 1994). Moreover, the results demonstrate indirect influences of alcohol-specific rules and alcohol availability on the best friend's drinking, indicating that parents seem to be able to affect their child's friendship selection processes.

The group of adolescents with stable friendships enabled us to examine whether adolescents and their best friends influence each other over time, and what role parents play in this process of peer influence, even when their child affiliates with the same friend for a longer period of time (in our case one year). The prospective findings show that adolescents and their best friends exert a small influence on each other's alcohol consumption over a one-year period. Interestingly, parents appear no longer capable of affecting their child's drinking. Thus, for parents it might be wise to undertake actions to prevent their teenager from drinking heavily or starting very early, and affiliating with (heavy) drinking friends, when they still are an important socialisation source for their child.

The pattern of findings in this study substantiates earlier studies on alcohol use among Dutch adolescents (for example Engels et al., 1999; Bot et al., 2005; Poelen et al., 2005). The effects of best friend's drinking over time – in stable and unstable friendships – were nevertheless not very strong. In terms of effect sizes, the absolute variance explained by best friend's drinking is limited. It is important to stress that also in many fine-grained prospective analyses predicting drinking over time with samples from other countries (see review by Bauman and Ennett, 1996; Jaccard et al., 2005), no support for a very strong effect of friends' substance use has been found.

Our results show consistent support for selective peer affiliation. The evidence for selection effects arises from the path from adolescent's drinking at the first wave to the friend's drinking at the second wave. One might argue that this path should be interpreted in terms of peer influence, namely that the study participants affected the peer's drinking. However, one should keep in mind that this subsample included adolescents who had different friends at the two waves. Furthermore, if the impact of adolescents on their friend's drinking is interpreted exclusively in terms of influence processes this would lead to the conclusion that our sample comprised an overrepresentation of adolescents with friends who are likely to conform to the alcohol use of their peers. The sample procedure we used makes this very unlikely (see Engels et al., 1999). Our findings are consistent with other studies showing substantial evidence for substance use being a source of selection processes in peer groups (Bauman and Ennett, 1996). One should however keep in mind that selection of friends can also be interpreted differently. Other studies revealed that 'selection' may take place even in ongoing friendships. Dishion and Skaggs (2000) examined the covariation between monthly bursts of substance use and contacts with substance-using friends. They showed that the period in which youth increased their drug use corresponded to the months in which they increased affiliations with substance-using friends. This implies that because most adolescents have a large peer group, they might select friends to spend time with on the basis of their preference to go out and drink.

New Directions

Studies systematically observing communication in friendships demonstrate that the content and structure of communication between close friends are related to the development of deviant behaviours, including drinking (Dishion and Owen, 2002). Furthermore, Bot et al. (2005b) showed that individual drinking levels in a bar are strongly affected by the average drinking levels within the group. Furthermore, we showed that relevant social influences on the consumption levels within a drinking occasion are primarily pressure and modelling by peers who are around in that setting. Friends' drinking does not play a substantial role, at least not when these friends are not apparent in the specific drinking context. In further analyses we also tested whether parental control and their own drinking (norms) affect young people's drinking when they are in a social context (bar lab) with peers; our findings showed that parental behaviours hardly affected drinking levels within this social setting. These findings clearly show that it is essential to rely not only on survey designs to test peer influences. Observational and experimental studies indicate that the use of surveys not only underestimates the role of peer influence in adolescent substance use, but might also not give a complete and insightful view on how and which peers affect adolescent and young adult drinking. We suggest that future research should combine longitudinal studies, survey studies and observational data to better elucidate how friends actually affect each others' drinking.

Findings from our study point in several directions for future research. In this study we have preliminary data showing that parents are affecting their offspring's friendship selection processes through communication, rule-setting and availability of alcohol. It would be interesting to scrutinise more explicit forms of parental management of friendship relations. Mounts (2000) identified several ways for parents to handle adolescents' peer relationships, such as talking about the consequences of being friends with particular (deviant) peers, prohibiting children to be affiliated with specific friends, or providing a home environment where adolescents are happy to bring their friends over. Focusing on these peer management skills leads to a better understanding of parents as friendship formation gatekeepers. In our opinion, future research should also not merely concentrate on the effects of parents on their children, but also on the effects of adolescents on their parents. Investigating bi-directional associations between parental practices and adolescent behaviour provides the opportunity to ascertain the actual effects of parents on their children, without ignoring the impact children have on their parents. Only a few studies have tested bi-directional relationships between parenting and adolescent alcohol use, and their findings actually support the idea that parents do react to the engagement in problem behaviour of their offspring (see Stice and Barrera, 1995).

Cultural Differences

One of the most interesting outcomes of the ESPAD project is the sharp cultural difference in drinking habits of young people in Europe (Hibell et al., 2004). If one concentrates on examination of variation in drinking habits between countries it is necessary to differentiate between overall consumption levels and specific risky drinking patterns. In most Mediterranean countries, people drink less per occasion, and are therefore less frequently intoxicated. So, people spread their drinking over many occasions per week or concentrate it in specific moments (like binge drinking on a Saturday night). Differences in drinking patterns evidently matter for cultural variation in health risks (for a discussion of cultural differences in youth drinking, see Engels and Knibbe, 2000). The question is whether differences in drinking patterns are related to differences in susceptibility to peer influences on drinking.

Thus, would the findings of our studies be different if we had examined peer influences on youngsters' drinking in other cultures? Unfortunately, to our knowledge, there are no longitudinal data available comparing peer influences on drinking in various European, or North American countries. However, a 1-year two-wave prospective study on early adolescent smoking, carried out in six European countries, showed remarkable marginal cultural differences in effects of peer's smoking (best friend and peer group) and parental smoking on smoking initiation (De Vries et al., 2003). In almost all of the six countries only limited effects of peer smoking on individual smoking onset were found. If the case is similar for drinking, we may not encounter strong differences between countries concerning the effects of peers in survey studies.

To go beyond speculation on cultural differences it requires survey and observational research on drinking in peer groups and friendships in other countries and cultures. To go one step further, we want to stress that when on an EU-level policy makers decide to advise countries to undertake actions (in terms of prevention and intervention), it is essential also to conduct cross-cultural studies on the precursors of drinking in various countries. If the causes for drinking diverge greatly across countries it might not be wise to undertake general actions focusing on decreasing drinking levels in adolescents and young adults.

In Conclusion

The results of this study provide evidence for the role of best friends in adolescent drinking. Evidence was also found for peer selection processes. Furthermore, we showed that parents not only affect adolescent drinking directly, but also indirectly through effects on friendship selection processes. Rule setting, communication and alcohol availability at home were multivariately related to best friend drinking.

Acknowledgment

This work was supported by the Netherlands Organization of Scientific Research (NWO 016-005-029).

References

Andrews, J.A. et al. (2002), 'The Influence of Peers on Young Adult Substance Use', *Health Psychology*, **21**, 349–357. [PubMed 12090677] [DOI: 10.1037/0278-6133.21.4.349].

Barnes, G.M. and Farrell, M.P. (1992), 'Parental Support and Control as Predictors of Adolescent Drinking, Delinquency and Related Problem Behaviours', *Journal of Marriage and the Family*, **54**, 763–776. [DOI: 10.2307/353159].

Bauman, K.E. and Ennett, S.E. (1996), 'On the Importance of Peer Influence for Adolescent Drug Use: Commonly Neglected Considerations', *Addiction*, **91**, 185–198. [PubMed 8835276] [DOI: 10.1111/j.1360-0443.1996.tb03175.x].

Bot, S.M. et al. (2005a), 'Friend's Drinking and Adolescent Alcohol Consumption: The Moderating Role of Friendship Characteristics', *Addictive Behaviours*, **30**, 929–947. [DOI: 10.1016/j.addbeh.2004.09.012].

Bot, S.M. et al. (2005b), 'The Effects of Alcohol Expectancies on Drinking Behaviour in Peer Groups: Observations in a Naturalistic Setting', *Addiction*, **100**, 1270–1279. [DOI: 10.1111/j.1360-0443.2005.01152.x].

De Leeuw, R.N.H. et al. (2006), 'Parents as Friendship-formation Gatekeepers: Parental Smoking-specific Communication and Adolescents' Friendships', under Review.

De Vries, H. et al. (2003), 'Influences of Parents and Peers on Adolescent Smoking Behavior in Six European Countries', *Health Education Research*, **18**, 617–632. [DOI: 10.1093/her%2Fcyg032].

Dishion, T.J. and Owen, L.D. (2002), 'A Longitudinal Analysis of Friendships and Substance Use: Bidirectional Influence from Adolescence to Adulthood', *Developmental Psychology*, **38**, 480–491. [PubMed 12090479] [DOI: 10.1037/0012-1649.38.4.480].

Dishion, T.J.,and Medici Skaggs, N. (2000), 'An Ecological Analysis of Monthly 'Bursts' in Early Adolescent Substance Use', *Applied Developmental Science*, **4**, 89–97. [DOI: 10.1207/S1532480XADS0402_4].

Engels, R.C.M.E. and Knibbe, R.A. (2000), 'Young People's Alcohol Consumption from a European Perspective: Risks and Benefits', *European Journal of Clinical Nutrition*, **54**, s52–s55. [PubMed 10805039].

—, R.C.M.E. and Willemsen, M. (2004), 'Communication about Smoking in Dutch Families: Associations between Anti-smoking Socialization and Adolescent Smoking-related Cognitions', *Health Education Research*, **19**, 227–238. [PubMed 15140843] [DOI: 10.1093/her%2Fcyg042]

—, R.C.M.E. et al. (1999a), 'Influences of Parental and Best Friends' Smoking and Drinking on Adolescent Use: A Longitudinal Study', *Journal of Applied Social Psychology*, **29**, 338–362. [DOI: 10.1111/j.1559-1816.1999.tb01390.x]

—, R.C.M.E. et al. (1999b), 'Predictability of Smoking in Adolescence: Between Optimism and Pessimism', *Addiction*, **94**, 115–124. [DOI: 10.1046/j.1360-0443.1999.9411158.x]

—, R.C.M.E. et al. (2006), 'Peer Group Reputation and Smoking and Alcohol Use in Early Adolescence', *Addictive Behaviors*, **31**, 440–449. [PubMed 16046078] [DOI: 10.1016/j.addbeh.2005.05.026].

Ennett, S.T. et al. (2001), 'Parent-child Communication about Adolescent Tobacco and Alcohol Use: what do Parents Say and Does it Affect Youth Behavior?', *Journal of Marriage and Family*, **63**, 48–62. [DOI: 10.1111/j.1741-3737.2001.00048.x].

Finkenauer, C. et al. (2002), *Self and Identity in Early Adolescence,'*, In *Understanding Early Adolescent Self and Identity: Applications and Interventions*. Brinthaupt, T.M. and Lipka, R.P. (eds), 25–56 (New York: State University of New York Press).

Gollancz, V. (1943), *The Pub and the People: a Worktown Study* (London: Mass-Observation).

Harakeh, Z. et al. (2005), 'Parental Rules and Communication: their Association with Adolescent Smoking', *Addiction*, **100**, 862–870. [PubMed 15918816] [DOI: 10.1111/j.1360-0443.2005.01067.x].

Hartup, W.W. (1996), 'The Company they Keep: Friendships and their Developmental Significance', *Child Development*, **67**, 1–13. [PubMed 8605821] [DOI: 10.2307/1131681].

Hibell, B. et al. (2004), *The ESPAD Report 2003: Alcohol and Other Drug Use among Students in 35 European Countries* (Stockholm: Swedish Council for Information on Alcohol and Other Drugs (CAN) and the Pompidou Group at the Council of Europe).

Huver, R.M. et al. (2006),'Are Anti-Smoking Parenting Practices Related to Adolescent Smoking Cognitions and Behavior?', *Health Education Research*, **21**, 66–77.

Jaccard, J. et al. (2005), 'Peer Influences on Risk Behavior: an Analysis on the Effects of a Close Friend', *Developmental Psychology*, **41**, 133–147. [DOI: 10.1037/0012-1649.41.1.135].

Jackson, C. et al. (1999), 'Alcohol-Specific Socialization, Parenting Behaviors and Alcohol Use by Children', *Journal of Studies on Alcohol*, 60, 362–367.

Kuntsche, E. and Jordan, M.D. (2006), 'Adolescent Alcohol and Cannabis Use in Relation to Peer and School Factors: Results of Multilevel Analyses', *Drug and Alcohol Dependence*, **84**, 167–174. [PubMed 16542799] [DOI: 10.1016/j.drugalcdep.2006.01.014].

Mounts, N.S. (2000), 'Parental Management of Adolescent Peer Relationships: What are its Effects on Friend Selection?' in *Family and Peers: Linking two Social Worlds*. Kerns, K. et al. (eds) (Westport, Conn.: Praeger), 167–193.

Muthén, L.K. and Muthén, B.O. (2006), *Mplus User's Guide*, 2th edn (Los Angeles, CA: Muthén and Muthén).

Petraitis, J. et al. (1995), 'Reviewing Theories of Adolescent Substance Use: Organizing Pieces in the Puzzle', *Psychological Bulletin*, **117**, 67–86. [PubMed 7870864] [DOI: 10.1037/0033-2909.117.1.67].

Poelen, E.A.P. et al. (2005), 'Trends in Alcohol Consumption in Dutch Adolescents and Young Adults', *Drugs and Alcohol Dependence*, **79**, 413–421. [DOI: 10.1016/j.drugalcdep.2005.03.020].

— et al. (2007), 'Best Friends and Alcohol Consumption in Adolescence: a Within Family Analysis', *Drug and Alcohol Dependence*, **88**, 163–173. [PubMed 17127016, 16039803].

Quigley, B.M. and Collins, R.L. (1999), 'The Modeling of Alcohol Consumption: a Meta-Analytic Review', *Journal of Studies on Alcohol*, **60**, 90–98. [PubMed 10096313].

Reifman, A. et al. (1998), 'Parental and Peer Influences on the Onset of Heavier Drinking among Adolescents', *Journal of Studies on Alcohol*, **59**(3), 311–317. [PubMed 9598712].

Sieving, R.E. et al. (2000), 'Do Friendships Change Behaviors, or do Behaviors Change Friendships?' 'Examining Paths of Influence in Young Adolescents' Alcohol Use',

Journal of Adolescent Health, **26**, 27–35. [PubMed 10638715] [DOI: 10.1016/S1054-139X%2899%2900056-7].

Stice, E. and Barrera, M. (1995), 'A Longitudinal Examination of the Reciprocal Relations between Perceived Parenting and Adolescents' Substance Use and Externalising Behaviors', *Developmental Psychology*, **31**, 322–334. [DOI: 10.1037/0012-1649.31.2.322].

Urberg, K.A. et al. (1997), 'Close Friend and Group Influence on Adolescent Cigarette Smoking and Alcohol Use', *Developmental Psychology*, **33**, 834–844. [PubMed 9300216] [DOI: 10.1037/0012-1649.33.5.834].

— et al. (2003), 'A Two-stage Model of Peer Influence in Adolescent Substance Use: Individual and Relationship-specific Differences in Susceptibility to Influence', *Addictive Behaviors*, **28**, 1243–1256. [PubMed 12915166] [DOI: 10.1016/S0306-4603%2802%2900256-3].

Van Der Vorst, H. et al. (2005), 'The Role of Alcohol Specific Socialization on Adolescents' Drinking Behavior', *Addiction*, **100**, 1464–1474. [PubMed 16185208] [DOI: 10.1111/j.1360-0443.2005.01193.x].

Van Der Vorst, H. et al. (2006a), 'The Impact of Rules, Parental Norms, and Parental Alcohol Use on Adolescent Drinking Behavior', *Journal of Child Psychology and Psychiatry*, **46**, 1299–1306.

— et al. (2006b), 'Parental Attachment, Parental Control and Early Development of Alcohol Use: a Longitudinal Study', *Psychology of Addictive Behaviors*, **20**, 107–116. [DOI: 10.1037/0893-164X.20.2.107].

Van Zundert, R. et al. (2007), 'Pathways to Alcohol Use among Dutch Students in Regular Education and Education for Adolescents with Behavioral Problems: the Role of Parental Alcohol Use, General Parenting Practices and Alcohol-specific Parenting Practices', *Journal of Family Psychology*, **20**, 456–467. [DOI: 10.1037/0893-3200.20.3.456].

Wood, M.D. et al. (2004), 'Do Parents Still Matter?' 'Parent and Peer Influences on Alcohol Involvement among Recent High School Graduates', *Psychology of Addictive Behaviors*, **18**, 19–30. [PubMed 15008682] [DOI: 10.1037/0893-164X.18.1.19].

Yu, J. (2003), 'The Association between Parental Alcohol-related Behaviors and Children's Drinking', *Drug and Alcohol Dependence*, **69**, 253–262. [PubMed 12633911] [DOI: 10.1016/S0376-8716%2802%2900324-1].

Chapter 7

Consumption beyond Control. The Centrality of Heavy Social Drinking in the Lifestyles of English Youth

Howard Parker

Introduction

There is no dispute that young people in many European countries are drinking more than their predecessors and that drinking for intoxication or drunkenness is a major driver. The UK is one country near the top of the drinking league on all measures as consecutive ESPAD studies have shown and as skilfully described by Barbro Andersson and Björn Hibell as well as Salme Ahlström, in, respectively, Chapters 3 and 4.

The ESPAD results for UK countries are fully supported by other national school surveys. In England, which this chapter will focus on, representative, time series surveys of 11–15-year-olds have shown that the proportion of adolescents who drank in the past seven days has remained fairly stable through time amongst boys but has been rising amongst girls for over a decade. In 2004, for instance, 44 per cent of 15-year-old boys drank in the last week but 46 per cent of girls did so as well. This is the first time more young women have reported recent drinking than young men.

More importantly, adolescents who drank in the past week in England now consume over twice the number of units as their age equivalents a decade ago. The amounts consumed have now plateaued at this far higher level. At age 15 in 2004 boys reported consuming a mean of 13.9 units in the past 7 days and girls 12.1 units (the highest amount recorded so far for females) (NCSR/NFER, 2005).

This chapter, however, rather than describe the quantitative nature of England's heavy youth drinking, takes this consumption reality as indisputable, and focuses on understanding the dynamics associated with young heavy drinkers' lifestyles and motives for regular drinking. It argues that explanations should be set in a broad cultural and consumption context which moves beyond both adolescence and alcohol in isolation. Firstly, focusing, as ESPAD does, on early adolescence is limiting. Drinking careers must be set in a life transitions paradigm. In the UK drinking rates increase into young adulthood primarily driven by early adolescent drinkers continuing to increase and sustain their drinking frequency and volume. Secondly, there is a clustering of smoking, drinking and drug use. Today's heavy drinkers, at say 18 years of age, are far more likely to be tobacco smokers (see also Jensen et al., 2003) and recreational drug users (for example cannabis, cocaine). Focusing on younger alcohol users is unsound without recognising the amplifying and confounding issues of poly-substance use. Certainly, in the UK across the last decade most young recreational *drug users* in regional studies were also *drinking* above recommended units (Egginton et al., 2002). Thirdly macro 'global' perspectives are required because heavy drinking and recreational drug use is found right across the socio-economic spectrum and across the globe. Patterns of alcohol and drugs consumption in the UK are similar to those in Australia for instance. Whilst traditional subcultural or 'risk factor' analyses remain salient for understanding problematic drinking and drug use amongst a socially excluded minority of young Britons, it is amongst educated and employed young Britons that sustained heavy, especially weekend drinking (and drug use) is disproportionately located. Any theoretical or conceptual tools must be macro in nature and be able to embrace the fact that university students and successful graduates are at the front of the nightclub queue having already consumed large amounts of alcohol, circuit drinking in the entertainment quarters of most cities in England every weekend. Regular heavy drinking, as part of a leisure repertoire related to the search for intoxication, is essentially normative in the UK amongst young people and our explanations must reflect this.

This chapter will rely on already published findings gleaned from two longitudinal studies and a large scale nightclub study undertaken by the author and colleagues at Manchester University focusing on alcohol, drugs and leisure. The North West England longitudinal study or *Illegal Leisure* cohort (for example Parker et al., 1998) followed several hundred conventional young people from when they were 13 years old in 1991 up to 2000–2001 when they were around 22 years old. The Northern Regions Study (Morris et al., 2002) followed over a thousand young people from 14 to 18 years of age, highlighting their drinking and drug use profiles across adolescence. The nightclub study (Measham et al., 2001) profiled over 2,000 young adults who attended nightclubs and dance clubs in Greater Manchester around the millennium.

There was welcome consistency in the key findings in each of these studies also reflected in overviews of the UK scene. The thrust of the analysis is that understanding 'youth culture' requires an increasingly trans-national perspective and much reliance on the modernity debate, 'risk society' and consumption theories. Micro analysis and factor or locality specific studies remain veracious but must be situated on this important backcloth. In many European societies for instance whilst socio-economic, rural-urban, gender and ethnicity axes remain important variables almost all young people now experience delayed transitions to full citizenship and adulthood. This process touches the majority and in similar ways – longer periods in education and training, less secure employment pathways, delayed marriages and parenting, exposure to the consumption of leisure and so on. The key point is that adolescent big drinkers are now sustaining their drinking careers for longer. This has implications for personal and public health and the management of the night-time economy in respect of the migration of tens of thousands of young adults to bar and clubland at the weekends. Recreational nightlife (Calafat, 2001) is a key locale of the consumption of leisure where 'time out' is purchased rather than self or family generated.

The Functions of Social Drinking

The dominant reasons why so many younger people are so committed to regular drinking are critical. There is a strong consensus in the literature as to the functionality of social drinking (for example Mäkelä and Mustonen, 2000; Health Promotion Agency, 2003; Joseph Rowntree Foundation, 2005).

In each of our three source studies we also found that heavy drinkers nominated more functions or positive attributes to regular alcohol consumption. Table 7.1 illustrates this based on the Northern Regions study (Egginton et al., 2002) but these findings are replicated in the *Illegal Leisure* cohort (see Parker and Williams, 2003).

We see that heavy drinkers (those drinking well above recommended levels in the cohort) as well as identifying more functions also emphasise the desire to get drunk and to 'wind down', relax and forget worries. Female heavy drinkers are particularly likely to attribute stress relief to heavy drinking. This is a clue to how drinking and temporary intoxication fit into the work hard – play hard lifestyles of post-modern times.

Drinking and Poly-Substance Use

Young Britons nominate similar functions for recreational drug use although distinguishing between substances which are defined as function specific. So ecstasy and now cocaine are associated with energy, dancing and self-confidence whilst cannabis is about relaxing, winding down and feeling mellow (Parker and Williams, 2001).

It is not surprising therefore to find alcohol and illicit drugs perceived by many as part of the same psycho-active basket. In all our indicative studies we find heavy young drinkers are far more likely to be smokers and illicit drug users. In the Northern Regions cohort at 17/18 years heavy drinkers were far more likely to be tobacco users (42.7 per cent) than moderate drinkers (who drank less than weekly recommended levels) (31.7 per cent) and light drinkers (12.6 per cent smokers) and non drinkers (10.2 per cent) (all at p = 0.001) (Egginton et al., 2002).

At 22 years of age the *Illegal Leisure* cohort was analysed in terms of their drug status. Over half were drug active (current drug users and opportunistic drug users) with the remainder either having given up drug use (ex-users) or having never tried a drug (abstainers). Table 7.2 shows not only that current drug users were more likely to be regular drinkers but they also drank more per episode than the other drug status groups. Over 90 per cent of current drug users drank excessively measured against recommended limits.

Table 7.1   Reasons for drinking alcohol in hierarchical order by drink status at 17/18 years

Drink status	Light drinker			Moderate drinker			Heavy drinker		
Gender	Male	Female	Total	Male	Female	Total	Male	Female	Total
N. size	101	82	183*	80	166	246	107	103	210*
Column percentage	%	%	%	%	%	%	%	%	%
Drink to celebrate	88	96	92	94	96	95	96	95	96
Drink for pleasure	79	74	77	86	77	80	92	88	90
Drink because like the taste	73	81	76	76	76	76	85	77	81
Drink because makes me feel good	51	54	52	68	50	56	65	57	61
Drink to wind down after work/study	45	38	42	59	39	46	66	50	58
Drink to get drunk	37	23	31	44	36	38	59	59	59
Drink to relax with friends	44	39	42	46	35	39	48	30	39
Drink to calm down if stressed	32	26	29	36	35	36	44	50	47
Drink to feel relaxed with opposite sex	38	35	37	43	29	33	42	33	38
Drink to forget worries	26	20	23	31	27	28	31	41	36
Drink for a sense of well-being	20	12	16	27	13	18	22	14	18
Drink to reduce inhibitions	17	10	14	23	14	17	21	15	18
Drink out of habit	4	4	4	13	10	11	22	22	22
Drink because there's nothing better to do	3	4	3	6	7	7	19	17	18
Drink to improve sexual performance	3	1	2	4	4	4	9	4	7

* Missing values: one light drinker and one heavy drinker did not indicate their reasons for drinking. Nominated from 17 options. Percentages rounded up.

Table 7.2   Alcohol profiles and consumption rates on last occasion by drug status at 22 years

Drug status	Current drug users	Opportunistic drug users	Ex-drug users	Abstainers	Total
N. size	130	146	73	113	462*
Column percentage	%	%	%	%	%
Ever had an alcoholic drink	100	100	99	93	98
Weekly drinkers	92	88	79	68	83
Every day to most days a week	35	20	17	9	21
2–3 times a week	43	53	47	44	17
Once a week	14	19	17	21	16
Less than once a week	9	10	14	20	13
Never drink alcohol now	0	2	6	7	3
N. size	126	143	69	99	437**
Units of alcohol consumed on last drinking occasion					
Half recommended alcohol units per day	4	6	3	11	6
Recommended alcohol units per day	5	15	13	23	14
Twice recommended alcohol units per day	24	25	26	27	25
Three times recommended alcohol units per day	23	15	22	16	19
Above three times recommended alcohol units per day	44	39	36	22	36
Mean alcohol units consumed on last drinking occasion	13	10	9	7	10

*   Missing values: n = 3 respondents are unclassifiable in terms of drugs status.

**   Missing values: n = 9 appropriately missing; n = 16 inappropriately missing; n = 3 respondents are unclassifiable in terms of drugs status.
Calculations based on recommended levels (UK) for males 3–4 units per day and for females 2–3 units per day.

At weekends alcohol and illicit drugs are routinely mixed by the nightclub crowd. In our study of over 2000 young clubbers in Greater Manchester drinking and the use of ecstasy, cocaine and cannabis was the norm. Six in 10 respondents were mixing alcohol and drugs on in-club survey nights (Measham et al., 2001). From these and consequent studies the notion of cultures of intoxication has emerged (Measham and Brain, 2005). Whilst primarily associated with the growth in heavy drinking amongst young people this concept is equally amenable to embracing poly substance use. The search for intoxication within the recreational scene is complex and 'layered' however constrained by commitment to the work hard – play hard lifestyle and the goal of disinhibited time out with minimum negative outcomes.

Cocaine and alcohol is now the dominant 'mix' for young adults and cannabis and alcohol for 'early onset' adolescents in respect of delivering altered states.

The Negative Outcomes of Regular, Heavy Drinking

In our longitudinal studies the earliest onset 'binge' drinkers (13–15-year-olds) reported negative outcomes associated with public drinking and getting into associated mishap and disorder including not being physically safe. This same finding has been recently reported by Coleman and Cater (2005). Most recently, in England very large 'gatherings' of mid adolescents, after school on Friday evenings, have become routine. These groups routinely indulge in public drinking, animated behaviour and cause low level public nuisance. As importantly there are numerous associated negative outcomes in terms of illness, unconsciousness, accidents and peer exploitation (Parker and Egginton, 2006).

With age, similar but more complex negative experiences occur when people go out to bars, clubs and parties. In short, our studies have consistently showed this process right through transitions from adolescence into post-adolescence and young adulthood.

The *Illegal Leisure* cohort, looking back, at 22 years of age, on their journey from adolescence into young adulthood provided important insights. Table 7.3 shows how the heavy drinkers reported more bad or negative experiences than moderate and light drinkers particularly in respect of being unable to remember part of the drinking-social event or becoming involved in a fight or argument. As importantly however, *all* the drinking status groups report extensive negative experiences. In qualitative interviews lighter drinkers actually nominated these unwanted experiences as a reason for not becoming or remaining a regular, heavy drinker. The heavier drinkers were far more sanguine perceiving these bad experiences and nights out gone wrong as part and parcel of intoxicated weekends. Essentially, they argued, if you go out or party regularly it is almost inevitable that you'll have the occasional night out ending in tears.

The most committed young go-outers in England are those that migrate to the bar-club scene of their local town or city at weekends from around 18 years of age. Numerous studies have identified the propensity for these young people to be involved in fights, assaults and to have to attend Accident and Emergency

Table 7.3 Negative post-drinking experiences since 18 years of age nominated at 22 years, in hierarchical order by drink status

Drink status	Light drinker			Moderate drinker			Heavy drinker		
Gender	M	F	Total	M	F	Total	M	F	Total
N. size	8	9	17*	14	32	46**	144	181	325
Column percentage	%	%	%	%	%	%	%	%	%
Unable to remember part of the evening, the next day	75	78	77	71	53	59	83	77	80
Felt so ill had to miss at least half a day's work/study	50	56	53	71	38	48	67	64	65
Unable to perform at work/study	50	78	65	50	53	52	59	54	56
Became sexually involved with someone who I wouldn't normally	38	44	41	64	25	37	48	38	42
Became involved in a physical fight or argument	25	33	29	36	28	30	52	36	43
Caused damage to friendship/relationship	0	33	18	43	19	26	35	26	30
Not taken contraception when having sex when usually I would	25	56	41	36	16	22	31	29	30
Caused damage to property	13	0	6	7	0	2	23	4	12
Had an accident when driving a car/motorbike	0	0	0	0	0	0	4	1	2
Other	0	11	6	7	0	2	8	4	6

* Missing values: n = 5 male and n = 5 female light drinkers did not indicate any post-drinking experiences.
** Missing values n = 4 male and n = 9 female moderate drinkers did not indicate any post-drinking experiences.
Nominated from 14 options.

Departments (Deehan, 1999; Thom et al., 1999) during these nights out. Many Emergency Room admissions are the consequence of becoming intoxicated and feeling ill or falling over. Whilst social drinking and going out are often perceived to strengthen bonding and friendships (Health Promotion Agency, 2003) there are occasions when friends and partners fall out. As Table 7.3 shows, this is subsequently regretted. Risky or unwise sexual encounters are also seen negatively in retrospect, especially by women.

Personal and Public Health

Given the obvious failure of primary prevention initiatives to discourage young Britons from adopting substance consumption-led leisure patterns (White and Pitts, 1998; Morris et al., 2002), the need for secondary preventation/harm reductions initiatives is apparent. There is already a framework for such experiments which is Europe-wide (for example the International Conference on Nightlife, Substance Use and Related Health Issues network). From a public health perspective we need public information and brief intervention programmes which are located in the realities of intoxicated weekends. We should start where the consumers are at and with the negative outcomes they report.

Whilst such initiatives should be poly-substance focused in the UK, there can be a primary alcohol focus in those countries where alcohol is the main issue. There might be three inter-linked themes. Firstly, we need an accurate factual public information agenda about drinking which embraces the positive functions of drinking in moderation as well as 'warnings' about sustained heavy consumption. Secondly, the largely social context of youthful drinking needs situating in an agenda about drinking events and settings particularly public 'under-age' drinking and nights out. This should focus on how to prepare for such events and how to stay safe, avoid trouble, look after drunk friends, get home safely, and so on. Such initiatives need to be informed by local context. In England the 'new' major public drinking concern is the teenage 'gatherings' phenomenon in public spaces on weekend nights to celebrate the end of the school week. Large numbers of teenagers meet up and drink in animated and sometimes disordered groups across the land. Currently, state responses are focused on enforcement and dispersal without any regard for the health and safety of the drinking gatherers. However the negative outcomes nominated by young adults such as risky sex, getting into arguments and fights, becoming ill or getting injured are equally salient for the adolescent public drinkers and should form part of the content of public information messages.

Self-assessment games or exercises can be helpful. A 'mid week' review could be promoted whereby the target audiences are encouraged to look at their immediate health, energy and concentration levels and how long it took to 'recover' from the weekend. 'Dependency' is poorly understood in this age and some simple questions and explanations might help increase understanding and the ability to identify morbidity or dependence as a consequence of drinking, smoking and recreational drug use.

Thirdly, the long-term health implications of sustained heavy drinking, smoking and drug use need presenting to younger populations. Young women in particular are undoubtedly storing up mid life health problems which need highlighting. The biggest difficulty for this public health message is that young people often dismiss such warnings particularly on the grounds that 'it won't happen to them' and that '"they" are always trying to scare us about poor diet, lack of exercise and what we should and shouldn't do and anyway we'll soon be 'settling down' and desisting from intoxicated weekends'. Traditionally, this has been the case but there are now signs that with delayed transitions and the dominance of work hard – play hard lifestyles moderation may no longer be bedding in for many even during their 20s.

Disorder, Safety and Public Health

Some European countries with this heavy youth drinking profile have developed alcohol strategies with a public health priority (for example Ireland). However, in England the media and political focus has been upon enforcement and the management of under-age drinking and social disorder associated with the alcohol led night-time economy as reflected in recent Alcohol Strategy.

This author would argue that both agendas need to be included but framed in the same policy paradigm. The rise in alcohol related disorder and the alcohol (and drug) consumption patterns of England's young adults are located in the same nexus. Disorder in terms of fights, assaults, trouble in bars, which peaks at the weekends (Deehan, 1999), flows from the same context as illness, accidents and injuries which occur on nights out drinking. It is the sheer scale of tens of thousands of young adults migrating to the entertainment quarters or parties and events to consume alcohol in crowded, animated venues which leads to the whole gamut of negative outcomes. Aside from individuals with a propensity to take risks and cause trouble, for the committed go-outers, occasional incidents or accidents are unwanted but accepted as inevitable, once in a while. In England there are political-governmental schisms which prevent this integration.

This search for intoxication is a cultural and consumption reality, a structural change which has taken many years to develop and aided by an on-going fall in the price of alcohol in real terms and a drinks industry happy to promote and cash in on a large targeted population of younger drinkers. England offers an example of how alcohol led recreation can come to dominate and become 'consumption beyond control'. In short there is no realistic prospect of government being able to reduce alcohol consumption or deflate the going-out market it has happily allowed to develop. The realistic and pragmatic option of managing the issue is thus slowly evolving.

Work Hard – Play Hard Lifestyles

About half of young Britons prioritise, with varying frequency, drinking in friendship groups which, from 18, migrate to going out 'to town' at the weekends. Licensed premises – the pubs, bars and clubs in town and city centres – provide the setting and the alcohol. We are thus seeing the nature of leisure evolving in line with the dominance of consumption. 'Time out' is thus in part purchased in post-modern times.

In our studies the biggest drinkers and recreational drug users are having equally successful transitions to adulthood and full citizenship. Counter-initiatively they are, as measured in the *Illegal Leisure* cohort, earning more income than their more abstentious peers (Parker and Williams, 2003). This is a further reason to cast explanations of sustained heavy drinking in a lifestyles perspective. The go-outer population is rarely at home, prioritising socialising, retail therapy and visiting pubs and bars, with friends and indeed private home drinking during the week. Intoxicated weekends out are seen as vital to the desired harmony and good fit between work and play, concentration and relaxation, dealing with problems and worries and 'time out' from this process. All too well known in Greece and Spain these young adult Britons also see holidays abroad as the ultimate reward. On such resort holidays heavy drinking, drug use and sexual adventures are also priorities (Bellis et al., 2004; *Sunday Times*, 2005). Cheap flight long weekend hen and stag parties are the latest manifestation of this process of having a 'moral holiday'.

All this fits with the modernity debate about global consumption patterns in a runaway world and this is why national and increasingly international efforts to, in this case, pull back intoxication cultures cannot fully succeed. The measures required are not plausible or politically feasible in post-industrial market economies. Clearly there are numerous cultural, historical, religious and geographical factors at work in shaping the extent to which the consumption of leisure has bedded into youth cultures across Europe and indeed Australia where similarities with the UK are substantive (for example Duff, 2005). England is the extreme case but perhaps provides an exemplar of how global processes may impact on other similar societies in due course.

All this said, intoxicated weekends, except for socially excluded minorities, are also constrained by work hard – play hard lifestyles. The conforming, generally law abiding and employed nature of the 'going out' sector is in one sense a protective factor. This is why there is potential in secondary prevention initiatives which can focus on reducing negative outcomes, whilst acknowledging the functional nature of the social context of heavy drinking and 'time out'.

References

Bellis, M. et al. (2004), 'Recreational Drug Use in International Nightlife Resorts', *Addiction*, **98**, 1713–1721. [DOI: 10.1111/j.1360-0443.2003.00554.x].

Calafat, A. (2001), 'Risk and Control in the Recreational Drug Culture' (Palma de Mallorca: SONAR/European Commission, Irefrea Books).

Coleman, L. and Cater, S. (2005), 'Underage 'Binge' Drinking: a Qualitative Study into Motivations and Outcomes', *Drugs: Education, Prevention and Policy*, **12**(2), 25–136.

Deehan, A. (1999), *Alcohol and Crime: Taking Stock* (London: Policing and Reducing Crime Unit, Home Office).

Duff, C. (2005), 'Party Drugs and Party People: Examining the Normalisation of Recreational Drug Use in Melbourne, Australia', *The International Journal of Drug Policy*, **16**(3), 161–170. [DOI: 10.1016/j.drugpo.2005.02.001].

Egginton, R. et al. (2002), 'Going Out Drinking: the Centrality of Heavy Alcohol Use in English Adolescents' Leisure Time and Poly-Substance-Taking Repertoires', *Journal of Substance Use*, **7**, 125–135.

Health Promotion Agency (2003), *Attitudes and Behaviour of Young Adult Drinkers in Northern Ireland: a Qualitative Study* (Belfast: Health Promotion Agency).

Jensen, M. et al. (2003), 'A Prospective Study of the Association Between Smoking and Later Alcohol Drinking in the General Population', *Addiction*, **98**, 355–363. [PubMed 12603235] [DOI: 10.1046/j.1360-0443.2003.00304.x].

Joseph Rowntree Foundation (2005), *Under-age Risky Drinking: Motivations and Outcomes* (York: York Publishing Services).

Mäkelä, K. and Mustonen, H. (2000), 'Relationships of Drinking Behaviour, Gender and Age with Reported Negative and Positive Experiences Related to Drinking', *Addiction*, **95**(5), 727–736. [DOI: 10.1046/j.1360-0443.2000.9557278.x].

Measham, F. and Brain, K. (2005), 'Binge Drinking, British Alcohol Policy and the Culture of Intoxication', *Crime, Media, Culture*, **1**(3), 262–283. [DOI: 10.1177/1741659005057641].

Measham, F. et al. (2001), *Dancing on Drugs: Risk, Health and Hedonism in the British Club Scene* (London: Free Association Books).

Morris, J. et al. (2002), 'The Integrated Programme: An Evaluation of a Multi-Component Drugs Prevention Programme in North England 1996–1999', *Drugs: Education, Prevention and Policy*, **9**(2), 153–168. [DOI: 10.1080/09687630110099353].

NCSR/NFER (2005), *Smoking, Drinking and Drug Use among Young People in England: 2004* (London: National Centre for Social Research / National Foundation for Educational Research).

Parker, H. and Egginton, R. (2002), 'Adolescent Recreational Alcohol and Drug Careers Gone Wrong: Developing a Strategy for Reducing Risks and Harms', *International Journal of Drugs Policy*, **13**, 419–432. [DOI: 10.1016/S0955-3959%2802%2900154-8].

— and Egginton R. (2006), *Young People's Drinking and Drug Use in Salford: Better Managing a Complex Agenda.* Salford Council (restricted).

— and Williams, L. (2003), 'Alcohol, Cannabis, Ecstasy and Cocaine: Drugs of Reasoned Choice Amongst Young Adults in England', *The International Journal on Drug Policy*, **12**, 397–413. [DOI: 10.1016/S0955-3959%2801%2900104-9].

— and Williams, L. (2001), 'Intoxicated Weekends: Young Adults Work Hard–Play-Hard Lifestyles, Public Health and Public Disorder', *Drugs: Education, Prevention and Policy*, **40**(4), 345–368.

— et al. (1998), *Illegal Leisure: the Normalisation of Adolescent Recreational Drug Use* (London: Routledge).

Thom, B. et al. (1999), 'Identifying Alcohol-related Harm and Young Drinkers: The Role of Accident and Emergency Departments', *Alcohol and Alcoholism*, **34**(4), 910–915. [DOI: 10.1093/alcalc%2F34.6.910].

Sunday Times (2005), *Project Holiday: Report for the Foreign Office* (Report Published under Freedom of Information Act reported by Sunday *Times* 26.06.05).

White, D. and Pitts, M. (1998), 'Educating Young People About Drugs: a Systematic Review', *Addiction*, **93**(10), 1475–1487. [PubMed 9926552] [DOI: 10.1046/j.1360-0443.1998.931014754.x].

Chapter 8

Being 'Taught to Drink'. UK Teenagers' Experience

Martin Plant and Patrick Miller

Introduction

As shown in many of the chapters in this volume, drinking patterns and the levels of the effects of drinking vary enormously between different countries (see also Pittman and Raskin White, 1991; Heath, 1995). This has been demonstrated in international studies related to teenagers (Hibell et al., 2004), as well as adults (Bloomfield et al., 2005). Drinking cultures are very different. These cultural differences include variations in the extent to which alcohol consumption is considered acceptable or normative, and the way in which drinking by children and young people is regarded. During recent years there has been clear evidence that rates of heavy drinking among young people in the UK has been rising. This increase has been accompanied by increases in alcohol-related problems among the young and by a heightened level of public concern about the phenomenon of youthful periodic heavy or 'binge' drinking (Plant and Plant, 2005, 2006).

The picture has been further complicated by evidence of a particular increase in heavy drinking among teenage girls and young women (Plant and Plant, 2001; Plant et al., 2002; Plant and Plant, 2004; Plant, 2005). The latest ESPAD-study showed that girls aged 15 and 16 years in the UK were more likely than boys to report having 'binged' (defined here as having consumed five or more drinks three or more times in the past 30 days). This development was only noted in the British Isles (Ireland, the Isle of Man and the UK), and not in the other 32 countries that participated in ESPAD in 2003 (Hibell et al., 2004).

Preventing alcohol-related problems by health education has often been suggested as an important policy option (for example Cabinet Office, 2004; Plant, 2004). In spite of this, a huge international literature shows that, with very few exceptions (for example Midford and McBride, 2004; Poulin and Nicholson, 2005) past attempts to curb heavy drinking and alcohol-related problems amongst young people by health promotion or alcohol education in schools using many different approaches have been unsuccessful. Some have even been counterproductive (for example Foxcroft, 2003; Plant and Plant, 2006). Even so, it has been suggested that the family is a major influence on the development of the drinking careers of young people in relation to both drinking habits and attitudes to drinking (for example Raskin White et al., 1991; Plant, 2001; Engels, 2005).

As shown in the ESPAD-study, teenagers in some countries such as France, Portugal, the Netherlands, Italy, Malta, Romania and Switzerland report low levels of alcohol-related problems. Those in countries such as Denmark, the Isle of Man, Finland, Lithuania, Ireland, Latvia and the UK report much higher levels (Hibell et al., 1997, 2001, 2004). One of the many cultural factors that might influence the development of youthful drinking is whether or not parents actively teach their children to drink within a family setting. It would appear that this approach is more normative in some countries (such as Portugal or Spain) than others (such as the UK and the Nordic countries). It is possible that one reason why teenagers and other young people in some countries handle alcohol with few problems is rooted in how they are introduced to it by parents or other significant individuals.

In previous reports based on findings from earlier UK and French ESPAD surveys (Miller, 1997; Ledoux et al., 2002; Miller and Plant, 2003) the authors have shown a profound influence of parental monitoring and parental attitudes on psychoactive substance use by teenagers. This investigation showed that parental knowledge of where their sons and daughters spent their Saturday nights and parental rule or boundary setting were associated with teenagers drinking less heavily. The present chapter seeks to go a stage further by exploring whether or not the parents of UK teenagers had taught their children to drink and what effects this might have produced. In the UK part of ESPAD 2003 the teenagers were simply asked whether or not they had been taught to drink by their parents. This is elaborated below in relation to factors such as age of first drink, alcohol consumption patterns, perceptions of drinking and social background.

Method

Information about a wide range of alcohol-related variables was available from the UK ESPAD survey carried out in the spring of 2003.

The population surveyed consisted of pupils born in 1987 throughout the UK. Lists were available for the whole UK detailing the schools (both state and independent) and the total number of pupils in each. One hundred and forty-one schools were sampled from this list with probability proportional to size, thus resulting in a self weighted representative sample covering the whole UK. Participating schools then supplied a list of all their classes containing pupils born in 1987, and two of these classes were randomly sampled from these lists by the researchers. Next, the standard ESPAD questionnaire was administered to each class under 'examination' conditions. The instructions emphasised that each student had been randomly chosen, that the answers were anonymous and totally confidential, that participation was voluntary and that answers need not be given to questions which the subject found objectionable. On completion the respondent sealed the questionnaire into a separate brown envelope. After the administration the local organiser completed a sheet detailing the numbers of pupils present, the numbers absent and the reasons for absence. Local organisers were paid a small honorarium for their help.

The ESPAD questionnaire is divided into a core section used by all countries, optional modules used by some countries and individual questions specific to a single country. The core questions are about use of cigarettes, alcohol and illicit drugs including some questions concerning the family situation and also attitudes and beliefs about substance use. The extra modules included by the UK covered parental attitudes and control, daily activities, self-esteem, depression and anti-social behaviour. The question on parental teaching about alcohol was an extra item specific to the UK (and the Isle of Man). It took the following form: 'Did your parents teach you to drink?' with the options being 'yes', 'no' or 'I do not drink'.

It must be acknowledged that this single question could have been interpreted in many ways by the teenagers who were surveyed. Moreover, being 'taught to drink' may also include a number of quite different things. The latter might include brief advice, long discussions, demonstrations of how much to drink and how much not to drink, being advised never to drink or being told that a liberal approach to drinking is acceptable. The inclusion of just this undefined single question in the 2003 UK survey reflected the fact that the existing questionnaire was long enough for use in school classes. It was also decided to cover this issue in much greater depth in the UK component of the 2007 ESPAD.

Results

Of the 141 schools approached only 77 (70 state and 7 independent) were willing or able to participate in ESPAD. The reason given for non co-operation was usually that the school had taken part in other research projects and staff did not have the inclination or capacity to be involved in yet another. This 'survey fatigue' is an increasingly common general problem for social science research. There were no discernible differences in the types of school co-operating and not co-operating. Within the 77 co-operating schools, student co-operation was good. A total of 83.4 per cent of those in selected classes filled in questionnaires. In addition, 14.6 per cent were absent due to illness or for some other reason for which permission had been granted and 1.1 per cent were absent without explanation. After exclusion of students not born in 1987 and a rejection of questionnaires with implausible answers or too many missing responses, the remaining sample (2,023 students) included 1,082 boys and 985 girls. There was some internal non-response to individual survey questions. Because of this, the numbers presented below vary from item to item.

In response to the special question, 17.8 per cent of pupils answered 'yes,' their parents had taught them to drink, 74.9 per cent responded 'no' and 7.4 per cent claimed to be non-drinkers. The gender distributions within these three categories were virtually identical.

Drinking Frequencies, Quantities Consumed and the Age at which Alcohol
Consumption Commenced

Table 8.1 compares the pupils who reported having been taught to drink by
their parents with those who reported that they had not been taught to drink
on drinking frequencies. A highly significant difference appears on lifetime
consumption, but this was reduced when only recent consumption is considered.
No significant difference was found in the extent of binge drinking.

**Table 8.1   Frequencies of alcohol consumption in those taught and not taught
to drink by their parents**

Parents taught subject to drink	Consumed alcohol on more than 40 occasions in the lifetime	Consumed alcohol on more than 40 occasions in the past year	Consumed alcohol on more than 19 occasions in the past 30 days	Consumed five or more drinks in a row in the past 30 days
No	642/1,455 44.4%	275/1,438 19.1%	70/1,444 4.8%	867/1,493 58.1%
Yes	197/349 56.4%	93/346 26.9%	24/347 6.9%	217/355 61.1%
Fisher exact probability	< 0.001	0.002	0.139	0.308

The quantities of beer, wine and spirits consumed on the last drinking occasion
(excluding subjects who did not drink a particular beverage on the last occasion)
are set out in Tables 8.2 and 8.3 together with the ages of first consumption of
these beverages and first getting drunk. Compared to the untaught group, there
is a tendency for the taught group to consume alcohol at a moderate level rather
than at a low or high level. This is significant for beer and nearly so for wine
(Table 8.2). Concerning age of first use of alcohol (Table 8.3), it is very clear
that the taught group commenced earlier that the untaught group. There was no
significant difference in the age of first intoxication.

*Personal Perceptions and Experiences Concerning the Effects and Consequences
of Drinking Alcohol*

The questionnaire contained 13 items on perceptions about what would happen to
them personally when they consumed alcohol. These items included variables such
as feeling relaxed and getting into trouble with the police. These were measured on
a five point scale. These items can be conveniently split into two scales measuring
'good' and 'bad' consequences of alcohol consumption. On good perceptions there
is no difference between the groups (mean taught 22.68, mean untaught 22.64,
scale range 6–30, t = 0.12 NS). On the bad scale, however, the untaught have
more bad perceptions than the taught (mean taught 16.62, mean untaught 17.37,
t = 2.24, P = 0.026, scale range 7–35). Three further questions asked how much
the subject thought people harmed themselves (physically or in other ways) by

Table 8.2 Quantities of alcohol consumed on the last drinking occasion

		1*	2	3	4	
Beer	Parents did not teach subject to drink n = 742	129 17.4%	249 33.6%	154 20.8%	210 28.3%	$\chi^2 = 10.30$ P = 0.016
	Parents taught subject to drink n = 206	23 11.2%	92 44.7%	37 18.0%	54 26.2%	
Wine	Parents did not teach subject to drink n = 742	149 29.4%	214 42.2%	69 13.6%	75 14.8%	$\chi^2 = 7.27$ P = 0.064
	Parents taught subject to drink n = 206	33 24.3%	71 52.2%	21 15.4%	11 8.1%	
Spirits	Parents did not teach subject to drink n = 742	149 19.7%	323 42.7%	174 23.0%	110 14.6%	$\chi^2 = 0.53$ NS
	Parents taught subject to drink n = 206	37 21.5%	75 43.6%	37 21.5%	23 13.4%	

* Categories for the different beverages are as follows:
beer: 1 = less than one bottle or can, 2 = 1–2 bottles or cans, 3 = 3–4 bottles or cans, 4 = 5+ bottles or cans;
wine: 1 = less than one glass, 2 = 1–2 glasses, 3 = half a bottle, 4 = a bottle or more;
spirits: 1 = less than one shot, 2 = 1–2 shots, 3 = 3–5 shots, 4 = 6+ shots.

Table 8.3   Ages of first consumption and first intoxication

		11 years old or less	12 years old	13 years old	14 years old	Never or later than 14 years old	
Beer at least one glass	Parents did not teach subject to drink n = 1486	381 25.6%	295 19.9%	248 16.7%	193 13.0%	369 24.8%	χ^2 = 26.49 P < 0.001
	Parents taught subject to drink n = 354	132 37.3%	71 20.1%	61 17.2%	29 8.2%	61 17.2%	
Wine at least one glass	Parents did not teach subject to drink n = 1484	426 28.7%	307 20.7%	242 16.3%	174 11.7%	335 22.6%	χ^2 = 52.70 P < 0.001
	Parents taught subject to drink n = 353	167 47.3%	72 20.4%	45 12.7%	25 7.1%	44 12.5%	
Spirits at least one glass	Parents did not teach subject to drink n = 1479	126 8.5%	203 13.7%	344 23.3%	339 22.9%	467 31.6%	χ^2 = 14.19 P = 0.007
	Parents taught subject to drink n = 354	45 12.7%	55 15.5%	94 26.6%	78 22.0%	82 23.2%	
Intoxication	Parents did not teach subject to drink n = 1484	89 6.0%	149 10.0%	312 21.0%	373 25.1%	561 37.8%	χ^2 = 5.92 NS
	Parents taught subject to drink n = 354	23 6.5%	36 10.2%	94 26.6%	78 22.0%	123 34.7%	

a) having one or two drinks nearly every day b) having four or five drinks nearly every day and c) having five or more drinks each weekend. Each question was scored on a four point scale from 'no risk' to 'great risk'. Only on a) was there a significant difference, with 58.8 per cent of the untaught against 52 per cent of the taught believing that having one to two drinks almost daily involved at least moderate risk (Fisher exact probability 0.023).

Finally there was a series of 14 questions concerning actual problems, for example quarrels, loss of money, and sexual intercourse, experienced due to alcohol use. On summing the responses to this series and analysing using the Mann–Whitney U-test no difference was found between the taught and the untaught groups ($Z = 1.06$, NS).

Parental Attitudes and the Family Circumstances

Three variables relating to family circumstances and parental attitudes were investigated. Firstly the educational background of the parents was considered, dividing the sample into those whose mothers and fathers had at least some further education after school and those where this was not the case. Secondly, the subject's responses on whether or not their parents would approve of them getting drunk were analysed. Thirdly each respondent was asked how well-off the family was compared to other families. The original 7-point scale was dichotomised into 'better off than average' and 'the same or worse off'. Table 8.4 sets out the findings.

Those whose parents taught them to drink were clearly more likely to be in better-off families with their parents showing higher educational levels. The taught group was more likely than the untaught to say that their parents would approve or at least not mind their getting drunk.

Cigarette Smoking and Illicit Drug Use

The questionnaire contained seven point scales covering lifetime cigarette smoking, lifetime experience of any illicit drug and cigarette smoking in the last 30 days. The taught group was slightly less likely to indulge in cigarette smoking but there was no difference in the use of illicit substances (Table 8.5).

Results Controlling for Family Circumstances

Since a larger proportion of the 'taught' group come from better-off more middle-class families the question arises whether family circumstances could account for all the results found. To test this, logistic regressions were run, first entering mother's education, family financial status and mother's attitude towards the subject getting drunk, followed by the taught-untaught variable. The dependent variables examined were lifetime drinking frequency, past year drinking frequency, first consumption of beer, wine and spirits, bad alcohol perceptions, harm done by having one or two drinks almost daily, lifetime cigarette smoking and cigarette smoking in the past month. In every case the 'taught-untaught' variable remained

Table 8.4 Family circumstances and parental attitudes

	Father's educational level		Mother's educational level	
	Parents did not teach subject to drink n = 1472	Parents taught subject to drink n = 352	Parents did not teach subject to drink n = 1471	Parents taught subject to drink n = 354
At least some higher education	630 42.8%	185 52.6%	715 48.6%	215 60.7%
Secondary education only	641 43.5%	137 38.9%	624 42.4%	115 32.5%
Don't know	201 13.7%	30 8.5%	132 9.0%	24 6.8%
	$\chi2 = 13.39$ P = 0.001		$\chi2 = 16.80$ P < 0.001	

	Father's attitude to the subject getting drunk		Mother's attitude to the subject getting drunk	
	Parents did not teach subject to drink n = 1362	Parents taught subject to drink n = 333	Parents did not teach subject to drink n = 1433	Parents taught subject to drink n = 346
Would discourage it	813 59.7%	157 47.1%	976 68.1%	181 52.3%
Would approve or at least not mind	549 40.3%	176 52.9%	457 31.9%	165 47.7%
	$\chi2 = 17.20$ P < 0.001		$\chi2 = 30.59$ P < 0.001	

Family circumstances		
	Parents did not teach subject to drink n = 1458	Parents taught subject to drink n = 333
Not well-off	747 51.2%	157 44.5%
Well-off	711 48.8%	196 55.5%
	$\chi^2 = 5.19$ P = 0.023	

Table 8.5   Smoking and illicit drug use in the 'taught' and 'untaught' group

Lifetime cigarette smoking		Never	1–39 times	40+ times	
	Parents did not teach subject to drink n = 1488	553 37.2%	577 38.8%	358 24.1%	$\chi^2 = 7.01$ P = 0.030
	Parents taught subject to drink n = 355	158 44.5%	127 35.8%	70 19.7%	
Cigarette smoking in the last 30 days		**None**	**less than 1/ day**	**1+ per day**	
	Parents did not teach subject to drink n = 1491	1,003 67.3%	167 11.2%	321 21.5%	$\chi^2 = 6.15$ P = 0.046
	Parents taught subject to drink n = 355	260 73.2%	39 11.0%	56 15.8%	
Lifetime illicit drug use		**Never**	**1–39 times**	**40+ times**	
	Parents did not teach subject to drink n = 1496	867 58.0%	474 31.7%	155 10.4%	$\chi^2 = 2.59$ NS
	Parents taught subject to drink n = 355	220 62.0%	97 27.3%	38 10.7%	

significant after the entry of the control variables with probabilities ranging from 0.038 for harm done by one or two drinks almost daily to 0.008 for cigarettes smoked in the past month.

Discussion

This chapter describes a very limited and tentative investigation of a very complex topic. The results mainly serve to suggest some future lines of more detailed investigation. The large majority of drinkers within this UK sample of 15- and 16-year-old school students reported that their parents did not 'teach them to drink'. When comparing this majority to the minority, who reported having been taught to drink by parents, the taught group had, on the one hand, consumed alcohol more frequently during their lifetime, but, on the other hand, were more likely to have consumed moderately on their last drinking occasion. The main finding from this study is that the minority of teenagers who had been taught to drink by their parents (whatever that really means) were drinking more often than those who had not been taught. It should also be acknowledged that last drinking occasion is simply one variable, while an individual's drinking behaviour really needs to be considered using an array of different measures. The explanation for the more frequent drinking of those who had been taught to drink may lie in the finding that these teenagers started drinking earlier in life. But other research shows that an early debut does not prevent heavy drinking later in adolescence. On the contrary it has been reported, early beginners tend to drink more, and report more binge drinking and drunkenness at age 15–16 (and later) than late beginners (Hingson and Kenkel, 2004; York et al., 2004; Pitkanen et al., 2004). The study reported in this chapter indicated that experience of problems due to alcohol did not seem to be related to the 'teach to drink' variable. Nor were there any significant differences seen in 'binge' drinking over the past 30 days. This certainly does not support the view that teaching children to drink reduces binge drinking or alcohol-related problems. Findings may be consistent with the fact that there might be a group of teenagers who 'binge' and who are impervious to messages about safe drinking. Clearly many issues related to this subject require additional research. Some strong evidence suggests that beginning to drink early is likely to be a factor in heavy drinking later in life. It is possible that this is true in some contexts and cultures, but not in others. There is substantial, convincing evidence suggesting that formal school-based health promotion or alcohol education seldom reduce the quantities of alcohol that young people drink. Even so it is also clear that the probability that young people do drink heavily or with problems varies greatly amongst different countries. This may, of course, simply reflect such profound factors tied up with nationhood and culture that low level, moderate or sensible drinking cannot be exported to another setting simply by identifying a few isolated variables which in one culture are associated with moderate drinking. One important issue may be the influence of the drinking habits of parents, siblings and the significant others in a young person's life.

Unfortunately, this issue was beyond the scope of the investigation reported here. It clearly warrants further consideration.

This has been purely the first attempt by the authors to address an important question. As already stressed, this was a very limited enquiry. This showed that a minority of teenagers had been taught to drink. These individuals were found to be drinking more often at the ages of 15 and 16 years. This might have been mainly attributable to the more privileged socio-economic backgrounds of the teenagers who reported having received parental guidance in drinking. A more detailed approach would probably be more revealing. This could include examining the context, and form of any parental or other guidance for young people on alcohol use. A number of new questions are to being included in the UK part of ESPAD 2007. These will explore in greater detail factors associated with teenagers' early learning experiences of alcohol. Even then it is stressed, findings will only relate to a single country at a specific time and may not be generalisable beyond those confines.

Acknowledgements

The authors thank Jan and Jim Green and Dunedin Data Services (Edinburgh). This study was inspired by Björn Hibell and aided by Barbro Andersson of the Swedish Council for Information on Alcohol and other Drugs. It was carried out with encouragement from the Pompidou Group of the Council of Europe and the World Health Organization. Thanks also go to Mr Stephen Longmire, Professor Robin Means, Mrs. Judy Orme, Dr Jane Powell and Professor Steve West of the University of the West of England, Bristol and to the students and teachers in the participating schools for encouragement and support. The UK study was funded by the Wates Foundation and the University of the West of England, Bristol. Additional support was provided by the Joseph Rowntree Foundation, the Oakdale Trust, Butcombe Brewery Ltd. Dr George Carey, the Jack Goldhill Charitable Trust, R. & J. Lass Charities Ltd and the North British Distillery Company Ltd.

References

Bloomfield, K. et al. (2005), *Gender, Culture and Alcohol Problems: A Multi-National Study; Project Final Report* (Berlin: Charité Campus Benjamin Franklin).

Cabinet Office Prime Minister's, Strategy Unit (2004), *Alcohol Harm Reduction Strategy for England* (London: Cabinet Office).

Engels, R. (2005), 'Parenting and Adolescent Substance Use', presentation at Alcohol and Health Research Trust Seminar, Bristol, UK, 11 February 2005.

Foxcroft, D. (2003), 'Longer-term Primary Prevention for Alcohol Misuse in Young People: a Systematic Review', *Addiction*, **98**, 397–411. [PubMed 12653810] [DOI: 10.1046/j.1360-0443.2003.00355.x].

Heath, D., ed. (1995), *International Handbook on Alcohol and Culture* (Westport, CN: Greenwood Press).

Hibell, B. et al. (1997), *The 1995 ESPAD Report: Alcohol and Other Drug Use among Students in 26 European Countries* (Stockholm: Swedish Council for Information on Alcohol and Other Drugs (CAN) and the Pompidou Group at the Council of Europe).

— (2001), *The 1999 ESPAD Report: Alcohol and Other Drug Use among Students in 30 European Countries* (Stockholm: Swedish Council for Information on Alcohol and Other Drugs (CAN) and the Pompidou Group at the Council of Europe).

— (2004), *The ESPAD Report 2003: Alcohol and Other Drug Use among Students in 35 European Countries* (Stockholm: Swedish Council for Information on Alcohol and Other Drugs (CAN) and the Pompidou Group at the Council of Europe).

Hingson, R.W. and Kenkel, D. (2004), 'Social, Health and Economic Consequences of Underage Drinking' in *Reducing Underage Drinking: a Collective Responsibility. Background Papers*, National Research Council and Institute of Medicine (ed.), 351–382. (Committee on Developing a Strategy to Reduce and Prevent Underage Drinking, Division of Behavioural and Social Sciences and Education, Washington, DC: The National Academies Press).

Ledoux, S. et al. (2002), 'Family Structure, Parent-Child Relationships, Alcohol and other Drug Use among Teenagers in France and the United Kingdom', *Alcohol and Alcoholism*, **37**, 52–60. [PubMed 11825858].

Midford, R. and McBride, N. (2004), 'Alcohol Education in Schools' in *The Essential Handbook of Treatment and Prevention of Alcohol Problems*. Heather, N. and Stockwell, T. (eds) (Hoboken, NJ: John Wiley), 299–319.

Miller, P. (1997), 'Family Structure, Personality, Drinking, Smoking and Illicit Drug Use: a Study of UK Teenagers', *Drug and Alcohol Dependence*, **45**, 121–129. [PubMed 9179514] [DOI: 10.1016/S0376-8716%2897%2901345-8].

Miller, P. and Plant, M.A. (2003), 'The Family, Peer Influences and Substance Use: Findings from a Study of UK Teenagers', *Journal of Substance Use*, **8**, 19–26. [DOI: 10.1080/14659890306266].

Pitkanen, T. et al. (2004), 'Age of Onset of Drinking and the Use of Alcohol in Adulthood: a Follow-up Study from Age 8–42 for Females and Males', *Addiction*, **100**, 652–661. [DOI: 10.1111/j.1360–0443.2005.01053.x].

Pittman, D. and Raskin White, H., eds. (1991), *Society, Culture and Drinking Patterns Re-examined* (Brunswick, N.J.: Rutgers Center for Alcohol Studies).

Plant, M.A. (2001), 'Learning by Experiment' in *Learning about Drinking*. Grant, M. (ed.) (International Center for Alcohol Policies Series on Alcohol), 129–146 in Society, Philadelphia: Brunner/Mazel).

— (2004), 'The Alcohol Harm Reduction Strategy for England: Overdue Final Report Omits much that was Useful in Interim Report' ('Editorial'), *British Medical Journal*, **328**, 905–906. [PubMed 15087323] [DOI: 10.1136/bmj.328.7445.905].

— (2005), 'Trends in Drinking, Smoking and Illicit Drug Use among 15 and 16 year Olds in the United Kingdom (1995-2003)', *Journal of Substance Use*, **10**, 331–339. [DOI: 10.1080/19659890412331519452].

Plant, M.A. and Plant, M.L. (2004), 'Binge Drinking: What's Happening?', presentation at *Binge Drinking: Problems and Responses*, International Conference, Bristol, 26 November 2004.

— (2005), 'Bar Wars: Media Frenzy and Licensing Chaos under Tony Blair', paper presented at the 31st Annual Alcohol Epidemiology Symposium (Riverside, CA: Kettil Bruun Society), USA, 30 May–3 June 2005.

— (2006), *Binge Britain: Alcohol and the National Response* (Oxford: Oxford University Press).

— (2001), 'Heavy Drinking by Young British Women Gives Cause for Concern', *British Medical Journal*, **323**, 1183. [PubMed 11711415] [DOI: 10.1136/bmj.323.7322.1183].

Plant, M.L. et al. (2002), 'Drinking, Smoking and Illicit Drug Use amongst British Adults: Gender Differences Explored', *Journal of Substance Use*, **7**, 24–33. [DOI: 10.1080/14659890110110392].

Poulin C. and Nicholson, J. (2005). 'Should Harm Minimization as an Approach to Adolescent Substance Use be Embraced by Junior and Senior High Schools?', *International Journal of Drug Policy*, **16**, 403–414.

Raskin White, H. et al. (1991), 'Learning to Drink: Familial, Peer, and Media Influences' in *Society, Culture and Drinking Patterns Re-Examined*. Pittman, D. and Raskin White, H. (eds) (New Brunswick, N.J.: Rutgers Centre for Alcohol Studies), 177–197.

York, J.L. et al. (2004), 'Association of Age of First Drink with Current Alcohol Drinking Variables in a National General Population Sample', *Alcoholism: Clinical and Experimental Research*, **28**, 1379–1387. [DOI: 10.1097/01.ALC.0000139812.98173.A4].

Chapter 9

Alcohol Use among Danish Adolescents: a Self- and Social Identity Perspective

Kirsten Verkooijen, Gert A. Nielsen, Nanne de Vries
and Kim Bloomfield

Introduction

Cross-national studies have shown that the alcohol consumption of young Danes, and especially their rate of engagement in binge drinking and experience with drunkenness, is one of the highest in Europe (see Chapters 3 and 4 in this volume). The purpose of the study presented in this chapter was to gain a better understanding of the high consumption of Danish adolescents by examining the role of identity. An identity approach to behaviour suggests that people tend to engage in behaviours that agree with their self-concept (Stryker and Burke, 2000). Doing so is believed to assist in the formation of a coherent and persistent sense of self (Swann et al., 1992). Adolescents, being in a transition phase from childhood into adulthood, are more in need of a stable self-image than any other age group (Erikson, 1968; Tarrant et al., 2001), and may therefore be especially motivated to enact central aspects of their self-concept in their behaviour. Hence, an identity perspective may be particularly well suited for the study of adolescent drinking. Before we set out the specific research objectives for the present study, we will first discuss in brief previous research on identity and adolescent alcohol use.

Previous Research

Despite the strong theoretical link between identity and behaviour, surprisingly few quantitative studies have addressed the concept of identity in alcohol research (or in behavioural research altogether). This lack of attention may be due partly to difficulties in translating 'identity' into meaningful and valid items for survey questionnaires – a typical format used in quantitative research. Much of the work on the impact of identity on behaviour has therefore consisted of qualitative research. The little quantitative work that exists can be roughly divided into two main streams.

The first line of research has examined the role of 'self-identity' in the prediction of behaviour. Self-identity in this context has been defined as the extent to which performing a particular behaviour is a salient part of one's self-concept (Sparks and Shepherd, 1992). It has been hypothesised that the more important the behaviour is to a person's self-concept, the more likely this person is to engage in the behaviour. Hence, a teenager who thinks of him- or herself as a heavy drinker and sees this as important to his or her self-definition, would be more likely to engage in binge drinking and heavy alcohol consumption than a teenager who does not perceive him- or herself to be a drinker. Research on self-identity has been conducted mainly within the framework of the Theory of Planned Behaviour (TPB) (Ajzen, 1988), which is probably the most widely used social psychological model in the prediction of human behaviour. According to TPB, behaviour is primarily determined by people's intention to perform the behaviour. Intention, in turn, is predicted by people's attitudes, subjective norms, and perceived behavioural control. The model is assumed to be complete in that any other factors are believed to influence behaviour through the three primary determinants (Ajzen, 1991). Hence, supporters of TPB would argue that identity does not provide additional predictive value to the model. Nevertheless, a growing number of researchers have addressed self-identity in a TPB framework and the results of their studies have demonstrated consistently that self-identity provides a significant and independent contribution to the prediction of behaviour (for example Sparks and Shepherd, 1992; Terry and Hogg, 1996; Sparks and Guthrie, 1998; Conner et al., 1999; Terry et al., 1999; Fekadu and Kraft, 2001). Still, only two studies have investigated self-identity in relation to alcohol use. Conner et al. (1999) examined the role of self-identity in the alcohol consumption of British university students. The researchers assessed self-identity using five items (for example 'drinking alcohol is an important part of who I am'; 'I would feel a loss if I were forced to give up drinking alcohol') and found self-identity as a drinker to predict the intention to drink over and above the TPB variables. In an unpublished study, Morojele et al. (1997) found self-identity to be a useful predictor of binge drinking intentions for 10th grade South African students.

The second line of quantitative research has addressed the role of *social* identity, that is, that part of one's identity that is derived from being a member of a certain group or social category (Tajfel and Turner, 1979). Social identity theory emphasises the importance of group membership to people's identity formation and behavioural decision making (Tajfel and Turner, 1979; Hogg and Abrams, 2003). The influence of social identity on individual behaviour is assumed to be mediated by the perceived behavioural norms of the group. Group members tend to act in line with perceived group norms because these norms have become important for self-definition (Terry and Hogg, 1996). Indeed, research has shown that the more strongly one identifies with a given group, the stronger is the impact of the perceived group norm on self-definition and personal behaviour (Terry and Hogg, 1996; Terry et al., 1999; Johnston and White, 2003; Smith and Terry, 2003).

Group identification tends to be particularly strong in adolescence, and the formation of so-called 'crowds' is very apparent among this age group (Pombeni et al., 1990; Tarrant et al., 2001). Crowds consist of large numbers of young people who are held together by a distinguishable group characteristic, such as a typical clothing style, music preference, belief, or leisure time activity (Brown et al., 1986; Kinney, 1993). Typically, these groups are given social labels that refer to the group's characteristic, such as *nerds, populars* and *hippies*. Adolescents' affiliation with crowds is believed to provide highly salient social identities (Brown et al., 1986; Kuther, 2000; Tarrant et al., 2001). So far, only a few studies have investigated the link between adolescents' identification with crowds and substance use. The majority of these studies have looked at cigarette smoking (Mosbach and Leventhal, 1988; Sussman et al., 1990; Schofield et al., 2003), but some have involved multiple behaviours including alcohol use (Dolcini and Adler, 1994; La Greca et al., 2001; der Rijt et al., 2002). The general conclusion of these studies is that there is a strong association between crowd identification and adolescent substance use.

Previous research regarding identification with various youth groups, however, has mainly addressed American adolescents (for example Mosbach and Leventhal, 1988; Sussman et al., 1994; Brown et al., 1997; La Greca et al., 2001). This research has found, for example, that alternative or 'outsider' groups such as *burnouts, nonconformists* and *dirts* have higher rates of cigarette, alcohol and other drug use than other more 'conforming' groups such as *jocks, brains* and *hot shots* (Mosbach and Leventhal, 1988; La Greca et al., 2001). It thus suggests that the groups which are in some way seen (or see themselves) as alternative or deviant are those which are associated with higher rates of substance use. Further, a recent Dutch study also found that teenagers who affiliated with 'counter-culture' groups were more likely to have a positive attitude toward using recreational drugs and also to smoke and drink at higher rates than those who did not affiliate with such groups (Van der Rijt et al., 2002). However, for Denmark, it is not immediately apparent whether such group identification categories are directly applicable for use with Danish adolescents and whether these would predict alcohol use in the same way. Thus, the present study proposes tentative hypotheses regarding the influence of social group identification on the alcohol use of Danish adolescents.

The Present Research

The present study examined the roles that self-identity and social identity play in the alcohol consumption of Danish adolescents. A longitudinal study design was employed in order to investigate the predictive power of identity over time. It was hypothesised that both self-identity and social identity would significantly and independently contribute to the prediction of drinking behaviour. With regard to self-identity, stronger self-identification with high alcohol consumption was expected to predict higher levels of alcohol use. Regarding social identity, stronger identification was predicted to produce either higher or lower levels of alcohol use depending on the type of social group. The study included eight youth crowds, namely *sporty, pop, skate/hip-hop, quiet, computer nerd, techno, religious* and *hippie*. These groups had been identified through prior focus group discussions with representatives of the target population. Because Denmark is a relatively 'wet' country with an established reputation of teenage binge drinking, drinking as such may not be associated as strongly with a 'counter-culture' or 'deviant' identification as in North America. Rather, we propose that identification with a culture of 'partying' or recreation would be associated with more drinking. To this end, we could propose the tentative hypothesis that identifications with the pre-identified groups *pop*, *skate/hip-hop*, *techno* and *hippie* (that is those more associated with recreation without directly involving serious athletics), would be associated with higher levels of alcohol use than identification with the groups *sporty*, *quiet*, *computer nerd* and *religious*. It is hypothesised that these latter groups reflect a more conforming and/or health conscious lifestyle that would not involve partying and activities involving drinking to the same degree as the former groups.

Methods

Participants and Study Design

Longitudinal data were collected in two waves with an interval of one and a half years. The first data collection took place in autumn 2002 as part of the Danish MULD-project (monitoring of young people's lifestyle, see Nielsen et al., 2002); a national postal survey carried out by the Danish Cancer Society and the Danish National Board of Health. Initially, 6,000 boys and girls in the age of 16–20 years were invited to participate in the study. This sample was randomly selected from the Danish Population Register by date of birth. Completed questionnaires were received from 3,956 (response rate: 66 per cent) adolescents, 44 per cent males and 56 per cent females. Respondents who showed a positive identification (that is score 4 or 5) with either one or two of the studied social identity groups (n = 2,210) were again invited for participation one and a half years later (Time 2). At Time 2, questionnaires were received from 1,611 (73 per cent) respondents. Data from respondents with inconsistent answer patterns or missing data on gender or age (n = 52) were excluded from analysis. The final sample consisted of 1,559 adolescents; 560 (36 per cent) males and 999 (64 per cent) females. The mean age at Time 1 was 18.10 ± 1.42. Adolescents who participated in the follow-up were overall slightly older than adolescents who did not participate at Time 2 (t = –2.03, p = 0.04). Also, relatively more girls participated in the follow-up. However, when controlled for sex and age, adolescents who did and did not take part in the follow-up did not significantly differ on the drinking or self-identity measures assessed at Time 1.

Measures

Alcohol use   Weekly alcohol consumption was assessed by asking respondents to estimate how many alcohol units they consume during a typical week. As an example of alcoholic units, the number of standard Danish alcohol units for various alcoholic drinks was given. In addition, respondents were asked to state at how many occasions over the last 30 days they had been drunk. Here, the five answer categories were: 'once', 'once or twice', 'three to five times', 'six to nine times' and 'ten times or more'.

Self-identity   As a measure of self-identification with binge drinking, respondents were asked to state how much they agreed with the statement: 'high alcohol consumption is an important part of who I am'. This item was taken from a study by Sparks and Shepherd (1992), adapted to the topic of drinking, and translated from English into Danish. Answers were given on five-point scales: 'totally agree'-'totally disagree'. The scores were recoded so that higher scores reflected higher self-identification.

Social identity   Social identification with nine groups was assessed by asking respondents: 'If your friends would call you one of following names, to what extent would you agree?' This was followed by a list of nine group names: *sporty, pop boy/girl, skater/hip-hopper, bodybuilder, quiet boy/girl, techno freak, computer nerd, religious* and *hippie*. These group names were obtained through prior discussions with representatives of the target population. In all, nine focus group discussions, each involving six to eight students, were held at five different types of high schools (that is different vocational and other secondary schools). Participants were asked to mention well-known peer groups in Denmark. In addition, participants of later discussions were asked to comment on earlier mentioned crowds. The group names that appeared to be most prominent and consistent were included in the present study. Answers were given for each group name on a five-point scale: 'totally agree'-'totally disagree'. The scores were recoded so that higher scores indicated stronger social identification. Because identification with the subgroup *bodybuilder* was overall very low ($M = 1.24 \pm 0.58$), it was decided not to include identification with this group in the data analysis.

Data Analysis Strategy

SPSS software (SPSS 13.0, 2004) was used for the data analyses. Firstly, descriptive statistics were calculated for the drinking measures as well as for other relevant variables. Paired t-tests were conducted to examine potential differences between measures at Time 1 and Time 2. Next, two sets of hierarchical linear regression analyses were performed to test the efficiency of self- and social identity as predictors of both the frequency of last month drunkenness and weekly alcohol consumption. The first set of regression analyses involved a cross-sectional analysis of drinking behaviour at Time 1. The second set of regression analyses investigated the longitudinal effect of self-identity and social identity on respondents' drinking behaviour at Time 2. Age, in years, and gender were included as control variables in the regression models.

Results

Descriptive Analysis of Drinking Behaviour at Time 1

Less than 8 per cent of the respondents (8.2 per cent of the boys and 6.9 per cent of the girls) reported not drinking any alcohol. Adolescents identifying themselves as Islamic in religion (n = 26) reported not drinking (77 per cent) far more often than Protestants (n = 1,132; 6.0 per cent). Among drinkers, the mean age for drinking one's first alcoholic beverage was 13.6 ± 2.83 years, and for being drunk for the first time 14.4 ± 2.83 years. No major gender differences in these debut ages were found. Yet, current weekly alcohol consumption and frequency of last month drunkenness was considerably higher among males than females (see Table 9.1). Boys reported on average to consume almost 11 alcohol units per week, whereas girls reported a weekly consumption of about six units. The majority of the respondents (68 per cent) had been drunk at least once during the past month; 38 per cent had been drunk once or twice, 22 per cent three to five times, and 8.5 per cent more than five times. The Pearson correlation coefficient between weekly alcohol consumption and last month drunkenness was 0.62 (p < 0.001). Most adolescents considered their alcohol consumption as not being too high; only 7 per cent said they drink a little too much, and less than 1 per cent (n = 10) said they drink far too much. Yet, 12 per cent of the drinkers reported to have tried to drink less at parties. Drinkers' estimation of their best friend's alcohol consumption correlated strongly with their own consumption (Pearson's r = 0.73, p < 0.001). Moreover, they estimated their best friend's alcohol consumption during a weekend to be even higher than their own weekly consumption (paired sample t-test: t = –7.2, p < 0.001). However, few respondents (3 per cent) indicated feeling pressured by friends to drink more than they actually want.

Self-identity   The means and standard deviations for self-identity, as well as drinking behaviour and social identity, are shown in Table 9.1. Compared to girls, boys drank more alcohol units per week (t = 11.3, p < 0.001) and had more often been drunk in the last month (t = 6.9, p < 0.001). Weekly alcohol consumption and frequency of drunkenness increased slightly with age (Kruskal-Wallis χ^2 = 26.2 and χ^2 = 17.7, p < 0.001) (data not shown). Self-identification with high alcohol consumption was generally low: 1.45 ± 0.92 on a five-point scale. Girls identified less with heavy drinking than boys (independent t-test: t = 5.40, p < 0.001). Self-identity did not significantly differ among age groups.

Social identity   While the majority of the respondents (78 per cent) in the initial cross sectional sample (n = 3,956) showed a positive identification (that is indicated 'agree' or 'totally agree') with at least one group (40 per cent positively identified with one group, 25 per cent with two groups, and 13 per cent with at least three groups), the present longitudinal sample included exclusively respondents with either one (62 per cent) or two (38 per cent) positive identifications at Time 1. Girls identified significantly more strongly with *pop, quiet, religious* and *hippie*, whereas boys more strongly identified with *skate/hiphop, techno* and *computer nerd* (see

Table 9.1). No significant gender difference was observed for identification with *sporty*. *Sporty* was the subgroup with the highest mean identification score.

Table 9.1 Means and standard deviations of Time 1 measures and correlations with Time 2 measures

Time 1 measures	Girls		Boys		Overall		Correlation with Time 2
	M	SD	M	SD	M	SD	
Weekly alcohol consumption[1]	6.05	5.94	10.77	10.13	7.79	8.07	0.57***
Last month drunkenness[2]	1.96	0.89	2.30	1.04	2.08	0.96	0.51***
Self-identity[1]	1.35	0.83	1.62	1.05	1.45	0.92	0.34***
Social identity:[3]							
Sporty	3.13	1.43	3.22	1.49	3.16	1.45	0.78***
Pop	2.23	1.25	2.01	1.20	2.15	1.24	0.64***
Skate/hip-hop	1.36	0.80	1.63	1.15	1.46	0.95	0.62***
Quiet	2.52	1.40	2.48	1.32	2.51	1.37	0.67***
Techno	1.31	0.79	1.57	0.97	1.43	0.93	0.68***
Computer nerd	1.27	0.71	2.18	1.32	1.60	1.07	0.75***
Religious	1.66	1.08	1.57	0.97	1.63	1.04	0.64***
Hippie	1.71	1.17	1.47	0.92	1.63	1.09	0.69***

1 Measured in alcohol units.
2 Measured on a 5-point scale: '0', '1-2', '3-5', '6-9' and '10 or more'.
3 Measured on a 5-point scale: 'totally disagree' – 'totally agree'.
*** $p < 0.001$ *Note*. Correlations are expressed as Pearson r.

Prediction of Drinking Behaviour at Time 1

Table 9.2 shows the outcome of the regression analyses predicting frequency of drunkenness and weekly alcohol consumption at Time 1. Self-identity, controlled for sex and age, accounted for 7 per cent of the variance in drunkenness and 9 per cent of the variance in weekly alcohol consumption. The effect sizes of self-identity ($\beta = 0.22$ and $\beta = 0.26$ respectively) were significant (and higher than the effect of gender). Identification with the eight social groups turned out to be the strongest predictor of drinking behaviour. Entered at the third step,[1] it explained an additional 10 per cent of variance in drunkenness and 9 per cent of variance in weekly alcohol consumption. Although the group-specific effect sizes were small, they were significant and in the predicted directions: identification with *pop*, *skate/hip-hop*, and *hippie* were associated with more drinking, while identification with *quiet*, *computer nerd*, and *religious* predicted less drinking. Only identification

---

1 Social identification was added to the model as eight separate continuous variables. We performed the same analysis with social identification added as eight dichotomous variables (score ≥ 4 versus score ≤ 3). The outcomes were very similar.

with *sporty* and with *techno* was not significantly associated with drunkenness. Interestingly, the largest effects were found among those groups that predicted drinking behaviour negatively (for example *quiet* and *religious*).

Table 9.2   Hierarchical regression analysis predicting drinking behavior at Time 1

Step	Predictors	Last month drunkenness			Weekly alcohol consumption		
		R^2	ΔR^2	β	R^2	ΔR^2	β
1	Sex	0.03	0.03^{***}	-0.16^{***}	0.08	0.08^{***}	-0.26^{***}
	Age			0.08^{**}			0.08^{**}
2	Self-identity	0.10	0.07^{***}	0.22^{***}	0.18	0.09^{***}	0.26^{***}
3	*Social identity:*	0.20	0.10^{***}		0.27	0.09^{***}	
	Sporty			-0.03			-0.06^{*}
	Pop			0.08^{**}			0.07^{**}
	Skate/hip-hop			0.10^{***}			0.10^{***}
	Quiet			-0.21^{***}			-0.18^{***}
	Techno			0.03			0.11^{***}
	Computer nerd			-0.06^{*}			-0.09^{**}
	Religious			-0.10^{***}			-0.06^{*}
	Hippie			0.08^{**}			0.10^{***}

Note: the given betas were calculated after all variables had entered the model
*** $p < 0.001,$ $^{**}p < 0.01,$ $^{*}p < 0.05.$

Descriptive Analysis of Drinking Behaviour at Time 2

The average weekly alcohol consumption at Time 2, 10.7 ± 9.73 alcoholic units for boys and 6.0 ± 6.49 for girls, was comparable to that of one-and-half years earlier (paired t-test; $t = -0.26$, $p = 0.80$). Also the average number of last month drunken episodes did not significantly differ from Time 1 ($t = -1.00$, $p = 0.32$). Less than 30 per cent of the subjects had not been drunk during the past month, 40 per cent had been drunk once or twice, 22 per cent had been drunk three to five times, and 8 per cent more than five times. Again, boys reported higher weekly alcohol consumption ($t = 11.3$, $p < 0.001$) and more drunken episodes ($t = 5.81$, $p < 0.001$) than girls. Significant differences in age were no longer found. The correlations of all measures between Time 1 and Time 2 are presented in Table 9.1.

Self-identity   At Time 2, self-identification with high alcohol consumption was overall lower than at Time 1 ($t = 7.52$, $p < 0.001$). Again boys showed a stronger identification with high alcohol consumption than girls ($t = 8.36$, $p < 0.001$). The correlation between respondents' self-identification at Time 1 and Time 2 was not very high ($r = 0.34$, $p < 0.001$). Although this finding may (partly) be explained by a difference in questionnaire format between Time 1 and Time 2, in that more items in the questionnaire referred to self-identity at Time 2 (see remark in discussion), it also suggests that identifying oneself in terms of heavy drinking is rather unstable during adolescence, less stable, for instance, than the actual behaviour of heavy drinking.

Social identity   The correlations between the social identifications at Time 1 and Time 2 (Table 1) were substantial (Pearson *r* ranging between 0.62 and 0.78). Paired t-tests revealed that identification with the subgroups *sporty*, *pop*, *skate/ hip-hop*, *computer nerd*, and *religious* was slightly higher at Time 2 compared to Time 1, while identification with *techno* was lower at Time 2. Identification with *quiet*, and *hippie* had not changed significantly.

Prediction of Drinking Behaviour at Time 2

Table 9.3 presents the summary statistics of the hierarchical regression analyses that tested the ability to predict drinking behaviour one-and-a-half years later from self-identity and social identity at Time 1, taking into account drinking behaviour at Time 1. Respondents' drinking behaviour at Time 1, entered after sex and age, explained respectively 24 per cent and 27 per cent of the variance in drunkenness and alcohol consumption at Time 2. After controlling for past drinking behaviour, self-identity, entered at the third step, still emerged as a significant predictor of drinking ($\beta = 0.06$ and $\beta = 0.05$), but now provided only an additional 1 per cent of explained variance. Social identity, entered at the last step, added another 2 per cent and 1 per cent of variance. Here we see that after the inclusion of past drinking (the most significant predictor of present drinking behaviour), the effect sizes of the various social identities have decreased. *Pop, hip-hop* and *hippie* identities remain significant in predicting last month's drunkenness while *quiet* and *computer nerd* remain significant for predicting reduced weekly consumption.

Discussion

The aim of the present research was to study the drinking behaviour of Danish adolescents with a special focus on self- and social identity factors. A first exploration of our data confirmed the results of previous studies: average alcohol consumption among Danish adolescents is high in relation to adolescent drinking in other parts of Europe and North America, and being regularly drunk is more the rule than the exception. Furthermore, this excessive drinking appears to start at a relatively young age. Worrisome is also the finding that hardly any adolescents view their own alcohol consumption as being (too) high, which indicates the broad social acceptance of excessive drinking among young Danes.

Consistent with our expectations, self-identity proved to be significantly associated with adolescents' alcohol use. Although adolescents' self-identification with high alcohol consumption was generally low, it did predict drinking

Table 9.3 Hierarchical regression analysis predicting drinking behavior at Time 2

Step	Predictors	Last month drunkenness			Weekly alcohol consumption		
		R^2	ΔR^2	β	R^2	ΔR^2	β
1	Sex (girls)	0.02	0.02***	–0.08**	0.08	0.08***	–0.15***
	Age			–0.05*			0.02
2	Drinking behavior T1[2]	0.26	0.24***	0.44***	0.34	0.27***	0.49***
3	Self-identity (T1)	0.27	< 0.01**	0.06**	0.34	< 0.01*	0.05*
4	*Social identity (T1)*:	0.29	0.02***		0.35	0.01**	
	Sporty			0.06*			0.01
	Pop			0.05*			0.01
	Skate/hip-hop			0.05*			0.03
	Quiet			–0.04			–0.05*
	Techno			–0.01			<0.01
	Computer nerd			–0.03			–0.06*
	Religious			–0.04			–0.03
	Hippie			0.09***			0.03

Note: The given betas were calculated after all variables had entered the model.
*** $p < 0.001$, **$p < 0.01$, *$p < 0.05$.
1 Last month drunkenness and weekly alcohol consumption respectively.

behaviour, that is, adolescents were likely to report higher levels of drunkenness and alcohol consumption if high alcohol consumption was an important part of their self-identity. Also, independent of self-identity, social identity was significantly associated with adolescents' drinking behaviour. Identification with the subgroups *pop*, *skate/hip-hop*, *techno*, and *hippie* were linked to an overall higher frequency of drunkenness and weekly alcohol consumption, whereas identification with *sporty*, *quiet*, *computer nerd*, and *religious* was associated with lower levels of alcohol consumption. Yet, with the exception of the quiet and religious subgroups, alcohol use was high among all groups and the group-specific effect sizes were relatively small. A similar observation was made by Van Der Rijt et al. (2002) who studied alcohol use among various Dutch teenage subcultures. They also found that alcohol use was rather common in all studied subcultures. The researchers argued that since alcohol use is rather socially acceptable, it provides less of an opportunity to express a rebellious (counter-cultural) identity than, for instance, smoking and drug use. What is interesting to notice with our results is that the group identifications with the strongest correlations to drinking behaviour were in general negative and were among those groups that could be considered 'conservative' or at least non-rebellious, that is *religious* and *quiet*. Thus, where differences in drinking behaviour tend to stand out among Danish youth are in the direction of drinking less rather than more.

In the cross-sectional model, self-identity and social identity accounted together for 17 per cent of the variance in last month drunkenness and 18 per cent of the variance of weekly alcohol consumption. These proportions are fairly high given that an extremely well-developed model such as the Theory of Planned Behaviour has been found to account on average for 27 per cent of the variance in behaviour (Armitage and Conner, 2001). The present study included a second wave of data collection with the purpose of investigating whether self- and social identity are able to predict changes in adolescents' drinking behaviour over time. The results confirmed that both self- and social identity provide some prediction of drinking behaviour one and a half years later. Although the independent effect sizes were small, they were significant even when controlling for past drinking behaviour. This is a notable finding since drinking behaviour proved to be relatively stable, which makes it difficult to demonstrate strong predictors of behavioural change. Moreover, although the correlation of self-identity measured at Time 1 and Time 2 was statistically significant, it was still low (partially due to methodological factors – see discussion below), indicating with respect to the other results that self-perceptions of heavy drinking are less stable than actual drinking behaviour.

Study Limitations

A substantial limitation of the study was that it relied on self-reported single-item scales as indicators of self- and social identity. Especially the measurement of self-identity could be improved. The questionnaire administered at Time 2 included two additional items referring to self-identification with high alcohol consumption, but for comparative reasons these were not considered in the data analysis. The inter-item correlations between the applied self-identity item and the two extra items were rather weak (Cronbach's $\alpha = 0.59$ and $\alpha = 0.41$), indicating a low reliability of the construct. As a consequence, the predictability of self-identity to drinking behaviour may be susceptible to differences in its measurement. Future research should aim to develop a multi-item self-identity scale that reflects the construct best. Regarding the assessment of social identification, it should be noted that, even though social identification proved to be relatively stable over a one and half year period, group characteristics may change over longer periods. To keep up to date with these changes the groups need monitoring over time (Sussman et al., 1994). Furthermore, one may want to consider examining social identification not with scale variables but rather as separate groups. An advantage of the present study is that respondents were not forced to choose a group. On the other hand, one may question the value of investigating the strength of identification with non-relevant groups. Finally, a shortcoming of the present study is that it does not provide any information on the background of the specific subgroups and the possibly different (symbolic) meanings of alcohol use to each group. Further research, particularly qualitative in nature, could complement the current findings in this respect.

Implications of the Findings

Although the Theory of Planned Behaviour has proven successful in predicting health related behaviour (Godin and Kok, 1996; Armitage and Conner, 2001), health interventions based on the theory's premises have shown to be only moderately effective or even ineffective (for example de Vries et al., 2003). Therefore, it may be worthwhile to explore new avenues within health promotion. From an identity perspective, young people engage in activities that fit the image of the kind of person they are or want to be. An identity approach to reducing adolescent alcohol use thus would take into account the developmental needs of adolescents and the functions that heavy drinking serves in that respect. For instance, interventions may aim to discourage the formation of excessive drinking identities and encourage the development of identities that stand for more moderate alcohol use. Furthermore, health promotion activities may benefit from an approach that tailors messages to specific social groups. As our data suggest, not all youth are equally likely to engage in heavy drinking. Moreover, youth crowds may be practical targets for health promotion programs since they make up very recognisable groups. Thus, an identity approach offers an invitation and unique challenge to health promotion specialists to create new and innovative interventions that may have the actual potential to change behaviour by appealing to the specific identities of youth.

The results of the present study provide some indication that an identity approach may be a fruitful strategy in the prevention of excessive drinking among young people. However, the implications of the present findings are still speculative at this point. More research is obviously needed before definite conclusions can be drawn. Given the rather weak assessments of self-identity in the current study, future studies that apply multiple-item measures of this construct are warranted. While social identity is extensively described by social identity theory, the self-identity construct, with its origin in both sociological and psychological literatures, is not as well-defined (Fleming and Petty, 2000). Furthermore, to investigate the determinants of changing alcohol use, it is advisable to study younger adolescents whose drinking behaviours are less established. Additionally, although we noted that social identification proved to be relatively stable over the study period, other research suggests that influences of identity on behaviour appear to be most powerful during the early adolescent years (for example Brown et al., 1986). Future studies should therefore examine younger age groups to determine which behaviours are still malleable and how they may be influenced so that, for example, age of initiation may be postponed or in this case binge drinking may be delayed or attenuated. Finally, on a theoretical note, the precise nature of the link between self-identity and social identity needs further investigation. Although research on self-identity and social identity has developed as separate lines of research, one could argue that self-identification with a particular behaviour in essence refers to social identification with the group of people that perform that behaviour (Deaux, 1996; Terry et al., 1999). Under this interpretation, self-identification with 'heavy drinking' implies nothing other than identification with the group 'heavy drinkers'. Future research may wish to explore further the relationship between the two theoretical constructs.

References

Ajzen, I. (1988), *Attitudes, Personality and Behaviour* (Buckingham, UK: Open University Press).

— (1991), 'The Theory of Planned Behavior', *Organizational Behavior and Human Decision Processes*, **50**, 179–211. [DOI: 10.1016/0749-5978%2891%2990020-T].

Armitage, C.J. and Conner, M. (2001), 'Efficacy of the Theory of Planned Behavior: a Meta-Analytic Review', *British Journal of Social Psychology*, **40**, 471–499. [PubMed 11795063] [DOI: 10.1348/014466601164939].

Brown, B. et al. (1997), 'Transformations in Peer Relationships at Adolescence: Implications for Health-related Behavior' in *Health Risks and Developmental Transitions during Adolescence*. Schulenberg, J. et al. (eds) (Cambridge: Cambridge University Press).

— et al. (1986), 'The Importance of Peer ("crowd") Affiliation in Adolescence', *Journal of Adolescence*, **9**, 73–96. [PubMed 3700780] [DOI: 10.1016/S0140-1971%2886%2980029-X].

Conner, M. et al. (1999), 'Alcohol Consumption and the Theory of Planned Behavior: an Examination of the Cognitive Mediation of Past Behavior', *Journal of Applied Social Psychology*, **29**, 1676–1704. [DOI: 10.1111/j.1559-1816.1999.tb02046.x].

De Vries, H. et al. (2003), 'The European Smoking Prevention Framework Approach (ESFA): Short-term Effects', *Health Education Research*, **18**, 649–663. [PubMed 14654499] [DOI: 10.1093/her%2Fcyg033].

Deaux, K. (1996), 'Social Identification' in *Social Psychology: Handbook of Basic Principles*. Higgins, E.T. and Kruglanski, A.W. (eds) (New York: Guildford), 777–798.

Dolcini, M.M. and Adler, N.E. (1994), 'Perceived Competencies, Peer Group Affiliation, and Risk Behavior among Early Adolescents', *Health Psychology*, **13**, 496–506. [PubMed 7889904] [DOI: 10.1037/0278-6133.13.6.496].

Erikson, E.H. (1968), *Identity, Youth and Crisis* (New York: Norton).

Fekadu, Z. and Kraft, P. (2001), 'Self-identity in Planned Behavior Perspective: Past Behavior and its Moderating Effects on Self-Identity-Intention Relations', *Social Behavior and Personality*, **29**, 671–686. [DOI: 10.2224/sbp.2001.29.7.671].

Fleming, M.A. and Petty, R.E. (2000), 'Identity and Persuasion: an Elaboration Likelihood Approach' in *Attitudes, Behavior, and Social Context: the Role of Group Norms and Group Membership*. Terry, D.J. and Hogg, M.A. (eds) (Mahwah: Lawrence Erlbaum Associates, Inc), 171–199.

Godin, G. and Kok, G. (1996), 'The Theory of Planned Behavior: a Review of its Applications to Health-related Behaviors', *American Journal of Health Promotion*, **11**, 87–98. [PubMed 10163601].

Hibell, B. et al. (2004), *The ESPAD Report 2003: Alcohol and Other Drug Use among Students in 35 European Countries* (Stockholm: Swedish Council for Information on Alcohol and Other Drugs (CAN) and the Pompidou Group at the Council of Europe).

Hogg, M.A. and Abrams, D. (2003), 'Intergroup Behavior and Social Identity' in *Handbook of Social Psychology*. Hogg, M.A. and Cooper, J. (eds) (California: Sage).

Johnston, K.L. and White, K.M. (2003), 'Binge-drinking: a Test of the Role of Group Norms in the Theory of Planned Behavior', *Psychology and Health*, **18**, 63–77. [DOI: 10.1080/0887044021000037835].

Kinney, D.A. (1993), 'From Nerds to Normals: the Recovery of Identity among Adolescents from Middle School to High School', *Sociology of Education*, **66**, 21–40. [DOI: 10.2307/2112783].

Kuther, T.L. (2000), 'Moral Reasoning, Perceived Competence, and Adolescent Engagement in Risky Activity', *Journal of Adolescence*, **23**, 599–604. [PubMed 11073700] [DOI: 10.1006/jado.2000.0346].

La Greca, A.M. et al. (2001), 'Adolescent Peer Crowd Affiliation: Linkages with Health-risk Behaviors and Close Friendships', *Journal of Pedriatic Psychology*, **26**, 131–143. [DOI: 10.1111/1532-7795.00036].

Morojele, N.K. et al. (1997), 'Predicting Binge Drinking Intentions of South African Adolescents', presented at the 41st International Congress on Alcohol and Addictions on the Prevention and Treatment of Drug Dependencies (Cairo, May 1997).

Mosbach, P. and Leventhal, H. (1988), 'Peer Group Identification and Smoking: Implications for Intervention', *Journal of Abnormal Psychology*, **97**, 238–245. [PubMed 3385077] [DOI: 10.1037/0021-843X.97.2.238].

Nielsen, G.A. et al. (2002), '*Unges Livsstil* og *Dagligdag* 2000: *Forbrug af Tobak, Alkohol, og Stoffer*', '[Lifestyle and Everyday Life of Young People 2000: Use of Tobacco, Alcohol and Drugs]', (Copenhagen: Danish Cancer Society and National Board of Health).

Pombeni, M.L. et al. (1990), 'Identification with Peers as a Strategy to Muddle through the Troubles of the Adolescent Years', *Journal of Adolescence*, **13**, 351–369. [PubMed 2074289] [DOI: 10.1016/0140-1971%2890%2990029-7].

Schofield, P.E. et al. (2003), 'Youth Culture and Smoking: Integrating Social Group Processes and Individual Cognitive Processes in a Model of Health-Related Behaviors', *Journal of Health Psychology*, **8**, 291–306. [PubMed 14670209] [DOI: 10.1177/13591053030083001].

Smith, J.R. and Terry, D.J. (2003), 'Attitude-behavior Consistency: the Role of Group Norms, Attitude Accessibility, and Mode of Behavioral Decision-making', *European Journal of Social Psychology*, **33**, 591–608. [DOI: 10.1002/ejsp.172].

Sparks, P. and Guthrie, C.A. (1998), 'Self-identity and the Theory of Planned Behavior: a Useful Addition or an Unhelpful Artefact?', *Journal of Applied Social Psychology*, **28**, 1393–1410. [DOI: 10.1111/j.1559-1816.1998.tb01683.x].

Sparks, P. and Shepherd, R. (1992), 'Self-identity and the Theory of Planned Behavior: Assessing the Role of Identification with "Green Consumerism"', *Social Psychology Quarterly*, **55**, 388–399. [DOI: 10.2307/2786955].

SPSS for Windows, Release 13.0 (2004) (Chicago: SPSS Inc.).

Stryker, S. and Burke, P.J. (2000), 'The Past, Present, and Future of Identity Theory', *Social Psychology Quarterly*, **63**, 284–297. [DOI: 10.2307/2695840]

Sussman, S. et al. (1990), 'Group Self-Identification and Adolescent Cigarette Smoking: a 1-year Prospective Study', *Journal of Abnormal Psychology*, **103**, 576–580. [DOI: 10.1037/0021-843X.103.3.576].

Sussman, S. et al. (1994), 'Group Self-identification and Adolescent Cigarette Smoking: a 1 year Prospective Study', *Journal of Abnormal Psychology*, **103**, 576–580. [PubMed 7930058] [DOI: 10.1037/0021-843X.103.3.576].

Swann, W.B. et al. (1992), 'Why People Self-Verify', *Journal of Personality and Social Psychology*, **62**, 392–401. [PubMed 1560335] [DOI: 10.1037/0022-3514.62.3.392].

Tajfel, H. and Turner, J.C. (1979), 'An Integrative Theory of Intergroup Conflict' in *The Social Psychology of Intergroup Relations*. Austin, W.G. and Worschel, S. (eds) (Monterey, CA: Brooks/Cole).

Tarrant, M. et al. (2001), 'Social Identity in Adolescence', *Journal of Adolescence*, **24**, 597–609. [PubMed 11676507] [DOI: 10.1006/jado.2000.0392].

Terry, D.J. and Hogg, M.A. (1996), 'Group Norms and the Attitude-behavior Relationship: a Role for Group Identification', *Personality and Social Psychology Bulletin*, **22**, 776–793. [DOI: 10.1177/0146167296228002].

Terry, D.J. et al. (1999), 'The Theory of Planned Behavior: Self-Identity, Social Identity and Group Norms', *British Journal of Social Psychology*, **38**, 225–244. [PubMed 10520477] [DOI: 10.1348/014466699164149].

Van der Rijt, G.A.J. et al. (2002), 'Smoking and Other Substance Use as Distinct Features of Teenage Subcultures', *Journal of Adolescent Health*, **31**, 433–435. [PubMed 12401430] [DOI: 10.1016/S1054-139X%2802%2900394-4].

Chapter 10

Conclusion: Changing Drunken Component or Reducing Alcohol-related Harm

Margaretha Järvinen and Robin Room

Since societies, like individuals, get the sorts of drunken component that they allow, they deserve what they get (MacAndrew and Edgerton, 1969).

This book has analysed youth drinking in Europe and especially drinking focused on intoxication. A central theme in many chapters has been the question how the variations and dynamics in adolescent drinking should be conceptualised and explained. What does the European map of adolescent drinking look like; why are some youth cultures more focused on drunkenness than others; why is it that a 'new culture of intoxication' seems to have manifested itself in many countries; and what factors can explain the differences in drinking patterns among youths within a country? In this concluding chapter we summarise the central findings of the book and discuss the question of what can be done about hard adolescent drinking.

Intoxication Cultures and Non-Intoxication Cultures

As shown in many chapters, the traditional classification of European countries into spirits countries, beer countries and wine countries is not directly applicable to youth drinking cultures (cf. the chapters of Room and Ahlström). For one thing, adolescents in traditional 'spirits countries' like Finland or Sweden do not drink more spirits than their peers in wine-producing countries. For another, adolescents in France and Portugal do not drink more wine than adolescents in Scandinavia or the UK (Hibell et al., 2004). In fact, beer is the preferred beverage among boys in all western European countries except Greece, Malta, Greenland and the Faroe Islands (where spirits dominate). Among western European girls, beer is the dominating beverage in half of the countries, while spirits dominate in the rest, with no systematic differences between northern and southern Europe. In no European country is wine the dominant beverage among adolescents. With such ambiguities in the traditional European wine-beer-spirits pattern, we must seek other classifications if we want to conceptualise the geographical variations in youth drinking cultures.

The other traditional classification of European countries into 'wet' vs. 'dry' – where 'wet' stands for the drinking cultures of southern Europe (low prevalence of abstainers, high integration of alcohol in everyday activities) and 'dry' describes the drinking cultures of northern Europe (high prevalence of abstainers, low integration of alcohol) – also has its limits when it comes to adolescent drinking. As shown in Room's chapter, young people in Scandinavia and the UK are not more inclined to abstain from drinking than young people in southern Europe, *nor* do adolescents in wine-producing countries report 'integrated drinking' (here: drinking at home) more often than their counterparts elsewhere in Europe. Furthermore, when Danish and British adolescents, for instance, both drink alcohol more often and in greater amounts on each occasion than do adolescents in southern Europe, it seems illogical to call their drinking pattern 'dryer' than the drinking patterns of French or Italian adolescents.

Instead of these classifications we have used a division of youth drinking cultures into 'intoxication cultures' and 'non-intoxication cultures'. The most obvious representatives of the former group are the UK, Ireland and Denmark (with Finland, and on some measures Sweden following closely behind), while Portugal and France (but more surprisingly, also countries like The Netherlands and Belgium) are examples of the latter group. The most important measure distinguishing the two groups of countries from each other, as shown in Andersson and Hibell's chapter, is the variable *self-reported* drunkenness. A high rate of self-reported drunkenness, more than any other measure of heavy drinking (including binge drinking) is the trademark of youth drinking in northern and north-western Europe, and also the variable that best predicts the level of alcohol-related problems in a country. Accordingly, adolescents in the UK, Denmark, Ireland and Finland report the highest levels of negative drinking consequences (quarrels and fights, accidents, problems in relation to parents, friends and school, sexual problems, and so on). Characteristic of young people from these countries is also that they have exceptionally high positive expectations of alcohol (they expect to feel relaxed, feel happy, have a lot of fun when drinking) and very low negative expectations (they do not fear to get into trouble, feel sick, do something they would regret, and so on as much as adolescents in other countries do).

The fact that self-reported drunkenness is a better predictor of alcohol-related problems than is binge drinking or average alcohol consumption per drinking occasion, indicates that drunkenness has another cultural meaning in northern/ north-western Europe than in other countries (cf. Room's chapter in this volume). At similar levels of physical intoxication, young people from different parts of Europe obviously enact very different forms of psychosocial intoxication. And obviously it is the active engagement in psychosocial intoxication or 'determined drunkenness' (cf. Parker's chapter in this volume), rather than consumption of a certain amount of alcohol per se, that lies behind the high rates of negative alcohol consequences in the UK, Ireland and Scandinavia. The youth cultures of northern Europe evidently have very weak collective mechanisms for regulating drunkenness. A visible psychosocial intoxication is a condition actively sought in many settings, a condition young people expect from each other – see the description of drunkenness as a 'collective tribute to the fellowship' in Gundelach and Järvinen (2006) – and not something they suppress, avoid or condemn.

Drunkenness – Not Only for Boys

Another characteristic distinguishing intoxication cultures from other cultures is that the gender differences in drinking tend to be relatively small (cf. the chapter by Ahlström). Although boys drink alcohol more often and in larger quantities than girls in all European countries, the gender ratios in the north/north-west are small – especially for drunkenness. There are differences though *within* the group of intoxication cultures (British and Finnish girls are exceptionally 'equal' with boys when it comes to drunkenness rates) and *within* the group of non-intoxication cultures (French and Portuguese girls are less 'equal' than girls in other southern European countries). Also, the analyses in Ahlström's chapter show that gender equality in drinking differs depending on how traditional a certain beverage is in a country. In 'beer-countries' like Denmark and the UK, the gender differences are larger in beer-drinking than in spirits- and wine-drinking. In wine-producing countries on the other hand, the gender differences are largest in wine drinking. A similar pattern of beverage-specific gender differences has been demonstrated for adults. In a comparative study of men's and women's drinking in 13 European countries, Bloomfield et al. (2005) show that the gender ratio for spirits drinking was largest in Finland (a former spirits country) while the gender ratio for beer drinking was largest in the Czech Republic (a traditional beer-country) (Bloomfield et al., 2005). In general, the gender ratio among adults was smallest for wine in most countries – in France, however, the gender ratios for spirits and beer were smaller than the gender ratio for wine.

Obviously, the gender ratios in drinking – for adolescents as well as adults – have something to do with gender roles/stereotypes and gender inequality in different societies. The European pattern of gendered drinking and equality, however, is not easy to decipher. On the one hand, Bloomfield et al. (2005) found a strong *general* correlation between adult gender ratios in drinking in the 23 countries (13 European countries, 10 non-European) included in their study and different measures of women's position in society (the measures of gender equality were picked from the World Values Study and the International Social Survey). The higher women's position in a country, the smaller was the difference between male and female drinking. On the other hand, Leifman et al.'s (2002) six-country survey of adult drinking habits showed no clear European pattern indicating smaller gender differences in the relatively gender-equal northern countries than in southern Europe (cf. Room's chapter). As already mentioned, Ahlström's analyses in the present volume lend some support to the presumed association between adolescent drinking ratios and gender equality. The gender ratios in both drunkenness and average consumption of alcohol *tend* to be smaller in intoxication countries than in other countries, but the gender equality hypothesis cannot explain why, for instance, Denmark has a higher gender ratio than the UK, or Greece has a lower ratio than France.

Determined Drunkenness as Mainstream Behaviour

As shown in several chapters in this volume, heavy drinking is not a marginal phenomenon to be found in certain sub-cultures, among enclaves of 'problem youth' or among adolescents from poor socioeconomic backgrounds. On the contrary, determined drunkenness seems to be a mainstream phenomenon, occurring in all social classes, in larger cities as well as in the countryside, among girls as well as boys – and a phenomenon that is much more determined by cultural factors, parenting styles and attitudes towards drinking than by socio-economic factors.

Parker's chapter in this volume analyses the increase in young Britons' drinking during the last two decades as associated, not with social marginalisation, but with a mainstream 'work hard – play hard' life style. The heavy drinkers and recreational drug users of Parker et al.'s studies are young people well integrated in the educational system and the labour market, who regard intoxicated weekends as vital to the desired harmony between work/school/concentration and time out. Parker describes a leisure world increasingly focused on consumption – including the consumption of alcohol and drugs. The 'new culture of intoxication' in Britain is not dominated by young people from rebellious subcultures or poor socioeconomic backgrounds but by normal youths with successful transitions from childhood to adulthood.

That adolescent drinking and drunkenness is spread across all social classes – and that young people from medium and high-affluent families are over- rather than under-represented in the vanguard of adolescent drinking – is demonstrated in Richter et al.'s chapter. Based on data from the HBSC-study (Health Behaviour in School-Aged Children in 29 countries), the chapter shows, first of all, that the socio-economic circumstances of the family only have limited effect on adolescent drinking and drunkenness. For girls, parents' occupation and family affluence had very little effect on alcohol consumption, and only in a few countries. For boys, the effect of family affluence (but not of parents' occupation) was somewhat bigger. Boys from affluent families reported more frequent drinking and more drunkenness than boys from low affluence families. Three-fourths of the 29 countries included in the study showed tendencies in this direction, although the results were not always significant. The main conclusion of Richter et al.'s chapter is therefore that parental socio-economic status is not among the most important factors for explaining adolescents' drinking behaviour, but that the results from the HBSC study point in the direction of affluent families' children (especially boys) drinking most.

Another contribution to the discussion of adolescent drinking as mainstream vs. marginal/subcultural can be found in Verkooijen et al.'s chapter. Using data on Danish adolescents, the authors analyse the relationship between drinking/drunkenness and young people's association with different subcultures and identity categories: pop, skate, techno, hippie, computer nerd, religious, quiet boy/girl and sporty. Social identification with the categories pop, skate, techno and hippie was associated with higher weekly consumption and frequency of drunkenness, whereas identification with sporty, quiet, computer nerd and religious were associated with lower levels of consumption. Yet the effects were relatively small for all categories except for the quiet and religious subgroups. Thus, where differences in youth drinking behaviour tend to stand out in Denmark is in the direction of drinking less rather than more. Verkooijen et al. also analysed the influence on drinking/drunkenness of the respondents' self-identity as a drinker (statement: 'high alcohol consumption is an important part of who I am'), showing a significant but rather weak effect. Interestingly, self-identification with the statement was rather low. Few respondents were of the opinion that they drink too much; 7 per cent said they 'drink a little too much' and 1 per cent said they drink 'far too much'. This may be compared to the fact that 21 per cent of the boys and 13 per cent of the girls in Denmark drink more than the maximum limits recommended for *adults* by the Danish National Health Service (20 units of alcohol per week for men, 14 for women) (Ringgaard et al., 2005).

Parenting and Adolescent Drinking

Parents' attitudes and behaviour are among the most important factors when it comes to explaining differences in adolescent drinking. First, as described in the chapter by Engels et al., there is substantial evidence for the direct effects of parents' own drinking on adolescent drinking. The larger the parents' own consumption of alcohol is, the more their children tend to drink. Second, parental rules on adolescents' drinking is one of the most important alcohol-specific socialisation practices. Studies from several countries have demonstrated a strong association between lax parental rules and adolescent drinking, and that alcohol-specific rules in the family postpone the age of drinking onset. Third, Engels et al. demonstrate how parents, through rule setting and availability of alcohol in the household, may affect selective peer affiliation among their children. In other words, parents not only influence their own children's drinking behaviour through alcohol rules and attitudes towards alcohol, they also influence what company their adolescents seek and whether the friends of their children are heavy-drinking adolescents or not. Given that friends tend to adapt their drinking to each other's drinking, this adds extra strength to the influence of parents on their children's alcohol use. Adolescents with lenient alcohol rules drink more than other adolescents and seek heavy-drinking friends who inspire them to drink even more, while adolescents with strict rules associate with other cautious drinkers, thereby consolidating their own moderate alcohol behaviour.

Underlining the potential influence of parents, a US study found that implementation of a programme of parental information and counselling about binge drinking before their child entered university (typically at about age 18) did result in reduced drinking and problems, at least in the short term (Turrisi et al., 2001). Similarly, a longitudinal study from Iceland showed that parental styles experienced by teenagers at age 14 predicted their drinking patterns at age 17 (Adalbjarnardottir and Hafsteinsson, 2001). Adolescents with 'permissive' parents were more likely to drink heavily at age 17 than were adolescents from 'authoritarian' families and the relation remained strong even after controlling for several influencing factors, such as the effects of parents' and peers' alcohol use and the adolescents' own previous use. However, a cautionary note is struck by some researchers (Kerr and Stattin, 2000; Stattin and Kerr, 2000), who point out that influences between teenagers and parents go in both directions, so that parental looseness about drinking may reflect the earlier behaviour of their children; some parents may simply have given up on attempting to control their wayward offspring.

The influence of parents' behaviour is analysed in the chapter of Plant and Miller as well. The starting point for their chapter is the hypothesis that 'integrated' drinking (the family/dinner drinking pattern of southern Europe) leads to fewer negative consequences and that parents' teaching their children to drink moderately at home could be a way of making them drink in less destructive ways. Testing this association in Britain, Plant and Miller analysed the differences in drinking patterns between adolescents who said their parents had taught them to drink (18 per cent of all) and other adolescents. The study showed that parental teaching first and foremost was associated with drinking frequency and onset of drinking. The 'taught' group started to drink earlier than the others and consumed alcohol more often than the 'untaught' group. They also held less negative attitudes towards alcohol and tended to regard drinking as less risky than the untaught group. As regards binge drinking and problems experienced due to alcohol use (quarrels, loss of money, unwanted sex), there was no difference between the groups. In conclusion, this study shows that sensible adolescent drinking habits do not follow automatically from parents teaching their children to drink at home. Whatever parental 'teaching' meant for the respondents in the study of Plant and Miller, it obviously did not have the effect of making their drinking habits more Mediterranean.

Tackling Adolescent Drinking and Alcohol-Related Harms

When discussing the question how to influence adolescent drinking and make it less hazardous it is important to note that drinking of young people generally reflects the context of adult drinking norms in a country (cf. Room, 2004; Bullock and Room, 2006). As stated many times in this book, there is a relationship between the geographical patterns of adolescent drinking and adult drinking – in terms of drunken component, gendered drinking patterns, and so on. This relationship – cf. the quote from MacAndrew and Edgerton at the beginning of this chapter about 'societies deserving the drunken component they get' – is the point of departure for the following discussion of prevention efforts and control policy in relation to adolescent drinking. Trying to do something about adolescent drinking without also attending to adult drinking means ignoring the cultural practices and frames which structure adolescent drinking, and is also certain to strike adolescents as hypocritical. In this context, it is recommended that the reader examine recent comprehensive reviews of the effectiveness of alcohol policies (for example Babor et al., 2003; Chapter

7 of Anderson and Chisholm et al., 2004; Anderson and Baumberg, 2006) to supplement our discussion of the effects of some general strategies particularly on young people.

Controlling Alcohol Availability

Among the various strategies to prevent alcohol problems, measures which control alcohol availability by price or conditions of sale belong to the group with the strongest evidence of effectiveness (Babor et al., 2003). Often the effect of these measures is stronger on teenagers than on older drinkers. For instance, the removal from sale in Swedish grocery stores in 1977 of beer between 3.6 and 4.5 per cent alcohol by volume, a measure particularly motivated by concern over youth drinking, did indeed have its strongest effect in reducing harms among teenagers, although it also had some effect on rates of harms for older drinkers (Ramstedt, 2002).

There is also substantial research evidence that young drinkers are especially sensitive to alcohol prices. The introduction of special taxes on 'alcopops' – sweet premixed drinks particularly orientated to young drinkers – in Switzerland, Germany, France and New Zealand has had dramatic effects on beverage choices among young drinkers, but the effects on total youth consumption have not been clear. However, it is clear that tax and price policy measures applied more generally are not only effective in reducing alcohol consumption among young people but also in reducing alcohol-related injuries and death, for instance highway mortality (Coate and Grossman, 1988; Grossman et al., 1995), although most of the studies on the effects of pricing specifically on youth have been conducted in the USA. In reviews of research on adolescent drinking and alcohol policy (see for instance, Grube and Nygaard, 2001), taxation/price increases have been singled out as an effective way of reducing adolescent drinking.

Another type of control which has been repeatedly evaluated and found effective is limits on minimum drinking age. Here, again, much of the research evidence comes from the US (or Canada), though there are also studies showing effects from Australia, and more recently from New Zealand (Huckle et al., 2006; Kypri et al., 2006) and Denmark (Møller, 2002). The studies show that increasing the minimum age of drinking (in the case of Denmark, adopting a limit) is an effective way of reducing both adolescents' consumption and alcohol-related problems. Sometimes the effect of a minimum drinking age on alcohol-related harms may be more through changing the location and circumstances of drinking than by changing the amount of drinking (Hingston et al., 1983)

Much of this research has focused on the raise of drinking age to the uniform 21 years in different American states, showing considerable decreases in the alcohol use, fatal traffic crashes, DUI (driving under the influence) arrests, and so on among young people. A legal drinking age as high as 21 years would probably be impossible to implement in most European countries, where the minimum age is typically 16–18 years.[1]

The US has low minimum ages for driving but high minimum ages for drinking, and raising minimum driving ages has proved unpopular not only with adolescents but with their parents. In Europe, while minimum drinking ages are lower, as we have noted, the minimum driving ages are relatively high – generally at 17 or 18 (Room, 2004), often with stringent requirements for driver training. It is likely that these provisions hold down rates of alcohol-related traffic casualties among European teenagers.

Of course, changes in the European minimum ages for drinking alcohol cannot be effective unless they are accompanied by enforcement and are backed up by the population. An example from Denmark may illustrate the point. In July 2004 the minimum age limit for off-premise buying of alcohol was increased from 15 to 16. The change was evaluated in a study comparing survey data on 13–16 year olds' drinking habits and ways of getting alcohol in May 2004 with similar data one year later (Jørgensen et al., 2006). The evaluation showed a marked decrease in off-premise purchase of alcohol among 15-year olds (the target group for the law change), and no significant changes in the other age-groups. While 43 per cent of the 15-year-olds had bought alcohol in a shop in 2004, the corresponding number in 2005 was 23 per cent. This decrease, however, was counteracted by the fact that one-fourth of the boys and one-third of the girls now received alcohol from their parents, and that this proportion showed a significant increase from 2004 to 2005. Obviously, a considerable number of Danish parents did not agree with the arguments behind the law change saying that 15-year-olds should not have an easy access to alcohol. Although there is a tendency towards decreased drinking (as regards both drinking frequency and binge drinking) among 15-year-olds from 2004 to 2005, the changes are very small. The conclusion of the evaluation is, therefore, that changes in age limits cannot stand alone, but should be accompanied by measures aimed at changing attitudes, in this case especially the attitudes of parents.

Education and Persuasion

Education, particularly school education, tends to be the most widely accepted approach to reducing youthful drinking and its harms. But research reviews of evaluations indicate that information campaigns or educational programmes alone do not successfully influence drinking behaviour (Paglia and Room, 1999;

---

1 The geographical patterns in Europe is that the Nordic countries (except Denmark) have the highest minimum age (18–20 years depending on beverage), followed by the Eastern European countries (18 years for all beverages), while the traditional beer-countries (such as Germany, the UK, Denmark) have somewhat lower age limits (16–18), and the wine-producing countries of southern Europe (Italy, France, Spain, Portugal) have 16 as their general age-limit. The extremes when it comes to European age limits are Luxembourg (no age limits at all) and Iceland (20 years for all beverage types) (cf. Ahlström and Österberg, 2004/05).

Babor et al., 2003). Educational programmes typically expose young people to a few hours of anti-drinking or moderate drinking messages. As pointed out by Wagenaar and Perry (1994), this is counteracted by the fact that adolescents are exposed to the broader social environment of pro-drinking messages for the rest of their waking hours. Changing adolescents' attitudes towards alcohol through such programmes has little long-term effect as long as public policies, adult drinking, alcohol availability and acceptability, and alcohol advertising all point the other way. Again we are reminded of the fact that adolescent drinking cannot be tackled independently of the general cultural pattern of alcohol use and of policies surrounding alcohol consumption at large.

Foxcroft et al. (2003) report from a Cochrane Collaboration Systematic Review on the effectiveness of primary interventions for alcohol misuse in young people. Primary prevention was defined as 'projects that have services directed toward reducing the incidence or prevalence of alcohol misuse and related problems or influencing knowledge, attitudes and behaviours related to drinking beverage alcohol'. Of 600 papers/reports, 56 studies met the quality inclusion criteria, the majority of them (84 per cent) from the USA. Twenty of the 56 studies showed evidence of ineffectiveness. Of the rest, 15 studies reported partially effective short-term interventions (up to one year follow up), 12 studies reported partial medium-term effects (one to three years follow-up) and only three studies reported effective longer-term interventions. The effective programmes tended to have one thing in common: they did not focus on young people's drinking alone, but on the relationship between young people's drinking, parents and/or community. One of the most successful prevention projects in the review was the 'Strengthening Families Program' – a project for parents and their 10–14-year-old children, aiming at delaying the onset of alcohol use among children by enhancing parents' child management skills, parent-child communication and affective relationships. However, this is an expensive program which has primarily been directed at high-risk families, and might be defined more as an intervention in an 'indicated' population than as alcohol education.

Another type of project singled out by Foxcroft et al. is large-scale community-based interventions, aimed at changing alcohol-use patterns not only among young people but among people of all ages. Based on environmental interventions including strengthening of community awareness, responsible beverage service, preventing underage alcohol access, and so on, some such projects have had (modest) positive effects on high-risk drinking and alcohol-related injuries.

Lastly, in contrast to most of the other school education studies in the literature, which aim to prevent or at least delay any drinking, a well-conducted study in Australia used an explicitly harm-reductionist approach to school education (McBride et al., 2004). In the 32-month follow-up (17 months after the intervention finished), rates of hazardous drinking were converging between the intervention and the control groups, whereas earlier they had been lower in the intervention group. But rates of reported harm from one's own drinking remained 23 per cent lower in the intervention group. Thus, the intervention seemed to have an effect on alcohol-related harm even when its effect on levels of drinking was wearing off.

Reducing Alcohol-related Harm

Though there has been little in the way of formal evaluation, approaches to risk management and harm reduction which take into account the collective nature of much youth drinking and intoxication, deserve more attention than they have received so far.

One example is the responses of Norwegian police and civic authorities to a youth fiesta known as *russefeiring*. While the fiesta is not popular with adult officials, attempts to suppress it have been more or less abandoned. Each year's high school graduating class in much of Norway elects a committee to be in charge of the festivities, which occur between May Day, a traditional spring holiday, and the nation day on May 17. *Russefeiring*, described as a classic rite of passage by the anthropologist who has studied it (Sande, 2002), involves not only a great deal of drinking but also feats of risk-taking and daring. The local police and the students' organising committee meet ahead of time each year to negotiate the limits of these feats – what will be acceptable and what is not.

With such approaches, of course, the risk will not be zero, and such an approach may not be culturally acceptable everywhere. Thus, equivalent efforts in the USA such as 'Project Graduation' focus on providing an alcohol-free celebration (for example http://www.woodbridge.k12.nj.us/SchoolsHS/Colonia-HS/proj_grad_home.htm), apparently with some success in reducing casualties (Mowatt et al., 1985).

Other examples of harm-reducing strategies concern drinking and driving. The research literature is clear that strategies directed at younger drivers are effective in holding down alcohol-related traffic casualties. Low blood-alcohol limits for teenage drivers ('zero tolerance laws'), and license restrictions for young and inexperienced drivers, such as night-time driving curfews, have been shown, mostly in North American studies, to reduce rates of youthful alcohol-related crashes (Babor et al., 2003, pp. 165–166).

While a number of other harm reduction approaches have been tried, and often quite widely implemented, evidence for the effectiveness of many of them is scanty. Training bartenders and other servers not to serve the under-aged or the already drunk has proven effective in reducing rates of alcohol problems only when it is required by regulations and backed up by effective enforcement (Babor et al., 2003, pp. 142–145). A Canadian controlled study (Graham et al., 2004) showed that training tavern door staff ('bouncers') and servers in how to manage aggression and other problem behaviour had an impact in reducing alcohol-related violence – predominantly associated with younger patrons.

Intoxication, Youth and the European Union

In June 2001, the European Council adopted two Recommendations, one concerning the development of an EU Strategy on Alcohol, and the other concerning the drinking of alcohol by young people. The Recommendations were the outcome of a process which began with concerns when alcopops were introduced and promoted particularly to youth in European markets (Sutton and Nylander, 1999).

After considerable delay and much behind-the-scenes pressure from the alcohol industry (Ulstein, forthcoming), an EU Strategy was finally adopted as a Communication from the Commission in October 2006 (Commission, 2006). An Annex to the Communication reports on the implementation of the 2001 Council Recommendation on the drinking of alcohol by young people (http:// ec/europa.eu/health/ph_determinants/life_style/alcohol/documents/alcohol_ com_625_a3_en.pdf). Fifteen of the 25 member states, including all three Nordic members and a broad scattering of others, reported changes to the regulations on underage drinking or better enforcement of them. Austria, Cyprus, Latvia, Slovenia and The Netherlands reported changes in blood-alcohol limits for young or novice drivers, and Lithuania plans to follow suit. Germany, France, Slovenia, Sweden and Finland reported that they had introduced health warnings on alcoholic beverage containers or advertisements. All members reported increased educational activities.

The new Strategy continues a substantial emphasis on young people. Aim 1 is 'to curb under-age drinking, reduce hazardous and harmful drinking among young people, in cooperation with all stakeholders'. The discussion of this talks of 'worrying drinking trends among young people', including 'an increasing trend of binge-drinking by young people in many parts of the EU'. Confidently, the Strategy states that this 'can be effectively addressed through public policy', and mentions 'enforcement of restrictions on sales, on availability and on marketing likely to influence young people' and 'broad community action to prevent harm and risky behaviour … supported by media messages and life-skills training programmes', adding that 'the alcohol beverage industry and retailers can play an important role to ensure that alcohol is consumed responsibly'. Later in the document, 'young and novice drivers' are mentioned as more involved in alcohol-related road accidents, and 'a lower or zero Bac limit for these drivers' is recommended as an 'efficient policy'. Throughout, there is a recurring emphasis on 'broad and carefully implemented' education programmes.

In the document's favour, one might conclude, is its recognition of 'worrying' trends in intoxication among young people in Europe and its suggestions of a broad spectrum of measures and policies. Some of the measures it recommends, as we have noted – and some of the measures that EU members report already adopting – have a track-record of effectiveness. On the other hand, the overarching emphasis on alcohol education, while understandable in political terms, is unlikely to have the effects the Commission desires. At best, the Strategy must be seen as a way station towards future work on more effective policy formation.

Alcohol education, as it is practiced in most countries, means a few hours of mandatory alcohol and drug information in schools, a measure proven ineffective in a number of evaluation reviews. Alcohol education, in a broader sense, may also cover the attempts of national health services and other players on the public health scene to make the drinking patterns of Scandinavia, the UK, and so on more Mediterannean. This however is not an easy task. Throughout the centuries, the alcohol cultures of northern Europe have been described as 'excessive', 'uncivilised' and as characterised by 'drinking for the sake of drunkenness' (cf. Chapter 1 in this volume). However convincingly the alcohol cultures of the wine-producing countries have been presented as an ideal, and whatever policy measures the governments of the North have tried, the populations of these countries have not given up their 'intoxication cultures'. If anything, there are signs of a European development in the opposite direction: young people in southern Europe have allegedly started to drink with a focus on drunkenness. Huge differences remain though, between different parts of Europe. This insight – that the European differences in alcohol cultures are as old as recorded history, and that drinking patterns in one part of Europe cannot simply be changed by coping cultural elements from another part – should be incorporated in any European strategy of tackling adolescent drinking problems.

References

Adalbjarnardottir, S. and Hafsteinsson, L. (2001), 'Adolescents', Perceived Parenting Styles and Their Substance Abuse: Concurrent and Longitudinal Analyses', *Journal of Research on Adolescence* 11, 4, 401–423.

Ahlström, S. and Österberg, E. (2004/05), 'International Perspectives on Adolescent and Young Adult Drinking', *Alcohol Research and Health*, **28**(4), 258–268.

Anderson, P. and Baumberg, B. (2006), *Alcohol in Europe: a Public Health Perspective* (London: Institute of Alcohol Studies). http://ec.europa.eu/health-eu/doc/alcoholineu_content_en.pdf.

Babor, T. et al. (2003), *Alcohol: no Ordinary Commodity – Research and Public Policy* (Oxford: Oxford University Press).

Bloomfield et al. (2005), 'Gender, Culture and Alcohol Problems: A Multi-National Study', *Final Project Report* (Berlin: Institute for Medical Informatics, Biometrics and Epidemiology).

Bullock, S. and Room, R. (2006), 'Drinking Behaviour, Coming of Age and Risk' in Aggleton, P. et al. (eds), *Sex, Drugs and Young People: International Perspectives* (London and New York: Routledge), pp. 122–137.

Chisholm, D. et al. (2004), 'Reducing the Global Burden of Hazardous Alcohol Use: a Comparative Cost-Effectiveness Analysis', *Journal of Studies on Alcohol*, **65**, 782–793. [PubMed 15700517].

Coate, D. and Grossman, M. (1988), 'Effects of Alcoholic Beverage Prices and Legal Drinking Ages on Youth Alcohol Use', *Journal of Law and Economics*, **31**, 145–171. [DOI: 10.1086/467152].

Commission of the European Communities (2006), *Communication from the Commission to The Council … : an EU Strategy to Support Member States in Reducing Alcohol Related Harm* (Brussels: European Commission). http://eurlex.europa.eu/LexUriServ/site/en/com/2006/com2006_0625en01.pdf.

Foxcroft, D.R. et al. (2003), 'Longer-term Primary Prevention for Alcohol Misuse in Young People: a Systematic Review', *Addiction*, **98**, 397–411. [PubMed 12653810] [DOI: 10.1046/j.1360-0443.2003.00355.x].

Graham, K. et al. (2004), 'The Effect of the Safer Bars Programme on Physical Aggression in Bars: Results of a Randomized Controlled Trial', *Drug and Alcohol Review*, **23**, 31–41. [PubMed 14965885] [DOI: 10.1080/09595230410001645538].

Grossman, M. et al. (1995), 'Effects of Alcohol Price Policy on Youth: A Summary of Economic Research' in *Alcohol Problems among Adolescents: Current Directions in Prevention Research*. Boyd, G.M. et al. (eds) (Hillsdale, N.J.: Lawrence Erlbaum Associates), 225–242.

Grube, J.W. and Nygaard, P. (2001), 'Adolescent Drinking and Alcohol Policy', *Contemporary Drug Problems*, **28**, 87–131.

Gundelach, P. and Järvinen, M. (2006), *Unge, fester og alkohol (Youth, Parties and Alcohol)* (Copenhagen: Akademisk Förlag).

Hibell, B. et al. (2004), *The ESPAD Report 2003. Alcohol and other Drug Use among Students in 35 European Countries* (Stockholm: The Swedish Council for Information on Alcohol and Other Drugs).

Hingson, R.W. et al. (1983), 'Impact of Legislation Raising the Legal Drinking Age in Massachusetts from 18 to 20', *American Journal of Public Health*, **73**, 163–170. [PubMed 6849474].

Huckle, T. et al. (2006), 'Trends in Alcohol-Related Harms and Offences in a Liberalized Alcohol Environment', *Addiction*, **101**, 232–240. [PubMed 16445552] [DOI: 10.1111/j.1360-0443.2006.01326.x].

Jørgensen, M.H. et al. (2006): *Evaluering af forbuddet mod salg af alkohol til personer under 16 år*. (Evaluation of the Ban on Sale of Alcohol to Persons under 16 years old) (København: Statens Institut for Folkesundhed).

Kerr, M. and Stattin, H. (2000), 'What Parents Know, how they Know it, and Several Forms of Adolescent Adjustment: Further Support for a Reinterpretation of Monitoring', *Developmental Psychology*, **36**, 366–380. [PubMed 10830980] [DOI: 10.1037/0012-1649.36.3.366].

Kypri, K. et al. (2006), 'Minimum Purchasing Age for Alcohol and Traffic Crash Injuries among 15 – to 19-Year-Olds in New Zealand', *American Journal of Public Health*, **96**, 126–131. [PubMed 16317197] [DOI: 10.2105/AJPH.2005.073122].

MacAndrew, C. and Edgerton, R. (1969), *Drunken Comportment: A Social Explanation* (Chicago: Aldine).

McBride, N. et al. (2004), 'Harm Minimization in School Drug Education: Final Results of the School Health and Alcohol Harm Reduction Project (SHAHRP)', *Addiction*, **99**, 278–291. [DOI: 10.1111/j.1360-0443.2003.00620.x].

Møller, L. (2002), 'Legal Restrictions Resulted in a Reduction of Alcohol Consumption among Young People in Denmark' in *The Effects of Nordic Alcohol Policies: what Happens to Drinking when Alcohol Controls Change?*, Room, R. (ed.) (Helsinki: Nordic Council for Alcohol and Drug), 93–99 Research, NAD Publication 42). http://www.nad.fi/pdf/NAD_42.pdf.

Mowatt, C. et al. (1985), 'Project Graduation'. 'Maine', *MMWR – Mortality and Morbidity Weekly Report*, **34**, 233–235.

Paglia, A. and Room, R. (1999), 'Preventing Substance Abuse Problems among Youths: a Literature Review and Recommendations', *Journal of Primary Prevention*, **20**, 3–50. [DOI: 10.1023/A%3A1021302302085].

Parker, H. et al. (2001), *Illegal Leisure: the Normalization of Adolescent Recreational Drug Use* (London: Routledge).

Ramstedt, M. (2002), 'The Repeal of Medium-Strength Beer in Grocery Stores in Sweden – The Impact on Alcohol-Related Hospitalizations in Different Age Groups', in *The Effects of Nordic Alcohol Policies: what Happens to Drinking when Alcohol Controls Change?*. Room, R. (ed.) (Helsinki: Nordic Council for Alcohol and Drug), 69–78 Research, NAD Publication 42). http://www.nad.fi/pdf/NAD_42.pdf.

Ringgaard, L.W. et al. (2005), *Unges livsstil og dagligdag* (The lifestyle of youths and daily life) (København: Kræftens Bekæmpelse og Sundhedsstyrelsen) (The Danish Cancer Society and the Danish National Board of Health).

Room, R. (2004), 'Drinking and Coming of Age in a Cross-Cultural Perspective' in *Reducing Underage Drinking: A Collective Responsibility*. Bonnie, R.J. and O'Connell, M.E. (eds) (Washington, DC: The National Academies Press), 654–677.

Sande, A. (2002), 'Intoxication and Rite of Passage to Adulthood in Norway', *Contemporary Drug Problems*, **29**, 277–303.

Stattin, H. and Kerr, M. (2000), 'Parental Monitoring: a Reinterpretation', *Child Development*, **71**, 1072–1085. [PubMed 11016567] [DOI: 10.1111/1467-8624.00210].

Sutton, C. and Nylander, J. (1999), 'Alcohol Policy Strategies and Public Health Policy at an U level: The case of alcopops', *Nordisk Alkohol –* and *Narkotikatidskrift* (Nordic Studies on Alcohol and Drugs). 16, (English Supplement): 74-91.

Turrisi, R. et al. (2001), 'Examination of the Short-Term Efficacy of a Parent Intervention to Reduce College Student Drinking Tendencies', *Psychology of Addictive Behaviors*, **15**, 366–372. [PubMed 11767270] [DOI: 10.1037/0893-164X.15.4.366].

Ulstein, A., (forthcoming), 'No Ordinary Partner', *Nordisk Alkohol- och Narkotikatidskrift* (Nordic Studies on Alcohol and Drugs), English Supplement.

Wagenaar, A. and Perry, C.L. (1994), 'Community Strategies for the Reduction of Youth Drinking: Theory and Application', *Journal of Research on Adolescence*, **4**(2), 319–345. [DOI: 10.1207/s15327795jra0402_8].

Wilsnack, R.W. et al. (2000), 'Gender Differences in Alcohol Consumption and Adverse Drinking Consequences: Cross-Cultural Patterns', *Addiction*, **95**(2), 251–265. [PubMed 10723854] [DOI: 10.1046/j.1360-0443.2000.95225112.x].

Index